The Making of a Terrorist

The Making of a Terrorist

Alexandre Rousselin and the French Revolution

JEFF HORN

OXFORD
UNIVERSITY PRESS

OXFORD
UNIVERSITY PRESS

Oxford University Press is a department of the University of Oxford. It furthers
the University's objective of excellence in research, scholarship, and education
by publishing worldwide. Oxford is a registered trade mark of Oxford University
Press in the UK and certain other countries.

Published in the United States of America by Oxford University Press
198 Madison Avenue, New York, NY 10016, United States of America.

Library of Congress Cataloging-in-Publication Data
Names: Horn, Jeff (Historian), author.
Title: The making of a terrorist : Alexandre Rousselin and the French Revolution / Jeff Horn.
Description: New York, NY : Oxford University Press, [2021] |
Includes bibliographical references and index.
Identifiers: LCCN 2020022231 (print) | LCCN 2020022232 (ebook) |
ISBN 9780197529928 (hardback) | ISBN 9780197675540 (paperback) |
ISBN 9780197529942 (epub) | ISBN 9780197529959
Subjects: LCSH: Saint-Albin, A. R. C. de (Alexandre Rousselin de Corbeau), 1773–1847. |
France—History—Reign of Terror, 1793–1794—Psychological aspects. |
France—History—Revolution, 1789–1799—Biography. | France—History—1789–1815. |
Revolutionaries—France—Biography. | Nobility—France—Biography.
Classification: LCC DC146.S127 H67 2021 (print) | LCC DC146.S127 (ebook) |
DDC 944/.04/4092 [B]—dc23
LC record available at https://lccn.loc.gov/2020022231
LC ebook record available at https://lccn.loc.gov/2020022232

Paperback printed by Marquis Book Printing, Canada

Contents

Acknowledgments   vii

Introduction: A Romantic Remembers the French Revolution   1

1. Education for Change, 1773–1792   8

2. The Making of a Terrorist, 1792–1794   28

3. The Consequences of Terror, 1794–1796   66

4. Rehabilitation: Political, Literary, and Social, 1795–1815   99

5. Liberalism and the Press, 1816–1838   133

6. Remembering and Forgetting the French Revolution: Memories
   and Memoirs   168

Conclusion: Satisfactions and Regrets of a Life in Revolution   181

Appendix: Alexandre Rousselin and the Historians   187

Timelines   195

Notes   201

Selected Bibliography   227

Index   235

Acknowledgments

CHARLES GEISST, MY friend and colleague , challenged me to tell him the best story from my years of archival research. He pushed me to write for a broader audience. I decided to give it a try. A spring 2014 sabbatical and summer grants in 2014 and 2017 from Manhattan College provided the time and money to do research in Paris. I made heavy use of Columbia University's Baker Library and the O'Malley Library of Manhattan College's interlibrary loan service. History Department funds donated by Patty and Jack Stack supported the inclusion of additional images. I am grateful for their support.

Many people helped this project along the way. I consulted Charles Cavaliere, Steve Clay, Lynn Hunt, Laura Mason, and Isser Woloch on certain points. Thanks to Jeff Ravel, I had the opportunity to present some of the material on the Terror to the Boston French History Group and got wonderful feedback. The Dante Seminar at Manhattan College heard an early version of Rousselin's story and encouraged me to continue. Kelli Christiansen gave me a great deal of useful advice about potential audiences and the publishing market. The New York Eighteenth Century Seminar provided valuable readings of the material on Rousselin's formative years. On several occasions, the conferences of the Society for French Historical Studies and the Western Society for French History were venues to get comments on and reactions to discrete parts of most chapters.

The librarians and archivists at the Bibliothèque Nationale de France, Archives Nationales both in Paris and Pierrefitte, and the Bibliothèque Historique de la Ville de Paris were extraordinarily helpful in making exceptions to rules limiting access or allowing me to photograph materials. Danielle Chartier at Paris' Bibliothèque Thiers responded quickly to a request for information about an obscure reference and Xavier Darcos, Secrétaire perpétuel de l'Académie des sciences morales et politiques, gave permission for me to visit the collection.

My wife Julie encouraged me to look up Rousselin on genealogical websites where I found considerable information that was new to me. I wrote to the person who posted most of it: Bruno Cazelles, a descendant of Rousselin. Nine months later, I heard back from him. After a brief email exchange, he put me in touch with his aunt, Isabelle Castillon du Perron Lacorne, who invited me to Paris to consult her collection of documents. Madame Lacorne and her husband Michel provided a convivial setting for research and wonderful discussions ranging from Rousselin's life and legacy to the role of the Terror in French history to contemporary politics. They could not have been more gracious.

As always, my friends have read parts of the manuscript and given me helpful comments. David Andress, Bob Blackman, Charles Geisst, Paul Hanson, Colin Jones, and Marisa Linton shared their expertise and enthusiasm for the period. Scott Dennis, Nana Nkrumah, Frederick Schweitzer, and Kathleen White read the entire manuscript, asked probing questions, and assisted me in clarifying my ideas. David Troyansky commented on a second version of the manuscript with his usual grace and style. Len Rosenband was once again my "go-to" reader. He read the chapters as I wrote them and then the whole thing once I had a complete draft. Over the years, Len has taught me a lot about writing and about the craft of history. He made this a far better story. David Bell and Charles Cavaliere went out of their way to be supportive when it came time to find a press. I am also appreciative of Oxford University Press' anonymous readers, who provided a host of valuable comments. Susan Ferber saw the potential of the manuscript and has been a superlative editor.

Historians are only as good as their sources. That is particularly true for a biography. Trying to make a coherent, interesting, and relevant story from the bits and pieces of the surviving archival record was relatively easy in some sections and rather difficult in others. I spent a lot of time searching for additional documentation to fill in the gaps, but even after finishing the book, there are a frustrating number of things that I do not and likely will never know about Alexandre Rousselin. As I have come to learn, that is the joy and the pain of writing biography.

My fall 2015 "Age of the French Revolution" class at Manhattan College read parts of the manuscript and I told them many stories about Rousselin's life and career. Those students—Gabrielle Cervone, Chris DiRisio, Anthony Fischetti, Brendan Fitzpatrick, Katie Garnett, Aukai Gilliland, Richard Grace, Juli Jaeger, Jamie Kiriakos, Kylie Knee, John Maiocco, Maria McCaughey, Oscar Ortiz, Teodora Peric, Derek Smith, Nina Torres, and Sean Vignoles— were a wonderful sounding board. As a group they responded so positively to the project and got so excited about what the biography of one person revealed about the period as a whole that I knew I was onto something. Their encouragement kept me going when I was frustrated by a lack of documentation on certain points. This book is dedicated to that class and to all my students over the last thirty-five years. They continually remind me that the best history is often the best story. I hope you enjoy this tale; it's the best one I've got.

The Making of a Terrorist

Introduction

A ROMANTIC REMEMBERS THE FRENCH REVOLUTION

ALEXANDRE-CHARLES ROUSSELIN, COMTE de Saint-Albin, had a secret. It was a skull preserved in a glass jar of alcohol. From the mid-1820s he kept it in a hidden cabinet in the wall of his office in his Parisian townhouse, showing it only rarely to intimate friends and family members. The skull was Charlotte Corday's, the woman who murdered Jean-Paul Marat, the pioneering radical journalist and one of the major figures of the French Revolution, on 13 July 1793. In his youth, Rousselin had been a fellow radical and one of Marat's greatest admirers. For those few who saw it, the skull appeared out of place. It seemed a bit too gothic for this determinedly rational newspaper publisher and liberal political fixer.

Even more macabre was the story that made the rounds about a dinner party Rousselin hosted. He was retired by that point, but retained sufficient influence to get a high-ranking government minister to accept his invitation. Rousselin sweetened the deal by promising that they would dine with "a great lady of the Revolution."[1] Intrigued, the minister arrived to find a skull on the table veiled under a napkin. When asked about whose it was and how he got it, Rousselin reportedly discussed his esteem for Corday and her desperate act. That the story was almost certainly made up seems to have helped to spread the tale rather than undermined its credibility.

At the end of the nineteenth century the skull was acquired by Prince Roland Bonaparte from Georges Duruy, Rousselin's grandson-in-law. According to "family tradition," Rousselin had purchased it from an antiques dealer located on one of Paris' quays. Yet there was strong suspicion that Rousselin had used his position as confidential secretary to influential Revolutionary politician Georges-Jacques Danton to acquire the head, soon

The Making of a Terrorist. Jeff Horn, Oxford University Press (2021). © Oxford University Press.
DOI: 10.1093/oso/9780197529928.001.0001

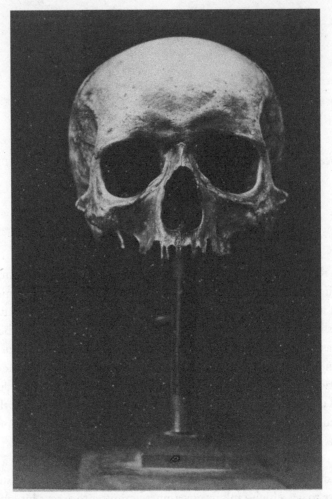

FIGURE I.I Charlotte Corday's skull from the Collection of Prince Roland Bonaparte. 6 phot. du crâne de Charlotte Corday provenant des collections du prince Roland Bonaparte, Bibliothèque nationale de France, département Société de Géographie, SG W-61.

after Corday was sentenced to death by the Revolutionary Tribunal that dispensed summary justice in July 1793 as part of the Terror during the French Revolution.[2] In turning over the curiosity to the prince to satiate that worthy's interest in the phrenology of a murderess, Duruy commented that he "would not be sorry to get rid of this anatomical item" because it "terrified" his wife. According to Duruy, Rousselin had written "a sort of philosophical dialogue" between himself and this remnant of Corday's remains that explored various motives for the murder.[3] Family members recalled Rousselin's familiar pose: sitting quietly, gazing out the window of his beautifully restored town-house at passersby on the rue du Vieille du Temple, just around the corner from the French National Archives. From that high perch he contemplated the past, his actions, and those of people he had known.

Rousselin's possession of the skull demonstrated his abiding interest in understanding why someone would resort to violence. At the same time, he sought to appreciate the political motives of the key figures in the French Revolution, both for his own reasons and to write their histories. These concerns reflected a lifelong fascination that typified many of his generation, at least those who survived the era's upheavals. The skull was a poignant re-minder of the violent consequences of Revolutionary action, both for victims and for perpetrators. It was also indicative of the emotional frenzy that gripped many people during the crisis atmosphere of the 1790s. This remnant of Corday symbolized the end of Rousselin's only partially realized hopes for a better world. In good Shakespearean fashion, the skull was also a focus for the attention directed at the past and the choices taken by the men and women who deliberately set out to change the world.

This account of Rousselin and Corday's skull begs some questions. Why would anyone want such a grisly token of the violence of the Revolutionary era? Why acquire it, and then why hide it? What was the aim of that dinner party? Did it actually happen? From a more philosophical perspective, what degree of obsession with the past is necessary for someone to talk to a skull and engage in a debate with it? Were these accounts just a bit of theater or something more psychologically meaningful?

Alexandre Rousselin also had a story he wanted told. For him to appear as the hero, he himself could not recount the last days of Revolutionary jour-nalist Camille Desmoulins and Danton before their execution for "modera-tion" in April 1794. So Rousselin bided his time and waited until somebody came to him asking for confirmation of reports they had heard, based on hints and clues that he had scattered in conversations with hundreds of people across the years. Only in 1834 did his subtle plan to get someone else to tell this tale bear fruit.

In 1794 the French republic was at war, both with itself and against most of Europe. To survive widespread civil unrest, runaway inflation, and inva-sion on every frontier, the French government resorted to a systematic effort to frighten and force the populace into following its dictates. This dreaded "Reign of Terror," or more accurately, the Terror, was directed by a relatively small group of militants in Paris grouped loosely into a faction known as "the Mountain." Implemented by a broader swath of the population, the Terror was instrumental in enabling France to survive the multifaceted crisis of 1793–94 and ultimately to go on the military offensive. But survival came at a steep price—perhaps 50,000 were executed during the Terror, of whom almost 40,000 had risen in arms against the republic. But the means and methods developed in 1793–94 persisted. Across the decade further deaths, estimated at nearly 300,000 and concentrated in the rebellious Vendée region of western France, followed. The Terror directed by the state did most of the killing in 1793–94, while everyday violence stemming from a politically radical but deeply divided nation experiencing war, civil war, and severe food shortages caused most of the deaths that came later. In a representative democracy, the decision of the Revolutionaries to deploy violence against the citizenry ultimately ruled out certain types of state action. The Terror alienated many, even most, French people from those who were supposed to represent them.

On behalf of the central government, Rousselin undertook two missions in 1793 to bring the Terror to provincial cities to drum up additional support for the war effort. Confident of the righteousness of his cause, Rousselin ordered the vandalism of churches, imposed a massive "tax on the rich," initiated house-to-house searches to find hidden grain and stores, and encouraged denunciations by members of the popular classes that led to the imprisonment of hundreds for their "moderation." Although these measures were not all that radical in that frenzied wartime emergency, Rousselin's activities led to his own imprisonment and narrow escape from the guillotine in the late summer of 1794. In short, he was a terrorist. But this was not the story that Rousselin wanted told.

Rather, Rousselin wanted his actions *resisting* the Terror to be remembered. After returning from his second mission, Rousselin recognized that the faction seeking to slow down or phase out the Terror was headed for the chopping block. He had hoped to rely on his patrons for protection, but both Danton and Desmoulins had been shunted aside. Political decisions were being made by others who were more willing to continue the Terror to ensure the survival of the Revolution.

By March 1794, it was clear that both men were vulnerable. Desmoulins made matters worse when he published a new issue of his inflammatory newspaper, *Le Vieux Cordelier*, which challenged the appropriateness of a policy of Terror and criticized one of its architects and a former close friend, Maximilien Robespierre. The existence of an even more radical faction than the one directing the government further destabilized the political situation.

The radicals were arrested, tried, and executed in March 1794. Rousselin saw what was coming and sought to alert his former employers of the storm about to break.

Not until 1834 did the story came to light. Pierre-Joseph-Marcelin Matton, a cousin of Desmoulins, intending to publish a little-known addition to *Le Vieux Cordelier*, decided to try to find "the generous citizen who, on the eve of the arrest of Camille [Desmoulins] and Danton, went to warn them about the threat to their lives." Matton followed the clues strategically dropped by Rousselin back to the man himself. To verify the story Matton spoke first to Anne-Françoise Duplessis, Desmoulins' mother-in-law, who corroborated it: "The day before the arrest, he [Rousselin] went back and forth breathlessly between Danton and Desmoulins, trying to get them to watch out for themselves."[4] Danton refused to take action or leave. Desmoulins concurred. Rousselin's warning was in vain: both were arrested early on 30 March 1794 and, after a brief show trial, guillotined on 5 April.

Matton was much impressed by Rousselin's actions in 1794 and even more by his "faithful sentiments and invariable principles" thereafter. He praised Rousselin for trying to save Desmoulins and Danton. This was the image of himself that Rousselin wanted propagated: someone who tried to save people from the Terror even when he too was threatened with denunciation. To spread this version of his actions, Rousselin had only to ensure that Matton's narrative based on Duplessis' testimony got the publicity it deserved—an easy task for a publisher of a popular, influential newspaper.

This account too raises questions. Why did Desmoulins and Danton ignore Rousselin's warning? What was his real relationship to the Terror? What was theirs? And why, four decades later, was Rousselin so concerned with his image and how the public viewed his actions during the French Revolution?

This biography can answer some, but not all of these questions. Situating the actions and words of an individual in the milieu of his times illuminates many issues and provides a sense of the lived experience, but as with all historical writing, motivations and conclusions are limited by the sources. Sometimes rhetoric or documented actions allow for a glimpse of the writer's emotions, but often only the context enables the full meaning of words or deeds to emerge. Alexandre Rousselin left hundreds of letters and reports, as well as considerable published work, many pieces of journalism, and numerous manuscripts, some of which eventually saw the light of day. Yet Rousselin's preoccupation with the past also led him to destroy documents that did not paint him in a flattering light. Other feelings and thoughts he never wrote down or shared with anyone else. At several key points in this account what Rousselin was thinking is unknown even if what he was doing, at least in public, is recorded. As a result, this biography relies on the views of others to fill in those gaps, especially in the first chapter. Bringing this complex man and his times to life requires close attention to Rousselin's position in a fast-changing society that was continually in transition.

Although little remembered today, Rousselin was an eyewitness and even a participant in an astonishing number of key moments during the Revolutionary era. In addition to serving as confidential secretary to Danton and Desmoulins, he fulfilled the same role for other influential politicians and generals including Paul Barras, Lazare Hoche, Jean-Baptiste Bernadotte, and Lazare Carnot. He worked closely with Joseph Fouché, Benjamin Constant, Adolphe Thiers, and Casimir Périer. Each of these individuals' importance will be discussed at the appropriate time, but the point is that Rousselin worked with or knew almost all of the central players of the period and wrote about them as an historian and chronicler of his time. Deeply engaged in Paris' popular politics, Rousselin was intimately involved with the elaboration of the Terror. For a year after his missions—and, in many ways, for the next five and a half decades—he was forced to devote himself to either defending his actions or destroying any trace of them. He was denounced, jailed repeatedly, and threatened with the guillotine. Thus he was not just a perpetrator, but also a victim of the era's excesses.

A longtime opponent of Napoleon Bonaparte, Rousselin came to support the return of the Emperor in 1815. With the Restoration of the House of Bourbon he returned to journalism, helping to found *Le Constitutionnel*, the bestselling newspaper in the world for much of the 1820s and 1830s. To protect the paper's liberal views, Rousselin waged a constant battle against government censorship. He helped put Louis-Philippe on the throne of France during the Revolution of 1830 and remained a close advisor. Along the way, Rousselin acquired a noble title from his foster father and built a fortune.

The path taken by this terrorist to survive the consequences of his actions and then to thrive as a liberal was highly unusual, but certain facets of his journey were shared with many of his contemporaries. Rousselin struggled to make sense of a chaotic time of transition in the aftermath of the collapse of the old régime. He came to believe that the new republic's harsh repressive measures were justified by the magnitude of the threat to the Revolution and participated both in the formulation of the Terror and its implementation. These actions shaped his life, but he never lost hope in a better world even when he scaled back his expectations for immediate change. After 1815,

Rousselin and other remaining Revolutionaries learned that even wealth and power could not insulate them fully from the consequences of their actions. It is the combination of a unique position and representative problems that makes the biography of this previously unknown man a chronicle of the age of the French Revolution.

I

Education for Change, 1773–1792

> *It was the best of times, it was the worst of times, it was the*
> *age of wisdom, it was the age of foolishness, it was the epoch*
> *of belief, it was the epoch of incredulity, it was the season*
> *of Light, it was the season of Darkness, it was the spring of*
> *hope, it was the winter of despair, we had everything before*
> *us, we had nothing before us.*
>
> —CHARLES DICKENS, *A Tale of Two Cities* (1859)

LITTLE IS KNOWN about Rousselin's family or early years. His father, François-Charles, was born in 1731 in Gancourt-St. Étienne, a desperately poor village of fewer than two hundred people in Normandy. François apprenticed as a dyer before moving 60 miles to Paris, where he quickly found work and settled in the working-class parish of Saint-Médard on the Left Bank. In November 1767, he wed Nicole-Antoinette Marchand, a twenty-year-old Parisienne who worked as a washerwoman. Alexandre was born (most sources agree) on 12 March 1773 in Saint-Médard.

The next part of the story is murky. According to divorce papers filed in 1794, sometime after Alexandre's birth, François left Nicole. When exactly or why precisely was left unsaid. Also unsaid was when Nicole began a new relationship that culminated in marriage to someone of much higher social status. How they met and began their improbable relationship would almost certainly be a tale worth telling, but there is not enough information even to speculate. In adulthood, Alexandre deliberately obscured what information did exist.

Antoine-Pierre-Laurent Corbeau de Saint-Albin became Nicole's lover and foster father to young Alexandre. Scion of an old noble family from Dauphiné in southeastern France, Laurent, born in 1750, was the younger son of a marquis. He joined the artillery at eighteen and rose steadily through the ranks. Laurent often supervised workers making cannon in military arsenals.

The Making of a Terrorist. Jeff Horn, Oxford University Press (2021). © Oxford University Press.
DOI: 10.1093/oso/9780197529928.001.0001

Gregarious, he was a popular figure with other officers as well as with enlisted men. When the Revolution broke out he was a captain, stationed in
Metz. His postings at garrisons far from Paris complicate determining when
Laurent and Nicole began their relationship. As his later writings illustrate,
Corbeau read widely and deeply in Enlightenment texts. He wanted Nicole's
son to be able to participate in such intellectual conversation and to fit in
with elite society. Corbeau paid for Alexandre to attend the prestigious
and expensive Collège d'Harcourt, located only a few hundred yards from
where Alexandre was born. Students matriculated between the ages of ten
and twelve, so Laurent's and Nicole's relationship began no later than 1785
and probably a few years earlier. Alexandre's precocious political involvement
rested on the educational foundations he received as a youth.

Founded in 1280, the Roman Catholic Collège d'Harcourt was among the
most famous schools in France. Graduates moved seamlessly to the University
of Paris thanks to a rigorous classical education that attracted both nobles and
members of the middle classes. Among its eighteenth-century alumni were
major figures of the Enlightenment including political theorist Charles-Louis
de Secondat, Baron of Montesquieu and editor of the *Encyclopédie* Denis
Diderot. The school taught skills and fostered contacts that launched and sus-
tained Rousselin's careers in politics, journalism, and the arts. Most students
boarded at the school until they were sixteen or eighteen. Alexandre probably
boarded so that his mother could travel with Laurent. Almost all the teachers,
administrators, and staff were clerics. Students were required to attend chapel
each morning and to hear weekly sermons. Religious thought and practice
permeated the student body.

For six years students focused on the languages, literature, and history of
the ancient world, primarily Rome and Greece. Courses were taught in Latin.
The first four years were spent mastering the language. The next two years
were devoted to composition, which stressed rhetoric, the art of persuasion,
as well as the logical flow of argument and ethical reasoning. Most students
also learned ancient Greek. French was taught as a five-year course parallel
to Latin instruction. This curriculum inculcated the standardized, formal
French of the law courts, not the daily patois spoken in the streets of Paris.
A classical education marked speech patterns for life.

Extensive nightly homework drilled the rules and patterns of Greek and
Latin, the chief instructional texts, into young scholars. Only a few French
works from the age of Louis XIV were part of the eighteenth-century
curricula in Parisian collèges. This education ensured that the models of antiquity were more familiar to graduates of elite educational institutions than

was information about the contemporary political scene. Students frequently presented their written essays orally and then endured the critiques of their classmates' wit and wisdom. At the end of each year, students took challenging exams that determined if they moved up to the next grade level. Of his days at d'Harcourt in the early 1760s, future bishop, diplomat, and prince Charles-Maurice de Talleyrand-Périgord recalled, "I had some success in my studies or so I came to believe.... I received little encouragement for fear that it would give too much happiness to my youth."[1] For students of a less distinguished background, like Alexandre Rousselin, d'Harcourt's pedagogical approach bequeathed a lifelong delight in praise and a relentless search for intellectual validation.

Roman history fascinated Rousselin. Biographers who emphasized societal and individual ethics, such as Livy, Tacitus, and especially Plutarch, inspired him. He recognized the dangers of despotism and the benefits of a republican form of government. The chief conclusion he drew from Roman history was the threat that corruption posed to social well-being. This training prepared him to interact with French elites of similar educational backgrounds. A common vocabulary and literary foundation allowed him to understand and swiftly bond with older men.

At this particular collège, resistance to the "despotic" actions of the Bourbon monarchy and the Roman Catholic Church was woven into everyday life. D'Harcourt was closely affiliated with Jansenism, a strain of Roman Catholicism widespread in seventeenth- and eighteenth-century France that had a profound impact on the outbreak and course of the French Revolution. It stemmed from the mid-seventeenth-century Bishop of Ypres (in modern-day Belgium) Cornelius Otto Jansen's posthumous defense of the ideas of St. Augustine of Hippo. Jansenism reemphasized the importance of original sin, and consequently of human depravity. This religious viewpoint focused on the need for strict morality, rigid conduct, and close adherence to the sacraments to combat the corruption of humankind.

Jansenism spread widely and became associated with Gallicanism, the idea that the Roman Catholic Church in France should be self-governing. Most Jansenists sought to constrain the authority of the French monarchy through the maintenance of laws and traditions that protected their "liberties." From the late seventeenth century, the theology taught and most of the sermons delivered at the Collège d'Harcourt rebuffed the repeated attempts of church and state to impose their linked authorities on individual consciences. In the name of Gallican liberties, teachers at d'Harcourt emphasized the rule of law while drawing attention to Jesuitical and monarchial corruption to undermine their prestige and power.

In the generation that made the French Revolution, many people influenced by Jansenism became profoundly anti-clerical. Alexandre Rousselin detested the clergy's privileges and exhibited a deep dislike of the Church's institutional power. A deist, he accepted the existence or even necessity of a "supreme being" or "first mover," but rejected the possibility that a "god" was involved directly in human affairs in the manner articulated by organized religions, like the Roman Catholic Church. Rousselin espoused a sort of natural philosophy or civic religion intended to inculcate virtue and good morals based on Jean-Jacques Rousseau's "The Profession of Faith of a Savoyard Vicar" in *Émile, or On Education* (1762).

More than any other thinker, Rousseau influenced late eighteenth-century French political aspirations. Rousseau's version of Enlightenment formulations made particular sense to people educated in schools like the Collège d'Harcourt. Rousselin and many other French revolutionaries were inspired by Rousseau "because he dared to speak the truth."[2] In fact, Rousseau was the sole *philosophe* referred to in Rousselin's speeches, letters, or writings. And those references were frequent. The masthead of every issue of the first newspaper that Rousselin oversaw (see chapters 2 and 3) ran Rousseau's aphorism from *The Social Contract* (1762): "As soon as someone says of the state's business, 'what does it matter to me?'—that state is lost."[3] In 1792–1794 many revolutionaries claimed Rousseau's mantle, long associated with universal manhood suffrage and direct democracy. They sought the reputation of speaking on behalf of the people to represent the "general will." Robespierre wrote that Rousseau "heralded" certain "great moral and political truths," but did not cite specifics from his works to support his policy proposals.[4] For many devoted readers, Rousseau's influence was felt more in terms of style of expression, symbolism, and the goals of political action than in any particular program, but it had a major impact on the worldview of French political actors in this era.

Rousseau's works reinforced Rousselin's fascination with Roman history. Rousselin strongly favored a greater democratic voice for the common man and believed that a republican form of government minimized both social immorality and inequality. He also embraced Rousseau's emphasis on the need for moral rectitude in politics. Rousselin's search for a more virtuous society was stimulated by Rousseau's disgust with the corruption of court, aristocracy, and clergy.

At the Collège d'Harcourt, Jansenism and the Enlightenment shaped young Alexandre Rousselin. In the classical world, he found an antidote to the shortcomings of contemporary society. He also developed the intellectual and social skills to blend in with the French elite. He believed the *philosophe*'s promise of social change and hoped that a topnotch education would grant him entrée into a regenerated society. He did not fear falling into the world of hack writers and disappointed intellectuals whose scathing, often profane attacks on the monarchy, church, and nobility that were also part of the Enlightenment.[5] Rousselin was confident that he could do well for himself by doing good for society.

In 1789 Rousselin was sixteen years old, about 5 feet 4 inches tall, with curly brown hair, a round face, narrow shoulders, and a prominent nose. His collège education gave him a taste for and skill with words, along with networks of students, teachers, and alumni who helped further his career. This training also made it clear to him that drastic changes were needed in French society. He later recalled, "The Revolution which appeared in 1789 as

FIGURE 1.1 Alexandre Rousselin in 1813. From the Isabelle C. P. Lacorne Family Archives, used with permission.

a sudden creation had already taken place in the mind."[6] Rousselin was edu-cated by the Roman Catholic Church and the Enlightenment, but when the Revolution began, he was not yet sure for what.

Like any recent graduate, Rousselin's prospects were shaped by the economy. A deep recession, exacerbated by a poorly executed commercial treaty with England and several poor harvests, cast a pall over a relatively healthy economy. France became the richest country on earth, thanks in large measure to the enormous riches derived from trade and an empire based on the practice of slavery. Cities expanded and the middle classes multiplied, though some parts of the country grew faster than others, widening cleavages that divided people, groups, and regions, as well as town from village. For people like Rousselin, the sudden reversal of long-term trends frustrated French expectations of prosperity, drastically heightening uncertainty.[7]

Fueled by the Enlightenment, dissatisfaction with the privileges held by the crown, the nobility, and the Roman Catholic Church, among others, permeated French society.[8] Widespread frustration with growing inequality sapped the government and its supporters of much of their influence. But until the economic downturn of the mid-1780s, pressure for change was per-fectly manageable.

The Bourbon state's inability to pay its bills, particularly those stemming from its global military commitments, precipitated a crisis. Privilege severely limited royal revenues and impeded the state's ability to tap the kingdom's growing wealth. By the mid-1780s, nearly half of the state's tax revenue went to service the debt. Nobles and clergy wanted a greater voice in governing the kingdom if they were to make more than nominal tax payments. Bowing to financial pressure, on 24 January 1789, Louis XVI officially summoned the Estates-General, France's long-dormant legislature, to meet. Composed of three estates—the clergy, the nobility, and the Third Estate, which made up about 96 of the population—this institution was to assemble that May to re-solve the fiscal crisis.

Despite the optimism surrounding the opening of the Estates-General, little was accomplished. The king and his ministers failed to convince the body to accept their direction. As the Estates-General ground to a stand-still, the delegates of the Third Estate seized the initiative. On 17 June, they declared themselves the "National Assembly" in the name of the people and invited noble and clerical deputies to join them. This measure appropriated the legitimacy and authority of the king. He rejected their declaration and closed the group's meeting hall. On 12 July, Louis dismissed those ministers sympathetic to the Third Estate, spawning fears of a royal coup. The army was expected to disband the National Assembly by force. The city of Paris, turbulent and anxious at the best of times, was awash with rumors and speculation about what would happen next.

Alexandre Rousselin was embroiled in Paris' ferment. In 1789, he was only sixteen years old and had just completed his studies. Many of the activists who sought to harness popular outrage to defend the National Assembly were known to him from the neighborhood near the Sorbonne on the Left Bank or from the cafés where students congregated. Two men in particular drew his attention: Camille Desmoulins and Georges-Jacques Danton.[9] Both emerged as important Revolutionary leaders, in part because of their participation in the events of July 1789. Rousselin became the confidential secretary of each man in turn. Unfortunately, he left no account of his own feelings, thoughts, or actions during that tumultuous summer as a distinctive Revolutionary milieu developed. It enmeshed Rousselin completely. Tracing the actions of Desmoulins and Danton also shows the personal courage that it took to become a Revolutionary and the fears that fed the anxieties of political activists.[10]

Georges Duval, a nephew of the headmaster who went to school with Rousselin, left a detailed account of an 11 July 1789 visit to the Palais Royal, one of the city's most important sites for political discussion. Owned by Louis-Philippe-Joseph, the duc d'Orléans, this entertainment venue, situated on Paris' Right Bank, was chock-full of cafés and bookstores. The duc's protection meant that radical ideas could be discussed without having to worry much about the police. According to Duval, a group of conspirators met in a back room of the Café de Foy around 9 p.m.[11] Led by Honoré-Gabriel Riqueti, comte de Mirabeau, a prominent member of the National Assembly, the conclave included Desmoulins and Danton. The key figure was Danton, who entered "pale and haggard. Was it from anger or fright?" wondered Duval. Danton announced, "I have come to tell you, messieurs, that it is necessary to prepare a great uprising to thwart the counter-revolution led by aristocrats!" Duval related that the group sought to direct popular attention toward the Bastille, the decrepit fortress guarding the city's eastern approaches that had become a political prison and thus a symbol of monarchial despotism. Desmoulins wrote his father about a special effort to win over as many soldiers as possible to the National Assembly's cause, particularly the regiments of French Guards who garrisoned the city: "Crowds attached themselves to any soldiers they encountered, crying, 'long live the Third Estate.' When they entered a cabaret, they drank to the health of the communes [municipalities]. Soldiers were led astray publicly."[12]

The next day, Sunday, 12 July, Desmoulins went to the Palais Royal at 3 p.m., condemning "our cowardice" to all he met. When three young men shouted, "To arms!" he joined them. Mounting a table, he was rapidly surrounded by a crowd estimated at 6,000 people. Overcoming his serious stutter, Desmoulins gave an impromptu speech warning the audience that the next step in the counter-revolution was "perhaps a Saint Bartholomew's [Day Massacre] for patriots." He echoed the appeal "to arms" and finished by proclaiming that the "infamous police" were watching him, but that regardless of personal danger, he would "call his brothers to liberty." Pistol in hand, Desmoulins declared, "at least they will not take me alive and if I die, I will die gloriously!"[13] Duval reported that the crowd was "electrified by his eloquence" and determined to do his bidding.[14] Desmoulins' listeners spearheaded the search for weapons and prevented mounted troops from entering the city. Monday, 13 July, saw the tocsin, the city's alarm bells, ring continuously as a large crowd seized weapons stored at the royal military hospital. Desmoulins grabbed a new musket, a bayonet, and two pistols.

FIGURE 1.2 Paris Guarded by the People (Night of 12–13 July 1789). Credit: Paris gardé par le peuple, nuit du 12 au 13 juillet 1789. Dessin pour le 11ème tableau du recueil des tableaux historiques de la Révolution française [T.H.R.F] (1791–1817), Musée Carnavalet D.7747.

On the afternoon of 14 July, in Desmoulins' report, the now-armed crowd converged on the Bastille. After meeting with the attackers, the governor decided to open fire before the mob could infiltrate the fortress. A cannon belonging to the French Guards made a breach, and the crowd poured in. The governor was captured and killed, his head put atop a pike and triumphantly displayed. With the help of supportive French Guardsmen, the people seized control of the city. Expecting a riposte from the troops camped nearby, Paris waited anxiously. Fires burned everywhere to make night into day. Desmoulins joined the restless armed patrols that sought out soldiers returning to barracks to convince them to sit out an attack on the city. This hothead wanted to attack Versailles "to take in all the aristocrats in one haul." More than a hundred members of the National Assembly arrived to lead the crowds and make sure that they knew what—and who—they were fighting for. Holding a "naked sword," Desmoulins acted as a bodyguard to one of these deputies. Writing on 16 July, Desmoulins declared his "inexpressible joy" at the People's "triumph" over the king and the aristocracy.[15]

Like Rousselin, Duval worked with Desmoulins and Danton and recognized both their strengths and their weaknesses. He later noted that Desmoulins had a "bilious complexion like Robespierre, a hard and sinister eye and an appearance that was more osprey than eagle." Some called him a "pretty boy, but those are only flatterers who had never seen him." Danton had "audacity and did not lack spirit, but was dying to become someone and did not demonstrate any scruples as to means." Duval reflected:

I had the occasion to know and appreciate Danton and Camille, having been one of their most active agents, one of their most reliable supporters in the district and later in the Cordeliers Club. No laborer carried more stones than these two in the construction of the revolutionary babel; they were not the least skillful, nor, to be sure, the least ardent.[16]

Alexandre Rousselin became far closer to both men than Duval. For Rousselin, Desmoulins' and Danton's efforts to make a revolution were more important than their flaws, either physical or psychological. They were leaders worthy of his support.

Lucie-Simplice-Camille-Benoît Desmoulins was born in 1760 in the town of Guise in Picardy, north of Paris. His father was a diligent lawyer who did not make much money. At fourteen, Camille received a scholarship to the Collège Louis-le-Grand in Paris where he was inspired by the history and

FIGURE 1.3 Camille Desmoulins. Credit: Pierre-Joseph Matton, *Le vieux Cordelier de Camille Desmoulins, seule édition complète. précédée d'un Essai sur la vie et les écrits de l'auteur* (Paris: Ébrard, 1834), frontspiece.

literature of republican Rome. He studied law, but his stutter and violent temper won him few clients. Living cheaply on the dole from his father, he spent long hours with his friends in cafés, often at the Palais Royal. Like many future Revolutionary leaders, he became a freemason in the Nine Sisters lodge.

In July 1789, Desmoulins published two important works of Revolutionary ideology and propaganda: *Free France* and *Speech of the Lantern to Parisians*. The former work was composed during the stalemate of the Estates-General, but his printer refused to set the type because its radical message was likely to be censored. The tract appeared on 18 July. It called for a democratic republic unencumbered by the "odious" privileges enjoyed by the king, nobility, and clergy. The latter piece was written from the perspective of a lamppost on the Place de Grève outside city hall where executions occurred. By shining a light on society's problems, Desmoulins hoped to illuminate the way forward to a better future. At the same time, Desmoulins celebrated Parisian mob violence as the epitome of patriotism.

That November, thanks to the (temporary) patronage of Mirabeau and then of hero of the American war Marie-Joseph Paul Yves Roch Gilbert du Motier, marquis de Lafayette, Desmoulins capitalized on his notoriety to begin a weekly newspaper, *Révolutions de France et de Brabant* (in modern-day Belgium then ruled by Austria), that ran until July 1791. He took on a co-author and co-editor, Roch Marcandier. Later Louis-Marie-Stanislaus Fréron, a friend from Louis-le-Grand who lived in the same neighborhood, became his collaborator. Although Desmoulins found it "easier to make a revolution that turns France upside down than to be a distinguished writer," he told his father that his goal "was not money, but the defense of principles."[17] Deeply anti-monarchial, the weekly situated the French Revolution in an international movement for change. Its no-holds-barred critique of contemporary politics heaped scorn on anyone who Desmoulins deemed insufficiently "patriotic." As a writer, Desmoulins achieved financial success. He acquired and furnished an apartment in the Cordeliers district and could finally afford to marry. Inflammatory rhetoric and republican ideals also earned Desmoulins considerable political influence especially among dedicated revolutionaries.

These committed activists also influenced Desmoulins. Jean-Paul Marat's newspaper, *L'Ami du peuple*, however, persuaded Desmoulins of the dangers stemming from the press exhorting the crowd to violence. In 1790, he wrote: "It is distressing to see the lantern used too frequently. It is a great evil if the people become too familiar with these games. Executions by the people are horrible." Despite his recognition that inciting popular violence "threatens us all," Desmoulins continued to stir the pot when it suited his immediate political goals.[18] He emerged as a major player in the battle for public opinion both in Paris and in the provinces. Desmoulins won many supporters, especially among Paris' "vigilant" Cordeliers club and district, who he described as "the fathers of the country, my neighbors."[19] He also attended the Breton Club that gave birth to the Jacobin Club.

Sometime during these first two years of the Revolution, Rousselin became Desmoulins' confidential secretary, likely early in 1790 when *Révolutions* was taking off. The intense teenager worked cheaply and seems to have developed a kind of hero worship of the impassioned journalist. All accounts, however, agree that over time their relationship evolved into friendship. Their similar educations—and equally fervent natures—probably allowed Rousselin to relate easily to the emotional Desmoulins.

In the late eighteenth century, a secretary was more than an assistant. In addition to doing paperwork secretaries were confidants, advisors, and trouble-shooters who often knew secrets as well as the latest political gossip.

The job required both the ability to reflect and to act. It was a perfect position for an adept observer with a well-developed capacity for work who hoped to become a participant in the great events of the day, like Alexandre Rousselin.

Desmoulins needed a secretary. In addition to writing about half of each issue of the weekly newspaper, as editor, he also oversaw subscriptions and all correspondence related to the paper's distribution, especially in the provinces. To keep his finger on the city's pulse and to provide fodder for his political tracts, Desmoulins frequently attended meetings at the Cordeliers and Jacobin clubs. He was also busy wooing his rich and beautiful soon-to-be-wife Anne-Lucile-Philippe Laridon Duplessis.

Although deadly serious as a propagandist, Desmoulins had a reputation for youthful exuberance and behavior. Even when short of money, he rejected fees from clients and often forgot to collect on debts. In public and private discourse alike, Desmoulins was always referred to as "Camille" while every single one of his contemporaries was known by their last names, a telling difference. Friends and rivals alike emphasized his childlike frivolity and innocence. During a debate at the Jacobin Club, his devoted friend Robespierre described Desmoulins as "naïve," "a spoiled child."[20] When they served together in the legislature, Bertrand Barère, observed that Desmoulins "has a great deal of spirit and too much imagination to have good sense."[21] No wonder Desmoulins needed somebody as energetic and organized as Alexandre Rousselin to help him manage his life.

Desmoulins was only the first of several eminent revolutionaries who made use of Rousselin's services as a confidential secretary. These individuals' reliance on him reflected their own youth and inexperience. A few revolutionaries— on both sides of the Atlantic—were older and more established, but most of the key figures were in their twenties with careers that were either just beginning or already stalled. Although determined to build a better world, these young men had to build reputations and powerbases in a rapidly shifting political and social milieu. At the same time, they needed to prove themselves to themselves if only to relieve their own anxieties about their capacities and place in the world. Doing all these things simultaneously, especially in the hyper-politicized atmosphere of Paris between 1789 and 1794, would have been daunting to far more practiced and successful individuals, much less the youthful strivers, who rose to prominence in that frenzied time. Rousselin was even younger than most other revolutionaries but shared their thirst for recognition, influence, and glory. But he understood that the path toward getting them involved helping his patrons realize their goals. Only then would he be able to share the opportunities afforded by the Revolution.

Desmoulins was among the most vocal advocates for change. He was an early advocate of replacing the monarchy with a republic. Louis XVI's botched attempt to flee the country in June 1791 changed perceptions drastically, accelerating the spread of radical ideas.[22] Desmoulins played a major role in that process, both in the press and in terms of practical politics. He headed a delegation from the Cordeliers Club that presented a petition to the Paris Commune (the municipal government) on 16 July 1791 asserting that the king's flight constituted "formal abdication of the constitutional crown entrusted to him."[23]

The next day a demonstration held on the Champ de Mars, the military parade ground in western Paris, turned violent when troops under Lafayette's command opened fire on the crowd. Danton fled to avoid arrest. Desmoulins remained in Paris, mostly in his apartment on the Place du Théâtre-Français, but he was noticeably less active. This is likely when Rousselin began to look for a more reliable, more influential patron, someone who might help him get a government job to pay the bills. The exact timing is unknown, but Rousselin seems to have gone to work for Danton not long after his return from England in September 1791. There were no hard feelings on Desmoulins' part. Rousselin remained an intimate of both men and their families.

AS ROUSSELIN'S EMPLOYER and patron, Georges-Jacques Danton provided a series of opportunities that transformed this ardent republican first into a more radical Revolutionary and then into a terrorist. In 1789–90 Danton was the most prominent member of the Cordeliers Club and district, as well as the section of Paris that was carved from it in 1790 known initially as Théâtre-Français. At his side, Rousselin had a unique vantage point to watch the Revolution unfold.

Like many talented and ambitious provincials, Danton's path led to Paris. Much of what we know of his early life comes from a biographical sketch written by Alexandre Rousselin. Born into a comfortable middle-class family in Arcis-sur-Aube in Champagne in 1759, Danton attended a Jansenist-influenced collège in Troyes, the provincial capital. He moved to Paris in 1780, where he found a position as a clerk while studying law. Possessed of a stentorian voice accompanied by a certain rhetorical flourish, thanks to his rigorous classical education, Danton was a formidable speaker. That he was a large man who was notably ugly made an impression. Noted Revolutionary politician Antoine-Claire Thibaudeau described him sympathetically: "I was very much struck by his height, and his burly athletic figure; by the irregularity of his features, which pitted scars left by smallpox still further accentuated."[24] Despite the fact that his legal career generated little income, Danton successfully wooed Antoinette-Gabrielle Charpentier, the daughter of the well-to-do proprietor of his favorite café. Rousselin described her attraction to Danton: "She admired his wit, which most people found too sharp; she admired his spirit, which most people felt was too ardent and impulsive; and the voice which seemed to most people loud and frightening *she found gentle*."[25] Danton received an impressive 18,000 livres as dowry. Supplemented by loans from relatives, Danton set up housekeeping and bought a potentially lucrative post as an advocate of the royal council in 1787. The Dantons and the Desmoulins socialized frequently. Their wives became close friends. Like Desmoulins, he joined the Nine Sisters freemason lodge.

Danton's apartment was on the second floor of a building on the rue des Cordeliers (now the rue de l'École de Médecine) not far from the Collège d'Harcourt. This area of the Left Bank comprised a single, large, close-knit neighborhood. Located west of the Latin Quarter, connected by bridge to the judicial establishment on the Île de la Cité and Right Bank, and next to the popular Théâtre Français, the Cordeliers district housed numerous lawyers, publishers, booksellers, and writers who mixed with the actors and others attached to the theater. Several major newspapers were written or printed there, not just Desmoulins' *Révolutions de France et de Brabant*. Freedom of the press and hatred of censorship united these professional groups. They followed the lead of the radicals who gathered at the Café Procope where Danton and Desmoulins held sway.

In July 1789, Danton mobilized his home district by playing on fear. To enlist his neighbors in the patrols that became the National Guard, he proclaimed: "Citizens, let us arm ourselves to repel the 15,000 brigands assembled in Montmartre, and the 30,000 soldiers who are ready to descend on Paris to loot the city and slaughter its inhabitants!"[26] According to Thibaudeau, who was present, Danton "presided with the decision, alertness, and authority of a man who knows his own power. He drove the District Assembly toward his chosen goal."[27] In October, Danton's leadership pushed the Cordeliers in playing a major role in stirring up and supporting the Women's March on Versailles that forced the royal family to live in the heart of Paris, essentially as hostages to the city.

Later that month, the Cordeliers intervened when radical journalist Jean-Paul Marat was indicted for libel. Danton proclaimed that to defend Marat's "ability to express his ideas," on 7 October the Cordeliers district "takes under its protection, all the authors in its jurisdiction, and will defend them with all its power." Marat soon emerged from hiding to take up residence. On 19 January 1790, the Cordeliers championed "patriot writers whose zeal, even if exaggerated, contributes to the triumph of the truth and strengthens the budding constitution." The district passed a resolution that nobody could be arrested within its confines without the approval of a special committee headed by Danton. Three days later, Lafayette sent three thousand men supported by cannon to arrest Marat. The Cordeliers' administration backed by detachments of other districts' National Guards refused. Somehow Danton convinced the police that the warrant was outdated and therefore invalid. While they dithered, Marat made his getaway to England and Danton became a name to be reckoned with in Parisian politics. Despite the opposition of the mayor and Lafayette, Danton became a municipal councilor in 1790 and was voted onto the departmental administration early in 1791 before becoming deputy public prosecutor of the Commune that December.[28]

Danton emerged as the heart and soul of the Society of the Friends of the Rights of Man and of the Citizen that met in the Cordeliers convent. Founded in April 1790, it sought to be the mouthpiece of the popular movement once the old districts were replaced by sections. This administrative reorganization of every city with more than five thousand inhabitants was the official response to the Cordeliers' ability to resist the authority of the Commune. The leadership of Danton, Desmoulins, and several other Cordeliers enabled the Club to seize a key symbolic position in the incipient Revolutionary political culture of the capital. Democratic republicanism was an emblem that the Cordeliers were proud to wear. As early as July 1791, the Cordeliers voted overwhelmingly to advocate for the establishment of a republic. Rousselin's apprenticeship in the practical and symbolic politics of the new political landscape occurred within the Cordeliers.

Danton's visit to England after the Champ de Mars "massacre" let people's tempers die down. Outrage over the king's flight fueled Danton's ever more frequent denunciations of Louis XVI. He referred to Queen Marie-Antoinette solely as "the Austrian woman." In the Cordeliers Club, Danton proclaimed, "By upholding a hereditary monarchy, the National Assembly has reduced France to slavery! Let us abolish, once and for all, the name and function of King; let us transform the kingdom into a republic!"[29]

Danton maintained his base in the Cordeliers, but increasingly devoted his time to the Jacobin Club. He became a national figure in the debates about whether to go to war and, once begun in April 1792, how to prosecute it. Influential Revolutionary politician Dominique-Joseph Garat described Danton in this period: "His imagination and the type of eloquence that it gave him, singularly appropriate to his face, his body, and his stature, was that of a demagogue. His glance at men and on events: sudden, clear, impartial, and true was based on the solid and practical caution that only experience can bring."[30] At his installation as an officer of the Commune, Danton pronounced his principles:

> Whatever my individual opinions concerning men and affairs may have been at the time of the Constitution's overhaul, *now that it is sworn*, I would demand the death penalty for any man—were he my brother, my friend, or my own son—who raised a sacrilegious hand to attack it. Such are my feelings in this matter. The general will of the French people, solemnly manifested by their adherence to the Constitution, will always be my supreme law. I have consecrated my entire life to the people. No longer will their enemies attack or betray them with impunity. Very soon they will rise up and purge the earth of all its tyrants, unless tyranny abandons the league it has formed against them. If need be, I will die in defense of their cause.

Overblown as this rhetoric may have been, it moved his audience. They interrupted him with a chorus of: "Yes, yes, we will die, too!"[31]

On Danton's behalf Rousselin drafted documents, contacted other leaders, and made précis of what was going on in the press and in the legislature. He also seems to have handled intimate details of Danton's finances and family arrangements. The young man was always on call because, even in the midst of a national crisis, Danton preferred the life of the bon vivant to the thankless task of being a dedicated public servant. Just as his efforts had let Camille be Camille, Rousselin enabled Danton to be Danton.

WAR SPLIT BOTH Paris' popular movement and the Jacobins. Journalist turned politician Jacques-Pierre Brissot led a faction determined to provoke a war with Austria as a means of coming to power. This circle hoped that adopting a war policy would gain them Louis XVI's support and unite the country behind the government. Known to history as the Girondins, contemporaries usually referred to this group as Brissotins. After the King appointed three Girondin ministers, war was declared on 20 April 1792. Louis XVI soon dismissed the Girondins, however, encouraging radicals to push for an insurrection to establish a republic.

A military crisis exacerbated tensions. Although begun with high hopes, the royal army was both disorganized and disheartened. After the French advance into modern-day Belgium was rebuffed, Austrian and Prussian forces crossed the border in strength, forcing the Assembly to declare *"la patrie en danger."* The French people responded with an unprecedented outpouring of

FIGURE 1.4 Georges Danton "The Prussians are at our gates!" François-Alphonse Aulard, *Danton*, 2nd ed. (Paris: Picard-Bernheim, 1884), 2.

patriotism. Louis XVI's actions that seemed to impede the war effort convinced ever more people of his "treasonous" intentions. The war was the Revolution's single most vital turning point; French defeats forced the pace of change, radicalizing politics precipitously.

The arrival in Paris of detachments of National Guards from across France to commemorate the anniversary of the fall of the Bastille tipped the balance. Among the most radical contingents were those of the cities of Brest and Marseille, both quartered at the Cordeliers. On 30 July, the Théâtre-Français section voted to include passive citizens (those disenfranchised by the Constitution of 1791 because they did not pay enough taxes) in their deliberations and to enroll them in the section's National Guard. This measure widened France's democracy and heightened the influence of the popular classes. François-Joseph Westermann, a former soldier and Danton's close friend, took the lead in planning a fresh insurrection.

A manifesto issued on 25 July by the Duke of Brunswick who commanded the armies allied against France was the straw that broke the camel's back.

In order to "terminate anarchy in the interior of France," protect the king, and liberate "the majority of the inhabitants" from "the excesses of a faction which subjugates it," Brunswick threatened to "exact an exemplary and ever-memorable vengeance" on the city of Paris. He held all "rebels," including members of the legislature and civilians, "personally responsible" for their "misdeeds and errors."[32] With the Prussians and Austrians on the march, these threats fostered a perfectly rational sense of urgency, even panic, among that broad swath of the population that sought to bolster the war effort.

Late on 9 August 1792, the crisis came to a head. Lucile Desmoulins recalled that "the tocsin of the Cordeliers rang, it rang for a long time."[33] Delegates of 47 sections (of 48) voted to form a new Insurrectionary Commune to raise an army of National Guards and overthrow the monarchy. Many Jacobins were involved or were at least supportive, but the Cordeliers led the way. Danton, Desmoulins, their circle, and their neighborhood led the insurrectionary movement both in the sections and in the Commune. Many memoirs by eyewitnesses attest to their leadership. A British physician attached to the Embassy, Dr. John Moore, wrote that the actions of the sections were "planned by a faction of which Danton may be considered the leader, and of which the divisional electors were the instruments."[34]

The National Guards stationed at the Tuileries palace melted away. Only the Swiss Guards remained to protect the king. Louis XVI and his family fled and took refuge with the Legislative Assembly. An hour later, a huge crowd spearheaded by National Guardsmen from Marseille, Brest, and the Théâtre-Français section stormed the palace, and killed almost all its remaining defenders.

Once assured of victory, the legislators suspended the king. Recognizing their own inability to manage affairs, the Legislative Assembly instead chose to disband. First, its members appointed a provisional Executive Council of six ministers. Next, they followed the Cordeliers' lead and abolished the distinction between active and passive citizens, giving all adult males the vote. Then the legislators called for elections to a National Convention that would take power as a governing parliament in September. Danton was elected overwhelmingly to be Minister of Justice. Marie-Jean-Antoine-Nicolas de Caritat, *philosophe* and former marquis de Condorcet, explained why he voted for Danton to join three Brissotin ministers in the transitional government: "We need a man who has the confidence of the people whose agitators have overturned the throne. I choose Danton, and I do not apologize. May his rise restrain the most despicable elements in a worthy, glorious and essential revolution."[35] Though he became indispensable "by the grace of cannon," his energy and audacity enabled Danton to dominate the new government emerging as de facto president of the council.[36]

The new minister made Desmoulins his chief administrative secretary. Rousselin performed the same service in confidential matters. Jules-François Paré, a longtime friend from collège in Troyes, became secretary of the council of ministers. Writing to his father, Desmoulins crowed, "Despite your prophesies that I will never accomplish anything, I have been elevated to the highest level for a man of our station." He concluded, "I believe that liberty has been strengthened by the revolution of 10 August. Now we must made France as happy and as flourishing as it is free. To that goal I will consecrate my watch."[37]

Many Cordeliers were dispatched to the provinces as emissaries, either of the Commune or of the Assembly, to explain the events of August. Marie-Jeanne, the wife of Brissotin minister Jean-Marie Roland and an important member of the group in her own right, described these envoys as "a swarm of unknown men, intriguers from the Sections, brawlers of the clubs, *patriotes* out of fanaticism, and even more out of self-interest, most of them with no livelihood except what they hoped to pick up from political agitation, but devoted to Danton their protector and imitators of his licentious habits and doctrines."[38] A second, more radical revolution had begun. New men with new goals and new methods were now in charge. Danton's patronage gave Rousselin high hopes of becoming an active participant in the great events of the day. Revolutions may run on paper, but secretaries generally do not see their deeds as measuring up to those of the heroes of the Roman republic.

Closer to home, Alexandre Rousselin had another heroic model of Enlightened principles in action to emulate. Early in 1789 his foster father, now known as Captain Laurent Corbeau, was transferred to Valence. The town had "six times as many unfortunates as usual" that hungry winter. Corbeau demonstrated an abiding concern for the destitute by working with the archbishop to arrange more charity and "provided an example with a very large [financial] sacrifice." Corbeau also "visited all the houses for the poor established by the clergy to see conditions for himself, and to provide help with discernment. He distributed food, firewood, or clothes depending on what a family needed."[39]

In 1791, Corbeau led a mission to prevent bloodshed between Catholics and Protestants in the Comtat Venaissin, a territory owned by the papacy. Pope Pius VI's condemnation of the Civil Constitution of the Clergy, which unilaterally established a constitutional church, deepened local enmities. Corbeau and a colleague sought to convince wavering communities to adhere to French law and reject the advances of "counter-revolutionaries." According to Corbeau, "reason can always be understood by the sound part of the people. Intrigue leads them astray only with difficulty because reason can always make them listen." The mission successfully defused the confrontation. Soon thereafter, Corbeau was elected president of Valence's Jacobin club.[40]

Once war began, Corbeau was given diplomatic duty by the commander of the Army of the Rhine, General Adam Philippe, comte de Custine. Corbeau's unenviable task was to convince the King of Prussia to leave the coalition facing France. He failed, but that did not dampen Rousselin's appreciation for the patriotism and Revolutionary sentiments of his foster father. He later wrote that Corbeau, "his closest relative," was "owed public recognition" as "a virtuous citizen" whose "simple and pure life was joined to a very Enlightened spirit capable of noble and elevated ideas." Rousselin celebrated that Corbeau "expressed ideas during his mission that were more extensive than his mandate" as worthy of emulation.[41] That Corbeau spent almost eighteen months in jail for his actions did not register with his adoring foster son.

Rousselin and his patrons experienced the initial stages of the French Revolution differently from most of its adherents. Their identification with the Cordeliers Club led the decisions and responses of Danton, Desmoulins, and Rousselin to reflect the priorities of the popular movement rather than the Jacobins. This crucial difference underscores the complex, and above all local framework in which the French Revolution was lived.

Danton's elevation to the position of Minister of Justice put his youthful confidential secretary close to the reins of power. Rousselin was not satisfied to be a secretary even to such an important figure as Danton. Although he clearly possessed a remarkable ability to get powerful men to trust him, he was no longer content to remain behind the scenes. Like his foster father, like Desmoulins, and like Danton, he wanted to act. And he wanted those actions to matter. That Rousselin, a man of many words, never wrote anything about himself that occurred before August 1792 is telling: the life he chose to remember began with the fall of the monarchy. Rousselin increasingly sought both power and the approbation of public opinion, though he was unsure how to get them. The next, more radical phase of the Revolution gave this ambitious young man his big break. For this young Revolutionary, it was indeed the best of times.

2

The Making of a Terrorist, 1792–1794

*The tocsin about to ring is not a signal of alarm: it sounds
the charge against the country's foes. To defeat them,
gentlemen, we must dare, and dare again, and go on
daring, and France will be saved!*

—GEORGES-JACQUES DANTON, September 2, 1792

THE OVERTHROW OF the monarchy on 10 August 1792, broke France's political moorings. Adrift, with no sure direction to navigate the dangerous shoals buffeting a nation at war, many French people reacted forcefully to uncertainty and fear. With the symbolic father's fall from grace, this band of brothers and sisters came to believe that violence was justified to secure the liberty promised by the Revolution. Since the taking of the Bastille in 1789, "the People" had repeatedly deployed force to claim and defend their rights. As popular sovereignty swelled in importance, Revolutionaries like Alexandre Rousselin recognized the essential place of the passions of the crowd. Some understood the role of the crowd as an expression of Rousseau's general will, while others focused pragmatically on the expediency of popular action. For radical republicans, the Revolution and all it represented was their lodestone. Its continuation was worth paying any price. In 1792–1794, this core belief led Rousselin and many of his contemporaries to develop and deploy violent means of protecting the Revolution. Simply put, that is why and how Rousselin became a terrorist.

When hostilities with Austria and Prussia broke out in April 1792, Rousselin was swept away by war fever. Like many young men inspired by the events of 1789, he was dedicated to defending the French nation. But not on the battlefield. Rousselin knew his talents ran in different directions. The France he wanted to protect would be run by talented commoners who had proven their leadership in the crucible of Revolutionary politics. His patriotism combined with a view of the main chance. The Revolution needed advocates like him: hard-working, fervent, and able. By demonstrating his

The Making of a Terrorist. Jeff Horn, Oxford University Press (2021). © Oxford University Press.
DOI: 10.1093/oso/9780197529928.001.0001

many qualities, the nineteen-year-old imagined himself earning public acclaim as one of France's greatest champions.

AS DANTON'S CONFIDENTIAL secretary, Rousselin witnessed the growing dedication to direct democracy practiced by the Cordeliers Club and their allies.[1] Much of the rhetoric articulated at the Jacobin Club supported this political stance. Rousselin became a Cordelier and an active participant in the Four Nations (later Unity) section (or ward) of Paris. The inhabitants of the city demanded popular sovereignty which encouraged the sections to become neighborhood councils that met regularly and took political positions on matters both great and small. The transition was driven by mounting discontent with the king's leadership and frustration over the course of the war. During the summer of 1792, the sections of Paris either received or seized the right to meet daily, to allow any citizen, not just those who paid more in taxes, to hold leadership positions and to control the deployment of its National Guard battalion. In Paris, the forty-eight sections emerged as rival institutions to the clubs, National Guard, and municipal administration. The personnel often overlapped, but the sections' symbolic claim to Rousseau's mantle, along with their ability to mobilize and direct a crowd, gave them a substantial presence in the politics of the capital.

The government's first tentative step toward a systematic use of fear and violence occurred in the aftermath of 10 August. As it had since 1789, the radical press heightened the public's anxieties. Constant warnings of "conspiracies" led by nobles or clergy who refused to take the oath to support the government inundated readers.[2] But the invective spewing from the quills of Jean-Paul Marat, Jacques-Réné Hébert, and Louis-Marie-Stanislaus Fréron, among a host of others, swelled after the fall of the king. Most of these rabble-rousing journalists championed popular sovereignty and were linked closely to the Cordeliers. On 17 August, the Legislative Assembly responded to growing public panic by establishing a special court to try political cases. The juries were elected by the sections. This court's judgments had no appeal and those found guilty were supposed to be guillotined immediately. The Paris Commune authorized a city-wide surveillance committee to seek out traitors to the Revolution and urged every section to create their own branch. The same institutional development occurred in most urban areas. Taken to placate Parisian public opinion, these measures became the institutional foundation of the emerging system of Terror.[3]

In September 1792, the tools of violence were wielded by unsteady hands. On 2 September, news reached Paris that forces commanded by the Duke of Brunswick, who had threatened to level the city if the royal family was hurt, had crossed the border in strength. Furious, terrified crowds in several radical sections supported by provincial National Guard contingents broke into several prisons and executed the inmates. Popular violence raged for five days. The government was both unable and unwilling to stop the killing. About 1,400 people died. Many of the victims were criminals, but 232 clergy who refused to take an oath to support the state were also killed, along with a number of Swiss Guards who had survived the assault on the Tuileries. Minister of Justice Danton stated, "Moderate measures of any kind are useless. The People's rage has peaked and would be dangerous to try and stop. Once its first fury is satisfied, we can get it to listen to reason." Paris' central surveillance committee published a circular asserting that the executions were "acts of justice that seem indispensable for halting, through terror, the legions of traitors hidden inside the walls. . . . The whole nation will hasten to adopt similar methods so necessary for public security."[4]

The war drove this rage and made it permissible. The Brunswick Manifesto intensified a long-standing fear of plots. An emotional response fueled by alarm over military defeats affected both the popular classes and elites. Anxiety about safety united both groups against a common enemy, but in such a way that their fears were mutually reinforcing. Without the imminent

FIGURE 2.1 The Massacres of 2–6 September 1792. Massacre à la prison de l'Abbaye du 2 au 6 septembre 1792, rue Sainte-Marguerite, actuels 137–166, boulevard Saint-Germain et rue Gozlin, 6ème arrondissement. Estampe des "Mémoires sur la Révolution". Musée Carnavalet G.28583.

threat of danger stemming from the war to propel ever more radical solutions to France's problems, it would have been impossible to create and maintain the political consensus that permitted the systematic use of violence against fellow citizens. War loosened social restraints: it made the inconceivable feasible. Without the war, there would have been no Terror.

Rousselin wrote his eyewitness account of the September Massacres in late 1794 when he was under constant threat of denunciation and prison. He discussed events in terms of Enlightenment philosophy, Roman history, and the events of 9 Thermidor, the coup against the faction led by Maximilien Robespierre in late July. He emphasized politics and not religion. Rousselin sought to settle scores and to justify the actions of his mentors, especially Danton. As for the rest of what people knew or thought they knew, Rousselin proposed to submit their views to "the guillotine of history" to identify the truth. The Massacres were "the work of some monsters." Only they were "responsible," claimed Rousselin, not "the People," and certainly not the Revolution itself. Despite the graphic intensity of the narrative, he argued that violence was intrinsic neither to popular action nor to democratic governments.

The French, "already republicans in spirit," feared that the overthrow of the monarchy on 10 August was "incomplete as long as so many nobles and clergy went unpunished." Deathly afraid of plots that threatened the Revolution, "the People of Paris" and National Guardsmen from Marseille and Brittany were determined to end the threat of "these accomplices of the tyrant" Louis XVI, wrote Rousselin. News from the frontier that the fortress of Verdun was besieged sparked the People's demand for "vengeance," which "spontaneously" spread across the city. Crowds shouted that "their cruelest enemies were not at Verdun, but rather in Paris, in the prisons." According to Rousselin, this response was "natural based on the circumstances," but "certain men . . . sought to profit from these feelings of terror to get the People to participate in a crime. That was how 'the ingenious invention' of prison conspiracies was born."

That soon-to-be bloody Sunday, Rousselin was at his National Guard post near the abbey of Saint-Germain-des-Prés, which had been turned into a prison. Around 2:30 p.m., he heard shouts. As a crowd swiftly gathered, four carriages arrived full of people arrested on suspicion of royalism. Initially, the group had been taken to the town hall to be interrogated by Jacques-Nicolas Billaud-Varennes, deputy public prosecutor, a former law clerk of Danton, but he sent them to the Abbey prison. As they got out of the carriage, one of the new inmates, inflamed by the jeering crowd, hit a National Guardsman from Marseille. "Furious, he drew his sword, jumped up on the footboard and plunged the blade three times into the heart of his attacker," Rousselin recounted. "I saw the blood spurt in huge bubbles. 'We should kill them all. They are villains, aristocrats,' screamed the crowd. The Guardsmen used their swords to cut the throats of the three companions of the one who had been sacrificed." The crowd lost control and slaughtered most of the newly arrested prisoners.

At five o'clock, Billaud-Varennes appeared. Dressed in a dark red outfit and black wig, he sauntered through the corpse-ridden courtyard and harangued the crowd: "People! You have destroyed your enemies. You have done your duty." Rousselin described this speech as "cannibal oratory." He asserted that Billaud-Varennes deliberately inflamed the crowd's passions, touching off a search for new victims. National Guard officer Stanislaus-Marie Maillard suggested, "There's nothing more to do here. We should go to the Carmes [prison]." After killing the prisoners there, Rousselin observed, "a group of slaughterers covered in blood and dust returned [to section headquarters next to the Abbey prison]. These monsters were *exhausted* by the carnage, but their *blood lust was not satisfied*. Breathlessly, they demanded *wine*: *wine* or death!" The civil committee of the Four Nations section hastily produced 24 pints seized from a nearby wine-seller. "Drunk, they contemplated with pleasure the corpses strewn about the courtyard," until Maillard again goaded them into action. He suggested establishing a "*fair* court." The crowd named him its president. He was aided by "a bunch of crooks" seemingly chosen in advance. The members of this "court" claimed that they were acting "in the name of the sovereign people" and that they had "received a secret mission from a higher authority." The crowd then forced its way inside the prison. Pushed by Maillard and his cronies, the commission began to try the Swiss Guards. After brief mock trials, each prisoner was, in turn, sentenced to "*la force*" and then murdered by the crowd. Prominent supporters of the king were brought before this court of public opinion and executed. The crowd roared its approval of this treatment of "the guilty" for their notorious "crimes." The "judges" robbed the victims before they died, seizing "wallets, watches, rings, diamonds, and cash. They put them in their pockets rather than in baskets or boxes," noted Rousselin. The commission adjourned at 2 a.m. on 3 September as "judges" followed the mob toward other prisons. Those who remained drank more and more. When they roused themselves from their drunken stupor later that morning, they murdered the remaining occupants of the Abbey prison without further ado.

Around noon on 3 September, Billaud-Varennes provoked the crowd once more. He promised everyone involved in purging the prisons an outrageous sum of 24 livres; that the section did not have the money bothered him not one bit. Rousselin set the scene as the killers demanded payment:

One came with a sword, another with a bloody bayonet, a third with a ruined pike covered with brains; another had pulled out a beating heart that he carried at the end of a broken halberd; yet another had cut off a man's virile parts which allowed him to make outrageous jokes to the women in the crowd. These were the trophies, the abominable justifications on which they based their menacing demands. "I cannot believe that I earned only 24 livres," said a journeyman baker, armed with a club. "I killed more than 40."

The crowd temporarily accepted that their pay would be delayed, so long as their participation in the events of 2 September was acknowledged and recorded. But they returned later and threatened the leaders of the section: "the money or your life." A wool merchant advanced half the funds to quiet the furor. With some cash in hand, the crowd dispersed until the next day when they successfully extorted the rest of the money from the central government.

With the benefit of hindsight, Rousselin identified three types of actors in the initial phases of the September Massacres. Those motivated by the "blind vengeance natural to the People" comprised one category. A second group was composed of "tigers," animals isolated from the People or even from mankind who had "an unquenchable thirst for blood." Finally, he distinguished "an order, a direction that was widely adopted." Having related what he had seen in gory detail, a clearly appalled Rousselin "allowed his reader to make judgments that the historian should not if he wishes to avoid suspicion of bias." The September Massacres were a harbinger of what was to come. The tone of the piece suggests that it was only in retrospect and after experiencing the Terror as both perpetrator and victim that Rousselin could deal with his anger and horror at the crowd's emotional reaction to fear. At the time, he was as swept away by the passions of the Revolution and the war as anyone else. Until the fall of 1794 Rousselin thought the Massacres necessary, though he regretted the slaughter of innocents. For young idealistic men like Rousselin, a willingness to accept the need for violence was essential to the practice of Terror.[5]

The September Massacres transformed public opinion. Public servants needed close ties to the centers of power. A struggle for authority, symbolic as well as real, was taking place at multiple levels, not all of which were visible to Rousselin or any other contemporary eyewitness. The inability of the central government to control the National Guard, the clubs, the sections, or the Commune so starkly revealed in September 1792 allowed these popular institutions to exercise tremendous authority in the capital and to drive government policy on many issues. At stake was the nature of the government to be formed in the aftermath of the destruction of the monarchy. Would the new regime be a direct democracy or a republic dominated by elites like the new United States of America? At the same time, different groups of politicians used an emotional appeal for further popular violence to win friends and influence people. Beginning later that month, the Brissotin or Girondin faction accused Danton and Marat, among others, of facilitating or at least permitting the Massacres. Another faction, increasingly referred to as the Mountain (*la Montagne*) or Montagnards, defended the role of the People as a reflection of the general will. The political free-for-all that followed shaped the course of the French Revolution.

During the September Massacres, Alexandre Rousselin held an official post for the first time. He was selected to be the secretary of the Four Nations section, presumably because of his close ties to Danton and experience as a private secretary. In that role, he was responsible both for inventorying the booty that his friends and neighbors looted during the slaughter and for paying inhabitants of the section to remove the cadavers of victims from nearby prisons. This grisly duty demonstrated Rousselin's growing notoriety and reputation for administrative competence.

A few weeks later, Danton resigned the ministry to take up the mantle of deputy in the legislature, the National Convention. First, Danton got Rousselin a job in the Ministry of the Interior. Unfortunately, no documentation regarding Rousselin's activities survives for the tumultuous time between September 1792 and April 1793. He may have been too busy working on behalf of Danton and the new government to record his thoughts. For many militants, the need to act overwhelmed the desire to reflect on the proclamation of the Republic, the trial and execution of Louis XVI, the rebellion in the Vendée region of western France, or the establishment of the Committee of Public Safety by the National Convention. Later, when he had the time and the emotional distance, Rousselin chose not to document what he had said and done during this critical period.

Regardless of what Rousselin thought, these events transformed French, European, and world politics. Establishing a democratic republic, charging Louis XVI with treason, and then executing the former king ratcheted up the stakes of political action. The Duke of Brunswick's threat of violence against civilians in Paris if Louis was harmed continued to reverberate. Guillotining Louis XVI brought several crowned heads of Europe into the fray. England, Spain, and the Netherlands joined the coalition against France, accentuating the military threat and thereby intensifying the domestic political crisis.

FOR MANY DEPUTIES in the National Convention and Parisian militants, the persistence of the Republic was tantamount to their own survival. They perceived anything or anyone who slowed or damaged the war effort as a fundamental threat. Fear of plots and conspiracies fanned by the radical press reached fever pitch after General Charles Dumouriez, closely allied with the Girondins, deserted to the Austrians in March 1793. In this atmosphere of violence and fear, possibilities for compromise and accommodation were increasingly ignored. Escalating conflict between Montagnards and Girondins brought to fever pitch in the crucible of war provided the context for Alexandre Rousselin's public political debut in the spring of 1793.

In one sense, factional rivalry between clusters of deputies known to history as Montagnards and Girondins propelled French politics in 1792–93. In the National Convention, competition between these factions focused on gaining support from the Plain, the largest, uncommitted group, who sat in the middle of the meeting hall. Outside that building, where the terms "Left" and "Right" first took on political meaning, a different kind of contest for authority occurred. Each faction sought to win the support of public opinion in the capital, which neither grouping ever fully channeled much less controlled. There was more than one "public" with multiple "opinions." But in the capital's Jacobins and Cordeliers clubs, in the sections, and in the National Guard units, the ideas and actions of Marat, Danton, and Maximilien Robespierre found the greatest favor.

Although Revolutionary rhetoric rarely matched the reality, the content of that rhetoric mattered to many French people, especially those willing to resort to violence.[6] The Republic was under threat and needed to defend itself, but it had the potential to be a paradise on earth. It might take time, but Robespierre sought to create a Republic of Virtue dominated by morality and equality. Robespierre shared this political vision not only with contemporaries like fellow member of the Convention Tom Paine, but also with a host of others inspired by Jean-Jacques Rousseau, like young Rousselin.

For that Republic of Virtue to materialize, the French republic had to survive the war. The French republic and "the People" were justified in resorting to radical measures to remove impediments, threats, and traitors. Robespierre later asserted that "Terror is nothing but prompt, severe, inflexible justice; it

is therefore an emanation of virtue. It is less a special principle than a conse-
quence of the general principle of democracy applied to our country's most
pressing needs."[7] Clearly, for those motivated by these long-term hopes and
short-term fears, this end justified those means.

An intellectualized, almost mythic notion of what the future might
hold did not always mesh with the more pragmatic demands of the mass of
"the People" of Paris. In 1792, the pressure on behalf of popular sovereignty
came partly from middle-class or elite politicians and writers who viewed
the French republic primarily through the lens of ancient history and the
Enlightenment. But they were not alone. Neighborhood activists who had
been engaged in the Revolution from the beginning became known as *sans-
culottes*. Literally meaning "without breeches," these radicals used dress to denote their different socioeconomic status. They did not have the leisure to
wear knee breeches or stockings; they worked with their hands and so wore
trousers. Many—probably most—sans-culottes were artisans or shopkeepers.
They ranged in status from the owners of large businesses to journeymen and
apprentices. The sans-culottes were not the urban poor, nor did they com-
prise the mob, but they could mobilize them on behalf of their goals. After
the overthrow of the monarchy, the appellation was applied to and sought
by workers or anyone else who championed the political role of "the People."
Anyone claiming to act on behalf of the general will had to take the needs
and emotions of the sans-culottes into account. Prominent in the sections,
the sans-culottes exerted considerable influence in most clubs, especially the
Cordeliers. Their support made and broke political careers. Many idealistic,
educated men like Rousselin identified with the sans-culottes. Not until the
spring of 1794 did educated elites fully understand the divergence in goals between those who sought popular sovereignty and others who hoped to create
a Republic of Virtue.

REPRESENTING THE UNITY section, Rousselin emerged as a leading voice
in Paris' popular movement. On 15 April 1793, he presented a petition from
thirty-five sections to the general council of the Paris Commune demanding
the ouster of twenty-two Girondin deputies from the National Convention.
Rousselin declared that the sections had the support of the "shared public
opinion of the entire department of Paris" in seeking "vengeance" against
"perfidious representatives" for their "crimes." The Girondin members of
the legislature had "sold the liberty and the dearest rights of the People" for
"money and lucrative positions" to their "accomplice," "the tyrant" Louis XVI,
who they tried to protect from the People's "justice" on 10 August. "Seeking

an offensive war," claimed Rousselin, the Girondins "displayed a false love of the [Republic's] laws in order to preach murder and assassination" by allying themselves with the traitorous general Dumouriez hoping to incite a "civil war." Enumerating the crimes of Jacques-Pierre Brissot, Pierre Vergniaud, Marguerite-Élie Guadet, and Antoine-Joseph Gorsas, the most influential of the twenty-two deputies, the petition demanded that the views of the sections of Paris "be communicated to all the departments . . . with a list of the majority of those representatives guilty of felonies against the sovereign people. As soon as the majority of the departments have given their support, these deputies will withdraw from the National Convention."[8] With this speech, Rousselin made a splashy debut on the central stage of Revolutionary politics.

The Girondins counterattacked by arresting Marat for inciting violence against them. Other militants including Hébert were also jailed. The Girondins convinced enough deputies to get the Convention to empower an extraordinary "Commission of Twelve" charged with containing popular agitation. While Montagnard deputies waffled, Parisian activists took matters into their own hands. Each section developed its own political stance. Some supported the Girondins, but most favored the Montagnards, with a few, like Unity, following the Cordeliers. Marat's acquittal by the Revolutionary Tribunal on 24 April, followed by Hébert's release from prison, emboldened delegates of the sections, the Commune, and the department of Paris to plot insurrection.

On 31 May, a Central Revolutionary Committee to which Rousselin was elected began to organize a coup against the Girondins. Across the city, the tocsin rang uninterrupted. To attract the hungry as well as the militant, the Commune promised to pay 40 sous (the daily wage of a Paris journeyman) to anyone who answered the call. National Guardsmen from radical sections commanded by François Hanriot surrounded the meeting hall of the National Convention as Rousselin delivered the Central Revolutionary Committee's demands to the legislature. Standing before the bar, he presented documents attesting to the legality of the sections' demands. To thunderous applause, Rousselin proclaimed that "the Spartans expressed themselves in few words, but they knew how to die for their liberty. Situated at the Thermopylae of the Republic, we, the People of Paris, also know how to die, but we will be avenged." He described the Commission of Twelve as "unjust, arbitrary, and despotic. It oppressed patriots by throwing them in irons hoping to slit their throats." In the name of "resistance to oppression," the sections petitioned that the Commission's members "should be sent before the Revolutionary Tribunal."[9]

How a twenty-year-old attained such an important position can be explained by a combination of Rousselin's ambition and ability and Danton's influence. The Commission's formulation of the "accusation against the liberticide faction" depended heavily on Rousselin, "who was known for having extensive knowledge on the subject" of the Girondins' misdeeds from his work in the Ministry of the Interior.[10] Several notable Revolutionary politicians asserted that the petition itself was written by Danton. Delivery by his young, almost unknown protégé gave him deniability and showed the breadth of opposition to the Girondins. The petition occasioned much debate but did not convince the deputies to act.

The Convention and the Committee of Public Safety sought to build consensus before taking action against the Girondins. On 1 June, the Commune forced the pace. It raised the incentive for armed citizens to show up to 6 livres (the daily wage of a successful master artisan) to maximize the weight of popular pressure. The next day, intimidated by the vengeful crowd that filled its meeting room, the National Convention voted to arrest twenty-nine deputies and two former ministers. The popular movement temporarily demobilized,

LE 31 MAY 1793.

FIGURE 2.2 31 May, 1793. Getty Research Institute, Prints of the French Revolution, 1774–ca. 1840.

but in the uncertain aftermath of these events, a number of the arrested deputies escaped.

The fall of the Girondins put the Montagnards in the driver's seat, a difficult and dangerous place to be in the summer of 1793. The value of the currency was in free fall, a rebellion erupted in western France centered on the Vendée, and war raged on every frontier. In emotional terms, the war, more than any other factor, goaded the Montagnards to act. Challenged by a militant popular movement in the capital, the leaders of the Montagnards were in an almost impossible position with few resources at their command.

That nearly unmanageable situation soon got far worse. The escaped deputies aggravated unrest in the cities of Bordeaux, Caen, Lyon, Marseille, and Toulon, provoking rebellions against the government in Paris. The leaders of this Federalist Revolt were dedicated republicans and Revolutionaries; they just had a different sense of who should hold the reins of power. Endorsing the North American model, the rebels wanted to lessen the political voice of the popular movement in Paris in favor of establishing a "federal republic" with weak centralized authority. This insurrection threatened the hegemony of the capital and the influence of the sans-culottes. With the army in tatters and fully deployed against invaders, the revolts could not be quickly quashed. From April to December 1793, civil war between republicans diverted resources from, and thus endangered, the military effort against France's foreign enemies.

The Federalist Revolt accentuated Paris' paranoia about conspiracies and potential threats to the war effort. It profoundly deepened the Revolutionary crisis by challenging the legitimacy of the Republic's leadership. Pressure on the central government to resort to extreme methods reached new heights.

At the time, Rousselin certainly said the right things about the Girondins' "treason" and the need for harsh methods to defend the role of "the People" in French politics. In a speech justifying the coup against Brissot and his friends given later that summer, he told his audience of sans-culottes, "Make no mistake, during a Revolution a moderate is always a traitor."[11] But it is worth remembering that the initial petition sought the "withdrawal" of the Girondin deputies, not their arrest nor their judgment by the Revolutionary Tribunal. Danton eventually came to regret that the Convention allowed itself to be swept along by the popular movement to move against the Girondins undermining the immunity of the legislators and opening the way for further purges. Rousselin too later came to the same conclusions (see chapter 6).

In the short term, however, for Rousselin, the fruits of Revolutionary action in the spring of 1793 were sweet. Whether he wrote the petition or not, he reaped the rewards of delivering it. To reflect his greater status, Rousselin was promoted from clerk to division chief, with increased responsibility in the Ministry of the Interior. He held this important administrative position for about two months before taking over coordinating the reports of Paris' police spies in mid-August. Rousselin preferred this post which gave him access to secret knowledge, and therefore power, at a time when paranoia ran amok.

SOON, A NEW opportunity came Rousselin's way when the Committee of Public Safety decided to take a more active role in shaping public opinion. To support the war effort, the Committee sought to correct the slanders and libels of "the multitude of counter-revolutionary newspapers as well as those papers that are inaccurate or insignificant." With a quote from Rousseau displayed just below the masthead, the *Journal of Public Safety*, a "republican newspaper," appeared on 3 August 1793.[12] The Committee gave editorial direction to Dominique-Joseph Garat, the Minister of the Interior, and Rousselin. Garat wrote the prospectus, but daily management fell to Rousselin. The *Journal of Public Safety* rejected factionalism. The prospectus declared: "Our party will be the Republic. We will try to save the People from idolatry, from selfishness, and from the scourge of destroyers of liberty by removing them from the French character."[13] Such emotional rhetoric marked contemporary public discourse and showed why compromise and moderation were so difficult to achieve.

The responsibility for editing a daily newspaper subsidized and distributed by the Committee of Public Safety demonstrated Rousselin's rapid ascent. After Garat was denounced and replaced as minister by Jules-François Paré, another of Danton's cronies, Rousselin's influence grew greater still. He pushed for the state to print 3,500 copies of "his" speech on 31 May for distribution to "National Guardsmen and Jacobins." Journalism also provided a financial windfall. Along with 300 livres a month in salary, plus expenses, Rousselin received considerable sums allocated as "incentives for patriot writers" to fight counter-revolutionaries. These funds significantly raised Rousselin's income, though his post as a division chief in the ministry paid a hefty annual salary of 8,000 livres. Despite formally giving up editorship of the journal in September, he retained control over its political direction—and continued to be paid—until the end of 1793. Rousselin resumed editing the paper in April 1794.[14]

Journalism merged Rousselin's literary pretentions as well as his search for political influence. Early in September, he panned both the acting troupe and a production of Revolutionary politician Nicolas-Louis François de Neufchâteau's play *Pamela* at the French national theater for being pro-English, pro-aristocratic, and pro-royalist. Rousselin's withering review reflected a common view among radicals that the government needed to act decisively. The National Convention's discussion of a deliberate policy of Terror occurred three days later.[15] The review censured the couplet, "Ah, persecutors are the most reprehensible/And the most tolerant are the most reasonable" as criticizing the government. Commenting that "the national theater provides a new rallying point for lackeys of the aristocracy disguised as honest men," amidst a "room filled with women who displayed a truly monarchial luxury," Rousselin demanded that "this seraglio be closed forever!" and replaced by a "club for suburban sans-culottes." The actors should be imprisoned until the return of peace, he believed. The review caused a public outcry compelling the legislature to act. On 3 September, the actors and playwright were arrested, albeit briefly, and the theater closed. In the Jacobin Club, Rousselin fanned the flames. He asserted that by letting the actors go free, the National Convention's Committee of General Security (which oversaw police matters) was being too lax.[16] The actors were arrested once more and remained imprisoned for over a year.

Denouncing opponents in the press or in the clubs was an increasingly effective means of achieving political goals. The ambition to build "republican spirit" by condemning "enemies of the state" fueled Rousselin's next public foray. After Danton gave a series of speeches in the Convention attacking the nobility, Rousselin anonymously published a collection of "original correspondence" by émigré nobles that vindicated the overthrow of the monarchy and all the measures taken against nobles and royalists. Readers, claimed Rousselin, would "see the true authors of our troubles. They would also understand that what some call crimes, saved the Republic." Émigrés "will reap the vengeance of genuine Republicans."[17] This book provided the raw material for many emotional articles in the *Journal of Public Safety*. A number of impassioned diatribes in the Unity section by Rousselin among others were printed to stoke the public's anger at "traitorous aristocrats."

Like his contemporaries, Rousselin recognized the importance of political symbols.[18] He gave two well-publicized patriotic speeches memorializing "martyrs of liberty." The assassinations of Louis-Michel Lepelletier in January 1793 and then Marat in July by Charlotte Corday roiled public opinion. To capitalize on public anger, various groups commissioned busts of the two martyrs to display in public meeting halls. Even more tragic than these two murders, said Rousselin, was the heroic death of Joseph Bara, a thirteen-year-old Republican "drummer boy" in battle against counter-revolutionaries in

FIGURE 2.3 Maryrs de la liberté: Le Peletier, Marat, and Chalier [ca. 1794]. Getty Research Institute, Prints of the French Revolution, 1774–ca. 1840.

the Vendée. While honoring the martyrs, he reminded his audience that greater sacrifices were needed to preserve the French nation from its enemies. To justify his claims, Rousselin asserted: "Jean-Jacques Rousseau dared to speak the truth. Jean-Paul Marat applied it. Through love of the People, the love of truth was revealed. He began a second, more dangerous, more useful evangelism that surpassed his model. He proposed to execute what his predecessor concluded." For Rousselin, demonstrating philosophic principles helped make a Revolution, but the implementation of ideas was even more honorable.[19]

A third published speech focused on the measures needed to preserve the Republic. Rousselin stated: "The constitution has my special devotion because it . . . is a powerful weapon in our hands against the aristocracy. At birth, our constitution depends on the 'revolutionary methods' that brought it into being." "Vengeance," he declared, "is the sister of liberty." But vengeance could not be just an expression of popular frustration and anger, it had to be for the right reasons, because "tyrants have a legion of docile assassins while 25 million free men in the Republic are still waiting for their Brutus." Despite real concerns about his safety and that of the city he loved, Alexandre Rousselin aimed to be Brutus, a virtuous man, a "friend of the People," who was willing to kill a friend in defense of the Republic.[20]

To fulfill his goals, Rousselin developed a finely honed ability to sense the prevailing political wind. That skill is vital to almost every politician, but the hothouse atmosphere of Paris during the French Revolution made it even more essential. How did a young man with his ear to the ground make such judgments? Meetings of his section, service in its National Guard, regular attendance at the Cordeliers Club, and occasional (though ever more frequent) appearances at the Jacobins provided constant input. He heard what people were saying about key figures and which issues of the day mattered most. Handling the correspondence for a major metropolitan newspaper, as he had done for Desmoulins and was now doing for the *Journal of Public Safety*, also supplied insight. Letters from distributors, subscribers, and readers contained their reaction to events and their coverage in the press. Coordinating the reports of the network of police spies in the Ministry of the Interior afforded a daily snapshot of what was happening across the city from the perspective of those charged with keeping the peace. Police spies paid particular attention to militants as they were the people most likely to act on their views. Thus, Rousselin was one of the best informed people in the capital, but his perspective was shaped by the popular movement. Small wonder, then, that he prioritized the desires of the sans-culottes and their articulation of the general will. In 1793–94, this well-educated activist viewed politics from below. His multiple institutional ties helped him judge who was behind public opinion, who was ahead, and who represented the People. That outlook enabled him to gain a position of power, but when the wind blew from a different quarter, that outlook on public opinion worked against him.

FOR ACTIVISTS LIKE Rousselin, the depth of the Revolutionary crisis required greater sacrifices by the entire French people, not just Parisians. Military demand for grain, horses, metal, gunpowder, money, and recruits had to be met. Persistent fears of aristocratic plots combined with Enlightenment anti-clericalism to make nobles and clergy almost automatically suspect. The National Convention dispatched numerous representatives on mission with extensive powers to the armies and to the provinces to deal with these concerns. Anxiety about treason and alarm over meager results from these missions led the Committee of Public Safety to send civil commissioners to watch the watchers. In the eyes of the men who directed the Revolution, Rousselin's political activities and administrative experience qualified him for this sensitive job.

On 1 October 1793, the Committee of Public Safety ordered the Minister of the Interior to send two commissioners to Provins, the administrative center of the Seine-et-Marne department, about 60 miles southeast of Paris. Their primary objective was to "requisition all grain and flour in the city" and the wagons to transport them to the capital. Provins was permitted to keep only a week's supply. The pressure to feed Paris was so great that the commissioners were given authority to "suspend administrators who opposed that measure." After consultation with the popular society, quasi-official clubs affiliated with the Jacobins of Paris that existed in most provincial urban areas, the commissioners could also replace officials provisionally with "zealous and Enlightened sans-culottes." To ensure that the food left Provins, the commissioners were given command of an armed detachment of Parisians, known as the "Revolutionary Army," already in the district.[21] Minister Paré, supported by member of the Committee Bertrand Barère, chose Rousselin. For this young man, the mission evoked Laurent Corbeau's successful 1791 mediation between Jacobin groups in the southeast. Success on this mission would please all the father figures in Rousselin's life.[22]

A rich wheat-growing area, the Seine-et-Marne faced famine because so much grain had been requisitioned to feed Paris and the Army of the Ardennes. Among the astonishing 11,000 men from the department who joined the army were several battalions of young volunteers. Without the muscle and popular support provided by these militants, local administrators struggled to enforce unpopular measures such as the appropriation of gold and silver from Roman Catholic churches. The dispatch of a large number of suspects to Paris to be judged by the Revolutionary Tribunal troubled many. The suspects ranged from ancien régime nobles to stalwart activists from 1789. A deep enmity between the Jacobin clubs of Provins and Melun, the department's largest towns, made a Federalist revolt a distinct possibility. Widespread food rioting and the ravages of brigands further destabilized the situation. That a representative on mission had been on the ground since mid-July signaled how unsettled the region was in the fall of 1793.

The Committee of Public Safety was dissatisfied with the management of affairs. Nicolas Maure and Pierre Dubouchet had been sent to get the departments of the Seine-et-Marne and Loiret to requisition grain in mid-July 1793 following up an unsatisfactory earlier mission in March. Maure spent only a few days in the Seine-et-Marne, but Dubouchet stayed for nearly three months. Born in 1737, Dr. Pierre Dubouchet was from Montbrison and represented an older generation of militant. Aligned with the Mountain, he voted to execute Louis XVI. He and Maure were deeply concerned about public spirit and the way "good sans-culottes" were being oppressed. Dubouchet reported that "in a number of places, if you show yourself to be a patriot, you will be denounced, menaced, mistreated, and even incarcerated" by "rich farmers, property-owners, former nobles and lords allied with priests to enslave and lead people in the countryside astray." Even before the Convention passed the Law on Suspects, on 15 September, Dubouchet began putting sans-culottes in charge. He gave Melun's surveillance committee oversight of the entire district and delegated extensive police power to three agents to ensure the victory of the faction supporting the Montagnards in the department's other districts. These "victories of the People" occurred just as the imprisoned Girondins were sent to the Revolutionary Tribunal on 3 October.

Dubouchet and his proxies replaced dozens of local administrators to forestall "counter-revolutionary plots." Revolutionary committees were created in several towns to enforce unpopular laws, especially the newly passed "General Maximum," which established wage and price controls. Serious shortfalls in the supplies sent to troops from the Seine-et-Marne who were fighting in the Vendée led Dubouchet and his men to accelerate their political purge. Moderates were replaced with the area's few radicals. Dubouchet also "invited" rich citizens to make a "patriotic contribution" to support indigent parents of soldiers serving at the front. Such measures spawned angry denunciations of the representative and his agents to authorities in Paris. Rousselin's mission was Paris' response.[23]

According to Dubouchet, Rousselin's arrival made quite a splash. He and Edme Fauchon, the other commissioner, came "in a carriage drawn by six horses." Rousselin was "accompanied by a whore, for his 'low pleasures.'" Dubouchet complained that "the commissioners had the authority to suspend and fire public officials independently of the People's representatives, rivaling the powers given by the National Convention to its own deputies, demonstrating . . . thoughtlessness by the Minister of the Interior." Since he and his colleagues had already conducted a political purge and dealt with the supply issue, Dubouchet simply did not understand the need for civil commissioners. He was "astonished" that Rousselin was "immediately surrounded by numerous guards. We [other public servants], good sans-culottes, shielded by our great and noble characters and invested with immense authority, have no need of a praetorian guard. We are protected by the affection of our brothers." As a final dig, he noted that Rousselin dined in splendor with a sort of "Asiatic pomp" while patriots went hungry.[24]

Rousselin had to respond to this "slander." In the *Journal of Public Safety*, he explained that his carriage had four horses and that they had taken a carriage only because they were "commanded to depart instantly." Rousselin defended the virtue of "a woman who I can affirm is honest" and asserted that the women of Provins were more endangered by Dubouchet's denunciations than his actions. The commissioners and a few notables ate with their innkeeper and his family for two livres a meal. His guards were fed for 40 *sous* each, which was "hardly scandalous" (though still expensive for the region), while Dubouchet ate "alone with his secretary and secret guests. Every day, an honor guard stood outside the door to the dining room as is done in Austria and used to be done at Versailles." Through manipulation of such seemingly minor symbols denoting social class were reputations made and lost during the Terror.[25]

Dubouchet and Rousselin engaged in a kind of one-upsmanship contest of radical rhetoric. Both publicly encouraged the practice of denunciation as necessary to maintaining public spirit. A steady stream of accusations also ensured that sans-culottes remained in charge. For the first time, however, Rousselin had the power to do more than just talk. This was the opportunity he had waited for. In Provins, he put his Enlightenment principles into practice while maneuvering for political advantage.

Soon after arrival Rousselin decided that the local officials appointed just weeks before by Dubouchet were neither sufficiently energetic nor good sans-culottes. He tried to fire them but ran afoul of the representative. Dubouchet's appointees continued to hold sway at the district level, but Rousselin's took over the municipality, Jacobin Club, and National Guard. In the Seine-et-Marne, conflicting orders from legitimate authorities sowed confusion, fostered faction fighting, and slowed the pace of acquiring and shipping grain to Paris.

Rousselin recognized that inculcating Revolutionary spirit went beyond the necessities of food procurement. Lingering signs of feudalism were, to Rousselin, an affront to the Republic. Silverware embossed with the arms of former feudal lords was seized. Coats of arms were removed from buildings, statues, and any other public place and replaced with the tricolored flag of the

Republic. When told about a man who had been clapped in irons for twenty-four hours in the dead of winter for having killed a partridge on a noble's land, Rousselin angrily recommended, "the implementation of the law of 'an eye for an eye.' All those former privileged found guilty [of such behavior] should be punished the same way." Whenever possible, Rousselin recalled the example of Brutus. At the same time, he emphasized Marat's maxim that "publicity is the safeguard of the People." He worked to "ennoble denunciation" to protect the rights of the People whom the "aristocracy" sought to destroy by turning them into slaves. Only by executing the Republic's laws and mandates, said Rousselin, could the inhabitants of Provins escape their past oppression.[26]

Dechristianization was an important part of the sans-culotte agenda in the fall of 1793.[27] In Provins, the popular society agreed wholeheartedly with Rousselin on the need to eliminate the remaining influence of the Roman Catholic Church, especially its clergy. Rousselin stage-managed impressive pageants intended to stimulate Revolutionary spirit.[28] When he learned that the popular society could not get a bust of Marat for its meeting hall, Rousselin had one sent from Paris. Getting carried away by his subject and perhaps on a bit of a power trip, Rousselin proclaimed that this martyr to liberty was the only one they should worship. At the dedication ceremony, Citizen Pichon, a former parish priest, was permitted to address the crowd. This was surprising because he had been turned down for the "civic certificate" from the popular society required to stay off the official list of suspects. In dramatic fashion, Pichon repudiated his status by handing over his priestly credentials to be burned. Other "memories of feudalism" were also fed to the flames. Pichon claimed that during his years as clergy, "in giving himself to the worship of altars, he had been in a state of stupor and sloth." To hearty sans-culotte applause, Pichon received his certificate and was allowed to rejoin the popular society. Another former parish priest named Letondeur abjured the priesthood that same day. Rousselin later lauded the "Revolutionary philosophy found among the sans-culottes of Provins . . . because the instant that priests are no longer paid, they will no longer exist, while the Republic will." In combination with the seizure of precious metals from the Seine-et-Marne's churches, it was impossible for the anxious local population to miss the anti-clerical, anti-religious message. Contemporaries noted the quickening pace of denunciations against nobles and clergy. In Rousselin, Provins' young radicals and Parisian soldiers in the Revolutionary Army found a role model, a protector, and a spur to action.[29]

That Rousselin exceeded his authority in Provins so greatly suggests that he assumed it to be his duty, perhaps based on the model of his foster father.

At the same time, his actions indicated a deep-seated belief that to succeed, the Revolutionaries had to do more than just mobilize sufficient men and munitions to defend the Republic. His behavior implied a supposition that the Revolution had to change hearts and minds to build a true consensus on how France should be organized and governed. For Alexandre Rousselin, to accomplish the straightforward aspects of his mission required inculcating a profound shift in Provins' political culture. In the heat of the moment, he could not and did not try to separate practical politics from the ideological imperatives proposed in Paris. Rousselin justified implementing the Terror as both legitimate and necessary.

After fewer than ten days in Provins, frustrated by losing many battles with Dubouchet, Rousselin returned to Paris. He went straight to the Jacobin Club, where he passionately denounced the representative on mission as a "disruptor" and then claimed all the credit for the successes of Revolutionary government in the Seine-et-Marne. The denunciation failed to gain traction because a friend of Dubouchet's read a letter from him rebutting the charges. A thoroughly unflattering description of Rousselin's actions from the straightlaced Dubouchet did not help the young man's case. Rousselin tried again in the *Journal of Public Safety*. He accused Dubouchet of "paralyzing the special mission entrusted to him" and of "assuming a dictatorship over releasing prisoners." The paper framed the issue in general terms:

> This denunciation raises the very serious question of whether a representative of the people by himself has the right to oppose a formal, calmly deliberated resolution of the executive council. Can that same representative arbitrarily and capriciously annul the Revolutionary actions undertaken by purified [surveillance] committees which only royalists wish to undermine?

In this contest for authority, Rousselin defended the executive and local "purified" committees against the "arbitrary" actions of a member of the legislature. Swift, energetic action to overawe and intimidate "royalists" and "moderates" was the only way to prosecute the war and save the Republic. Despite Rousselin's best efforts and tangible support for his allegations from a delegation of Provins' popular society, Dubouchet retained the National Convention's support. The deputy remained in the Seine-et-Marne until the end of the month.[30]

Rousselin crossed a line in October 1793. He went beyond radical rhetoric, local activism, and facilitating the plans and policies of his patrons. In

Provins, he evolved from a Revolutionary into a terrorist. He became a true "missionary of the Republic," a weapon in the hands of the government.[31]

THE REVOLUTIONARY LEADERSHIP wasted little time in deploying its new asset. On the surface, sending Rousselin on another mission made little sense given his public clash with Dubouchet and his unsuccessful denunciation of the representative. Clearly, however, Rousselin possessed unusual energy and was attentive to public spirit. A deputation from the popular society of Provins enthusiastically "praised his conduct" for "electrifying republican hearts with the liveliest sentiments of liberty." Based on his ability to excite these feelings, his powerful patrons, Barère, Danton, and Paré, chose Rousselin for an undertaking well-suited to his youthful zeal. On 5 November, the Committee of Public Safety decided to send a civil commissioner to Troyes, administrative center of the department of the Aube, "with all powers necessary to renew the constituted authorities, stop any malevolence, reestablish public spirit in the city, and bring it to the height of the Revolution." Two-hundred men of the Revolutionary Army were to accompany the civil commissioner and remain in Troyes as long as necessary. On 10 November, Rousselin was officially named to the post.[32]

Barère and Danton, who had been born and raised in the Aube, knew they were sending Rousselin into a hornet's nest. About 100 miles southeast of Paris, this department was close to the military frontier and was an important transportation and supply hub for the Army of the Ardennes. Troyes, an important textile manufacturing center, had thousands of unemployed workers. Raw material shortages and destabilized markets wounded the local economy. The entire region was considered a royalist stronghold. Only a handful of other departments were visited by so many representatives on mission (7) and civil commissioners (2) in the 23 months between the declaration of the Republic and the fall of Robespierre. Every one of these agents of central authority was frustrated by a populace profoundly divided along urban-rural lines. Committed republicans (usually referred to as sans-culottes) concentrated in Troyes were overmatched by more conservative rural elites who dominated the higher reaches of local administration. Radical measures that seemed to be so necessary in Paris did not seem pressing to the Aubois.

Rousselin's mission to Troyes reprised an earlier visit by Joseph Fouché, deputy of the Loire-Inférieure and soon-to-be notorious "butcher of Lyon," in June and July 1793. Two previous representatives on mission had limited success finding men for the army, prompting the Committee of Public Safety to send Fouché to "excite the patriotism of the citizens" and enroll volunteers to fight in the Vendée. Fouché expressed satisfaction with stepped up recruitment by the departmental administrators but hinted that they only behaved appropriately because he was looking over their shoulders. Luckily, the Aube did not merit the version of state-sponsored Terror that this dedicated Revolutionary unleashed on Lyon.

The Law on Suspects gave Troyes' sans-culottes a path to power. Revolutionary politics circumvented the demographic weight of the rural population. The surveillance committees of the eight sections formed a "central committee" that soon dominated the city. A "sans-culotte mayor," former teacher François Gachez, was duly elected. While passing through on mission to a neighboring department, deputy Antoine-Marie-Charles Garnier of the Aube formed a Revolutionary Committee of 12 for the district of Troyes and subordinated all other local authorities to it. This institutional end-run was deeply unpopular with departmental elites who, in protest, angrily brought the work of government to a standstill. Neither the apparent craving of many members of the Revolutionary Committee for high-salaried government jobs nor the imposition of several anti-clerical measures won them any supporters. In October 1793, the members of the Revolutionary Committee of 12 requested help from Paris to support the war effort. Rousselin was their only hope of staying in power.

On 15 November, the civil commissioner arrived in Troyes accompanied by only a few men, the bulk of the detachment of the Revolutionary Army did not appear until almost three weeks later. Rousselin immediately prepared a purge of local administration. As in Provins, he did not bother to find out about local conditions or the people involved, he wanted to change things immediately. The chief qualifications for public service were socioeconomic position and public adherence to a Rousseauist-Republican ideology. From the start, Rousselin confidently set out to implement a radical program. He claimed "to be the faithful mouthpiece of the People's will, and nothing more."[33] His actions in Provins hinted at what was to come. But in Troyes, Rousselin was no longer constrained by the presence of a representative on mission. Revolutionary measures would reshape public spirit in the Aube, one way or another.

Anti-clericalism and inversion of the social order were at the top of Rousselin's lengthy agenda. He immediately proclaimed the "suspension and suppression of all priestly functions." On behalf of hungry sans-culottes, Rousselin intended to "procure the means of existence for the poor by levying a tax on the rich" tied to the forced loan mandated by the National Convention on 3 September. He ordered the Revolutionary Committee to compile an initial list of royalist "fanatics." Seven suspects—all prominent local figures active during the early years of the Revolution—were jailed immediately. Their papers were seized to find evidence of "treasonous actions." Alexis Lerouge, a former judge, was imprisoned because "he consistently and effectively avoided [walking past] important Revolutionary sites," while solicitor Bonaventure-Jean-Baptiste Millard was charged with giving ammunition to royalist army deserters. Sans-culottes were encouraged to denounce "the rich of all classes." This mandate let people act out their social resentments and petty jealousies. The sections' surveillance committees were told to gather either damning or exculpatory "information on moderates, royalists, monopolists, especially former nobles" within twenty-four hours. "Without clearance from these committees," said Rousselin, "in my eyes, these men will be suspects."

On 29 November, Troyes' Revolutionary Committee, prodded by Rousselin, decided to jail "persons suspected of aristocracy, moderation, or actions contrary to the principles of the Revolution." But recognizing that adding to the eighty-three already incarcerated was, perhaps, too harsh for those who were guilty only of "negligence or bad faith," the Committee took advantage of the Law on Suspects to come up with an alternative: 206 were issued "red cards," which put them "under the surveillance of all good and true sans-culottes." Social inversion greatly increased the bitterness of the rich without providing much help to the sans-culottes. In the Aube, the climate of fear and suspicion fostered by Revolutionary government accentuated divides between rich and poor, urban and rural, radical and moderate that had been present since 1789.[34]

Charles-Antoine Nicolas, formerly comte de Lamotte-Valois, was a notorious symbol of the corruption of the old régime. His wife had been implicated in the Diamond Necklace Affair, an infamous incident in the mid-1780s involving Queen Marie-Antoinette and a Roman Catholic prince of the Church that revealed the depravity and venality of court life and helped to undermine faith in the monarchy.[35] Although condemned to a lifetime sentence rowing galleys, Lamotte-Valois had been freed with the Revolution. He was living quietly in Bar-sur-Aube when Rousselin issued a warrant for his arrest on 5 December 1793.

Four members of Bar-sur-Aube's surveillance committee and a policeman oversaw the arrest. The officials conducted an "exacting search, opening all the armoires and cupboards." The contents were brought into one room where a justice of the peace sealed them. Fleury and Charles Codant, officers of the Revolutionary Army, "put all the valuables, silver, and jewels in their pockets." Lamotte-Valois claimed that they also "stole a beautiful sewing kit with English implements, a very pretty knife embossed with gold, an expensive pair of pistols with silver engraving, a sack of gunpowder, two fine razors in a leather case, and a valuable pair of scissors," all of which were "subtracted from the goods under seal." The officers asked if Lamotte-Valois had a gold pocket watch. When he said it had been sold, Fleury "had the audacity to stick a hand into his vest to check." Before leaving, the officers took a double-barreled hunting rifle and a sword. On "the pretext that they were suitable for the military," they also appropriated several horses and took them to the nearby army depot. Lamotte-Valois spent almost a year imprisoned in Troyes. He never recovered the property taken from him during his arrest, though he made several attempts to take his revenge for the thefts and humiliation.[36]

The militancy of Rousselin's mission intensified after a whirlwind overnight visit by Danton. On 18 November, he and his family arrived in Troyes. After a long, private talk, Danton dined with his protégé and a few cronies. The next morning, several eyewitnesses later attested that Danton responded to a rumor about events in his hometown: "If I have time to return to Arcis, I will guillotine several people."[37] That same day, Rousselin ordered Troyes' churches closed. With his patron's support he inaugurated a new, more radical phase of the Terror in the department of the Aube. At the same time, Rousselin disbursed (or, more probably, passed along) a great deal of money to several of Danton's friends and relatives, all former priests. The irony was not lost on contemporaries.

Rousselin justified the use of state-sponsored violence in terms of both tactics and strategy. "Taken together, energy and speed assure the success of Revolutionary measures," he stated. "My invariable principle was to use force only against aristocrats, but the threat of force is often necessary to open the eyes of an abused people seduced by malicious intent." Radical methods were required to ferret out "traitors" and to "wake the administrators of the department of the Aube from their profound lethargy, their moderation, and their stagnant practices." With the unconscious condescension of a Parisian, Rousselin opined that the problem was an innate cultural conservatism: "I do not know whether to attribute the department of the Aube's slow and late steps in implementing Revolutionary measures to the nature of its people or to the climate." To overcome these handicaps and accomplish his mission, Rousselin was willing to employ extreme measures.[38]

As in Provins, Rousselin, with local help, orchestrated a series of public displays of anti-clericalism. An address to his "Revolutionary brothers" in the sections emphasized that "priests removed according to the People's wishes" must find employment. He commanded that "exterior signs of evangelism like the mass be replaced by explanations of the rights of man and the Republican catechism. Those who sing songs other than those of liberty will no longer be allowed to sing in public." To attract people to an extraordinary gathering in the enormous gothic cathedral of St. Pierre-St. Paul, Rousselin recruited trumpet players and drummers to parade through the streets announcing the meeting. The spectacle drew 8,000 people. After introductions, he pressed Auguste Sibille, the former constitutional bishop of the department, to come forward. To avoid denunciation, Sibille renounced his clerical status after forty-five years as a priest. Then a pair of Troyes parish priests was thrust into the nave, which was packed to the rafters with sans-culottes. The priests were told that "instead of performing their normal functions, they should combat obstruction of Revolutionary administration by giving political speeches. They must make every effort to destroy the fanaticism infecting Troyes to strengthen the Republic and improve happiness and peace in the city." The duo loudly promised to "do everything in their power to rouse Republican spirit." They also acknowledged, albeit unhappily, that they would be more effective if they abjured the clergy.[39]

At that moment, a large deputation from the parish of St. Remy arrived to support their beleaguered priest. They lauded his patriotism and wanted him to resume saying mass. The group's spokesman defended their request as protected by the constitution, which safeguarded an individual's right "to perform their job." The parish was upset that Revolutionary sentiment in the city had already led the priest to suspend religious services. They had been afraid to complain because they feared denunciation both individually and collectively.

Rousselin backpedaled. He stated that "it was never anyone's intention to stop the priest of St. Remy" from saying mass. Rather, "the priest himself had raised the question of whether to continue." "Priests are allowed to say mass," said Rousselin, "and those who wish to attend may do so on the *décadi* [the festival day of the ten-day-long Republican week]." But shops and businesses could close only on that day, not on the "former Sunday," he insisted. "Religious freedom," asserted the civil commissioner, "consists of not favoring any faith exclusively, since liberty is the only faith recognized by the Nation." A few minutes later, "the vicars of the parish of St. Pierre entered and attested that they were entirely devoted to the public good. They were willing to make all possible sacrifices, but they remained faithful to their religious opinions." The delegation was interrupted by Paul-François Bramand, the charismatic priest of St. Pantaleon, who "spoke in Republican terms." Bramand asked the gathered sans-culottes whether France should continue to have priests. The throng shouted back, "No! No more priests! No more skullcaps! Long live the Republic!" A group of women inquired if they could speak. When given permission, they repeated the same slogans to show the unanimity of the People. Rousselin then stated that "to respond in advance to malevolent slanders," such a momentous decision had to be made calmly. A vote must to be taken. Almost unanimously, the crowd raised their hands to affirm that the municipality would "no longer recognize" and "no longer pay" clerical salaries. The cathedral was officially renamed the temple of reason. Troyes' churches were closed definitively and given over to other functions.[40]

On 5 December, Rousselin issued new orders. Because of the confusion that might result from "a competition between divinities" after the erection of a "statue of liberty" in front of the temple of reason, "alterations" must be made to the former cathedral. "All exterior signs of a particular faith such as crosses, images, or statues were to be taken down or effaced within a week of the release of the decree." In addition, church bells could no longer ring to mark religious service. Instead the tocsin would sound only to "call the people in case of fire or some other object of general utility."[41] Catholic practice was still allowed in the department, as it was in France, but only in private.

Denunciations of clergy and former clergy accelerated over the course of the next week. Those who could demonstrate their Revolutionary bona fides were released, but most could not. The jails overflowed. A significant number of terrified former clergy went to work for the government. Many became Rousselin's accomplices and apologists. But most former clergy were either unable or unwilling to convince people of such a drastic change of heart and mind.

Members of the former first estate desperately sought to remain free however they could. The minutes of the Revolutionary Committee reported: "Desmoulins, former vicar of St. Pierre, deposed his clerical certificate and renounced priestly functions. Based on Rousselin's promise, he demanded a civic certificate and a passport." This request represented another blow for dechristianization. At the popular society, Rousselin reminded the public that "it had been decreed that protection, assistance, and passports were available to Catholic clergy who abjured the errors of fanaticism." He suggested that Desmoulins "announce publicly to the citizens at the passport office what he had come to do and Rousselin's promise." Three priests immediately stood up, "deposed their certificates, renounced their clerical functions, and demanded passports." On 18 December, a printed poster appeared with a "declaration" by fourteen "ministers of the Catholic faith in the city of Troyes." They proclaimed their appreciation for the "religious freedom" "protected by the constitution" and endorsed closing the churches.

They also supported Rousselin's donation of the decorations and vestments to the war effort, "because these things belong to the Nation." In the version of the Terror implemented in Troyes by Rousselin and the Revolutionary Committee, clerical status was dangerous.[42]

ROUSSELIN'S AGENDA WAS also social. A Revolutionary tax on the rich to support the poor was implemented in many places by representatives of the central state in 1793. Based on ability to pay, 373 Troyens had to contribute. Small landowners were assessed 200 livres, while a large manufacturer might be expected to contribute 50,000 livres. The assessments came to about 1.7 million livres. The difficulty of finding so much cash quickly led Rousselin to allow "the aristocracy of all classes" to pay their Revolutionary tax with goods or merchandise.

After three frustrating days of intense meetings about how to get people to pay their assessment, Rousselin made a fateful choice. He empowered the Revolutionary Committee to enact coercive measures to collect the tax. Those who did not pay within 24 hours owed double. After 48 hours, "villains" in arrears would be jailed.[43] Homes, businesses, and goods were sealed to facilitate the hunt for evidence of their treason. Rousselin authorized the sections' surveillance committees to visit the homes of recalcitrant citizens and search for hidden caches of gold and silver. Even if someone had already paid their tax, like the Widow Huez, but concealed precious metals were uncovered, the gold and silver were confiscated. Three days after mandating the tax, Rousselin extended the Revolutionary Committee's jurisdiction to the entire department. This expansion of the Revolutionary Committee's powers shaped the implementation of the Terror in the Aube and opened Rousselin up to charges of "tyranny" and "graft."

By emphasizing that the "rich," especially former nobles and clergy, were, simply because of their former status, suspect, Rousselin introduced the Terror to daily life in Troyes. Local administrators, judicial personnel, the Revolutionary Army, and militants in the surveillance committees were enlisted to visit homes, inspect papers, find witnesses, grill potential suspects, and catalog weapons, stocks of cash, and decorations made of gold or silver while verifying the "Revolutionary actions" of those whose socioeconomic standing made "good sans-culottes" doubt their loyalty.

Citizen Louise Finot was suspect because her husband was a well-to-do lawyer. The couple's papers were sealed. On 27 November, an agent of the Revolutionary Committee, a justice of the peace, and his clerk lifted the seals and read the documents. "Finding nothing suspect or contrary to the interests of the Republic or to its laws," they attested that "they had no further questions for her." Nerve-wracking as this was, others were far more at risk.[44]

Nicolas Pilon's frequent journeys gave him the opportunity to make contact with royalists or their agents, or so his interrogators insisted. Claiming that "business interests and a preference for the countryside" took him outside the city walls, he was astonished to return from a night at his brother's place to find his house sealed. He endured harsh questions about his three-month visit to another brother, a priest in the neighboring department of the Marne, as well as a brief trip south to Tonnerre. Two suspicious municipal officers inquired whether he had stayed with Nicolas Parent, a former legislative deputy accused of royalism, on his trips. They also asked how well he knew the heads of the local group of "royalists" who happened to be members of his National Guard unit. Questioned over and over again about where he went, whom he met, and why he left the city, Pilon responded briefly and negatively. He stated that he knew nothing about any of the counter-revolutionary acts referred to by the police. After eight hours of interrogation, the officers certified that Pilon told "the truth." To confirm their interview, they searched his home thoroughly and inspected his papers, but after finding nothing incriminating, the seals were lifted.[45] With hundreds of people engaged in this time-consuming fact-finding process, a well-founded fear of denunciation gripped the city. Productive work ground to a halt. A week after Rousselin's arrival, 105 people had been jailed in the Little Seminary, Danton's alma mater. Troyens (residents of the city) were too busy implementing the Terror, searching for protection, and dreading denunciation to unite against the outsider.

To guarantee that no one could miss the looming threat of Revolutionary justice, Rousselin wanted to construct a visible symbol of "the fundamental regeneration" of Troyes. He argued that "the aristocracy of all types" and "committed royalists" took advantage of lax criminal procedures to spread monarchial principles. "In the name of the People," Rousselin asked the Committee of Public Safety to approve erecting a guillotine. He also sought the authority "to establish a revolutionary tribunal as its indispensable accessory." A special jury of "patriots" could be elected immediately. Rousselin reported that "four or six eminently guilty heads must fall to the vengeance of liberty before the People will be convinced. Then equality will be cemented in place forever." In a follow-up letter, Rousselin proudly stated, "I have made terror the order of the day. It is deeply ingrained, and the city of Troyes will be saved." A guillotine was set up in front of the temple of reason replacing the statue of liberty and a revolutionary tribunal was formed. Neither went into operation, a fact that greatly annoyed the civil commissioner. Next, Rousselin and the popular society recommended that if a suspect's home displayed the tricolored flag of the Republic, it should be removed and replaced with an inscription reading "Enemy of the People." The Revolutionary Committee took it to an extreme. On the doors of nine houses, they had "Assassin of the People" painted in big yellow letters. Symbols became reality in a city in the grip of the Terror.[46]

While in Troyes, Rousselin kept in close contact with his constituencies in Paris, namely his patrons, his section, and readers of the *Journal of Public Safety*. A letter to the Committee of Public Safety describing public spirit in Troyes was reprinted in the paper. After appealing to patriotism, he wrote proudly, "the city of Troyes has been rid of priests. They have been suppressed forever." Asserting that the "Republican mass will lead people to forget the Catholic [version]," Rousselin "promised to bring an immense convoy of precious metals taken from churches to Paris." With an audience of sans-culottes firmly in mind, he wrote that the Terror "had nothing to do with vengeance

COMITÉ DE L'AN DEUXIÈME

FIGURE 2.4 Revolutionary Committee of the Year II. Getty Research Institute, Prints of the French Revolution, 1774–ca. 1840.

but was instead required by exact and rigorous justice." With the arrest of suspects well underway and the purge of aristocrats proceeding swiftly, Rousselin reported that "Troyes approaches Paris' heights." As he had learned in Provins, keeping Parisian public opinion engaged in his mission was vital to success.[47]

For Rousselin, a thorough purge of the departmental, district, and municipal administration was essential to both parts of his mission: uplifting public spirit in the Aube and supporting the war effort. Another shakeup was needed to follow up on the changes he made upon arrival. Almost all the officials in the department named earlier that fall were replaced by "patriots," especially "sans-culottes." Social origin and occupation remained more important qualifications than administrative competence or even literacy. To Paris, Rousselin complained constantly about the small number of "true Revolutionaries." Accordingly, he agreed to let his key adherents hold more than one post. Because the press of administrative duties made it impossible for these sans-culottes—both honorary and real—to work a regular job, Rousselin ordered his inner coterie of supporters to be paid five livres a day (a lawyer's daily wage in Troyes) from public funds, angering many, especially those involved in the administrative heavy lifting undertaken by the surveillance committees. Rousselin allowed the gothic, former basilica of St. Urbain to be used by the popular society and authorized spending 25,000 livres raised by a further "extraordinary tax on the rich" to make repairs *à la sans-culotte* to this temple of reason. These "repairs" and "alterations" to the Aube's gothic churches would come to be characterized as "desecration" and "vandalism."[48]

By mid-December 1793, the bloom was off the rose for Rousselin in Troyes. Accusations that he was a "hideous charlatan" who appropriated goods confiscated during domiciliary visits as well as cash from the tax on the rich were dangerous in a "Republic of Virtue." Individual and collective petitions claiming "wrongful arrest" and demanding discharge from prison were sent to Danton and members of the department's legislative delegation. Others protested the actions of the Revolutionary Committee and/or the agents Rousselin sent to bring the Terror to the department's five outlying districts. A notary named Guyot complained about the way decisions were made and justified in the name of public opinion. "What is public opinion?" he asked. "It should not be mistaken for the passion of a few agitators who under the mask of patriotism constantly deceive the People. They [the agitators] lead the People astray under the pretext of educating them about their real interests. Instead they profit from the People's credulity to satisfy their ambition and take their petty vengeances."[49] These charges challenged Rousselin's credibility. So too did the passage of the law of 4 December that slowed down the pace of centralization by limiting the powers of the Committee of Public Safety and the representatives on mission.

Several of Troyes' sections began to show renewed signs of independence. Increasingly, they refused calls for greater financial sacrifices, more lists of suspects, or cooperation with administrative requests, even those clearly related to the war effort. The key moment came when three sections loftily demanded that the Revolutionary Army leave the city to put down religious unrest in villages 20 miles to the west. Without them, Troyes' National Guard would be able to intimidate Rousselin and his allies. The civil commissioner later complained that he was excluded from meetings during this period. Official communications and even letters addressed to him were withheld. He was watched constantly, ostensibly for his own protection. To escape the guards at the door of his lodging, he had to leave "disguised as a woman."[50]

After ten days of watching his authority dwindle, Rousselin and Gachez left for Paris on 19 December. They planned to convince the Committee of Public Safety to dedicate a significant proportion of the proceeds of the tax on the rich to prop up the local economy. They also sought to persuade the Committee to activate the guillotine and revolutionary tribunal as a means of recovering power in Troyes.

The civil commissioner was in a difficult position. It was no longer possible to believe that his opponents did not know that they were undermining the war effort and therefore the Republic. Clearly many activists in the sections rejected his leadership because they did not think he represented the Revolution. Rousselin's subsequent behavior suggests what he thought about this challenge to his actions and beliefs. For him, there was only one way forward: Intensify the Terror. Many Revolutionary leaders in 1793–94 seem to have concurred. Rousselin charged down that slippery slope knowingly, perhaps willingly, despite the fact that it meant ignoring the wishes of the majority of citizens, if not necessarily the general will of "the People" of Troyes and the department of the Aube.

Jobs were essential to securing the support of Troyes' sans-culottes. The Committee of Public Safety accorded 400,000 livres to sustain indigent workers and encourage idled textile mills. But they declined to endorse any of Rousselin's more radical requests. The Committee hoped, with good reason, that this financial support would give the civil commissioner sufficient tools to win back the People's good will and galvanize the department's contribution to the war effort.

During the three days Rousselin was absent, some sections and the district administration took advantage of a flurry of rumors that he was in jail or headed to the guillotine to recover the initiative. Even after he returned, those moderate Troyens who resisted the militants associated with the Revolutionary Committee asserted that Rousselin's mission was over. That meant he no longer had any authority. Furious, the officers of the Revolutionary Army demanded authorization to treat Troyes like Fouché handled the defeated Federalist city of Lyon, by executing the leaders in ghastly fashion. Several municipal officials sought to divert a bloodbath by confronting Fleury, the commander of the detachment in the Aube. He agreed not to act unless requested to do so by the proper authorities. But the municipal officials overplayed their hand when they ordered the troops to commandeer grain from a village about ten miles away. Fleury refused, inflaming the situation still further. After his return from Paris on 22 December, the sections indicted Gachez, the deeply corrupt sans-culotte mayor and Rousselin's most important local ally.

The depth of Troyen opposition convinced Gachez to resign his post despite being "as pure as gold passed through a melting pot." Crowds of women and children either prevented Gachez from leaving his residence or attacked him when he went outside. To avoid further unrest, the municipality confined him at home, where he was protected by a picket of national guardsmen. Gachez was petrified that what he, Rousselin, and the Revolutionary Committee had done to hundreds of others was about to be done to him.

Numerous measures taken by the militants generated irate responses from some locals. Several shopkeepers demanded to be able to close on Sunday. Many expressed righteous anger over the lascivious nature of various public performances taking place in the temple of reason. A group dance around the former altar of the cathedral was criticized because it "expressed a public gaiety judged excessive."[51]

The leaders of the sections wanted to eliminate the radicals from local government just as they had been about to do when Rousselin arrived. To start a purge, they needed to regain control of the popular society. The moderates' first measure was to exclude women. Allowing women to speak and later to vote had been an essential part of the radicals' success. Over Rousselin's strong objection, his opponents sent a delegation to Paris asking for permission to conduct another shakeup. The sections prohibited anyone else from leaving the city. A ruse by Revolutionary Army officers enabled them to get a packet of documents including the civil commissioner's version of events out of the city. Refusing to wait, the moderates dismissed Rousselin's associates and appointees. This act demonstrated how far the civil commissioner's influence had fallen in Troyes. It is also a reminder that in certain circumstances, local solidarity could mitigate or even counteract the threat, much less the implementation, of state violence.

In Paris, however, Rousselin's Revolutionary credentials remained in good stead. Officers of the Revolutionary Army got to the capital after the delegates of the sections. But thanks to Rousselin's connections, they were heard first. On 25 December, speaking for the Committee of Public Safety, Barère announced to the Convention that "in Troyes, the merchant aristocracy, the most despicable of all, has raised its head. An envoy of the Committee of Public Safety did not suffice to impose order. We propose that you send a representative of the people . . . to enforce Revolutionary laws" in Troyes.[52] Representative Jean-Baptiste Bô of the Aveyron, another doctor, arrived on 28 December.

In a mere six days, Bô reversed the tide. His success demonstrated the gap in ability to get things done between an experienced representative on mission and a youthful civil commissioner. Although Bô expressed some "anxieties" about Rousselin's decree closing the churches, he concluded that "the empire of reason must prevail." Irate at being balked by the sections, Bô ordered the arrest of eighty-three activists. He accused them of unjustly resenting the tax on the rich and spreading bribes to recover their influence. His next step was to remodel the municipality, eliminating the office of mayor. Then he restored Rousselin's allies to their posts. No longer believing that the five- to six-hundred-member popular society expressed the will of "true sans-culottes," Bô dismissed them all. He entrusted twenty-five reliable men with the job of vetting a reconstituted group. Four prisoners were sent to Paris' Revolutionary Tribunal where they were executed a month later. Bô described his measures as a "vigorous" response to the Troyens' "counter-revolutionary views and actions," which he compared to the Federalists of Lyon and Marseille. The representative expressed his appreciation of Rousselin's fingering of the ringleaders of the protestors and praised "the wisdom and firmness of his deeds."[53]

To cap his "regeneration" of the city, Bô organized a civic festival on 2 January 1794 to celebrate the French recapture of Toulon and the Republic's military success in the Vendée. Earlier celebrations had been stillborn because of conflict between the Revolutionary Army and the National Guard. But Bô wanted to see "the People" and to let them see him. He was confident that "without the intriguers and their leaders, the mercantile spirit which dominates here will not test Revolutionary measures." A report to the

Committee of Public Safety written before the festival stated, "I guarantee the tranquility of the city of Troyes."[54]

The Revolutionary Army started the festival by planting a large liberty tree before the town hall. Nooses dangling from the branches enfolded symbols of royalty and portraits of foreign princes. As a crowd danced around a bonfire, feudal land titles seized from the files of local notaries were burned as token symbols of Revolutionary progress. Bô and Rousselin, accompanied by the departmental administration, and a detachment of the National Guard, marched to the altar of the Nation in the temple of reason where a "majestic Mountain" constructed of wood and plaster dwarfed both symbolically and physically, paper mache representations of the defeated cities of Toulon and Lyon. Bô gave a speech emphasizing the need for and benefits of sacrifices for the fatherland. In unsubtle terms, he arrogantly warned the large crowd of the dangers of fanaticism. Rousselin followed. He tried to resurrect Gachez' career, a goal endorsed by Bô. Angry murmurs led the representative to order the orchestra to drown out the audience. After a musical interlude, a procession along festively lighted streets returned to the town hall for more group dancing.[55]

Bô left soon afterward for Paris, accompanied by Gachez. The depth of local antipathy meant Gachez had no choice but to leave. Nervous about local opposition, Rousselin escorted the arrested activists from the sections to jail in the nearby town of Brienne. Then he returned to Paris, concluding his sojourn of about seven weeks. Rousselin "confessed that it is flattering and glorious for me to have witnessed Bô consolidating my work."[56]

The wealth of surviving documentation demonstrates the fear that motivated both representatives of the central state and their local opponents as they confronted the deep political and social cleavages that divided "the People" during this moment of crisis. Rousselin's hasty decisions, frenetic activity, and ad hoc policies were illustrative of a far larger group of mid-level operatives charged with implementing the Terror. His experience was mirrored in events all over France. Yet Alexandre Rousselin spent the rest of his life hiding his activities as a terrorist in Troyes along with what he sought to accomplish. Intensifying the Terror, but leaving locals in charge as Bô did, proved the difficulty of changing hearts and minds.

To understand the Terror, it is vital to see that many measures implemented by Rousselin and others like him strayed rather far afield from the war effort. Yet that is not the way they saw it. For the Revolutionaries the war against external enemies could be prosecuted far more effectively if the entire population united to embrace the values of the Republic. Thus, defeating France's internal enemies—those who divided and distracted the People—required thoroughgoing social change. The Revolutionaries believed that public spirit profoundly affected military matters and that only through Terror could those changes be implemented in time to save the Republic. Rousselin's experiences reveal the longer-term consequences of that dangerous expedient. This biography applies the "guillotine of history" to display those tensions and to consider their broader significance for French society and politics.

Among missionaries of the Republic, Rousselin was in the middle of the pack. At one end of the spectrum were Jean-Baptiste Carrier and Joseph Fouché. To decapitate the Vendée rebellion, Carrier formed a revolutionary tribunal at Nantes that guillotined numerous prisoners. Many more, especially priests and nuns, were put on boats that were then sunk in the Loire River.[57] Fouché and Jean-Marie Collot d'Herbois executed the leaders of the Federalist Revolt at Lyon by having cannon fire grapeshot at them. Others were guillotined or simply stabbed. Both these representatives on mission ordered the deaths of thousands. On the other end of the scale, some deputies focused on acquiring supplies for the army or gathering grain for Paris with a minimum of violence or involvement in local politics.

Most missions like that of Pierre Dubouchet in the Seine-et-Marne, fell somewhere in between. Dubouchet implemented Revolutionary measures such as dechristianization and the tax on the rich and he conducted purges to put sans-culottes in charge. Although hundreds were placed under suspicion during his three-month-long mission and dozens jailed, some for long periods, those suspected of serious crimes were sent to Paris to be judged. Nobody was killed in the Seine-et-Marne, though some citizens of the department were executed by Paris' Revolutionary Tribunal. The responsibility for any deaths was sloughed off on others. Although they clashed in Provins, Dubouchet's approach to implementing the Terror closely resembled what Rousselin did in Troyes.

Among the actions of other civil commissioners, it is the breadth of Rousselin's Revolutionary activities that stands out, not their depth or content. Acting as Robespierre's agent, nineteen-year-old Marc-Antoine Jullien, a contemporary figure who held a position similar to Rousselin's, denounced several representatives on mission, including Carrier for his barbarity and Jean-Lambert Tallien for his leniency in Bordeaux. Jullien purged that city's administration of all remaining Jacobins and participated in the execution of five Girondins. Rousselin's hands were far less bloody than those of many others sent to the provinces to wield the authority of the central state.[58]

Rousselin recognized the power provided by the institutions of the Terror, and their limitations. As civil commissioner, he dominated Troyes and the Aube, and watched it all slip away, only to recover his authority through a further intervention of the central government. That experience had to have challenged his self-confidence as well as his ideals. Rousselin understood the fickle whims of public opinion and the difficulty a small group of militants had keeping control of a large population even with the war to encourage solidarity. Bô condescended to Rousselin, but he salvaged the mission, enabling him to go home claiming that "the regeneration of Troyes has been achieved." Rousselin acknowledged that the situation would not last. After returning to Paris, he wrote a fifty-page "report" justifying his actions in the Aube. In addition to glorifying his accomplishments, the report warned: "Republicans and those who love liberty face 'new perils'" from "aristocrats allied together to destroy it." Rousselin still saw the Terror as necessary, but he predicted "storms" on the horizon.

A month after the civil commissioner left Troyes, the department, district, and municipality joined with the popular society to send delegates to the National Convention praising Rousselin and his mission. They enthused that "fanaticism, the inseparable accompaniment to despotism, no longer exists among us." Rousselin put the department of the Aube on a "truly Revolutionary path." After a recitation of his accomplishments, "the fruit of the great operations of civil commissioner Rousselin," the delegates observed, "Without doubt, deputies, slander is the serpent of a thousand forms whistling around such commendable conduct." In case "aristocrats" swamped the voice of sans-culottes, the delegates wanted to set the record straight. The Aube's delegates were applauded by the legislators. Their speech received "honorable mention" in the official bulletin.[59]

Rousselin was right to predict storms. Less than three months after his departure, the small cohort of overmatched militants lost control of the department of the Aube. Grasping the general will was an uncertain proposition at best. For Rousselin, the repercussions of being a terrorist lasted far longer than the missions. It has become a cliché that "revolutions devour their own."[60] The Troyens did their best.

Even before the intensification of the Terror in the summer of 1794, Alexandre Rousselin experienced the ups and downs associated with wielding Revolutionary power. The twin tasks of insulating himself from the consequences, while still maintaining his belief in the Revolution and its ideals, shaped the rest of his life. His conduct as a missionary of the Republic in the fall of 1793 represented a turning point for Rousselin. Now and in some ways forever, he was a terrorist. He was twenty years old.

3

The Consequences of Terror, 1794–1796

*A Special Criminal Court shall be established at Paris
to take cognizance of all counter-revolutionary activities,
all attacks upon liberty, equality, unity, the indivisibility
of the Republic, the internal and external security of the
State, and all plots on behalf of the re-establishment of
monarchy or of any other authority hostile to liberty,
equality, and the sovereignty of the people, whether the
accused be civil or military functionaries or ordinary
citizens.*

—DECREE OF THE NATIONAL CONVENTION
ESTABLISHING THE REVOLUTIONARY TRIBUNAL
(10 March 1793)

*They are calling for me. Just now the Commissioners of
the Revolutionary Tribunal have been questioning me.
All they asked me was: "Had I ever conspired against the
republic?" What a mockery! Is it possible that the purest
republicanism can be so insulted? I foresee the fate that
awaits me.*

—CAMILLE DESMOULINS, April 1794

REVOLUTIONS RUN ON networks. In 1793–94, France's chief political networks were rooted in and held together by ideology, patronage, friendship, residence, and shared experience.[1] Many other forms of association and community also bound people together. Networks channeled political and personal action, especially during the crisis facing the Republic that birthed the Terror. In the Brunswick Manifesto of July 1792, France's enemies proclaimed that they would "inflict an ever memorable vengeance by delivering over the

The Making of a Terrorist. Jeff Horn, Oxford University Press (2021). © Oxford University Press.
DOI: 10.1093/oso/9780197529928.001.0001

city of Paris to military execution and complete destruction, and the rebels guilty of the said outrages to the punishment that they merit."[2] Fear linked to the war motivated both crowd action and more formal politics in complex, inherently unstable ways. The reactions of frightened men and women created tensions within and between diverse networks. For missionaries of the Republic like Alexandre Rousselin, political networks were critical to their ability to survive the consequences of having enforced the Terror in the provinces.

What happened when a primary network collapsed? When Rousselin returned to Paris from his mission in Troyes, his safety and position depended heavily on his patron, Georges-Jacques Danton. However, he quickly recognized Danton's declining influence. In 1792–93, Rousselin had had other sponsors like Bertrand Barère and Jules-François Paré. At the same time, he had built networks in his section, within the Ministry of the Interior, and, more broadly, through his journalism and public speeches. But all these ties rested on the firm foundation of Danton's backing. In the spring of 1794, Rousselin watched helplessly as his mentor went to the guillotine.

Danton's precipitous fall emboldened a group of formerly suspect Troyens to denounce Rousselin. Anticipating their action, he spent the spring of 1794 in a determined effort to attach himself to different patrons and networks amidst the rapidly shifting kaleidoscope of Revolutionary power relations. This hunt led Rousselin to participate in assembling the coalition that ultimately brought down Maximilien Robespierre on 9 Thermidor of Year II (27 July 1794).

The fall of Robespierre is considered one of the turning points of the Revolution. How did he go from the pinnacle of influence to a relatively isolated figure? What was his relationship to the Terror? Such questions have been at the heart of debates over the meanings of popular politics and Revolutionary violence from the very start. Rousselin's experience provides a new vantage point on this important moment and highlights the key role of factional struggle and political networks in the evolution of the Terror. At the same time, the shift in his position from perpetrator to victim of the Terror, a process that extended long past 9 Thermidor suggests that this iconic date was far less of a turning point than has often been claimed.[3]

RETURNING FROM TROYES was hardly the triumph of Rousselin's boyhood dreams. He had to be saved by the intervention of representative on mission Jean-Baptiste Bô. Rousselin recognized the consequences of the fickle nature of public opinion during a Revolution. But the greatest threat to his position was Danton's mounting isolation from the centers of power. Rousselin attended the Jacobin Club where he watched and waited to see what would happen. He also resumed overseeing the Ministry of the Interior's Parisian spy network and editing the *Journal of Public Safety*.

During the late winter of 1794, Rousselin published a self-congratulatory *Report* of his mission in the Aube as a lengthy pamphlet. It quoted reports of his zeal and effectiveness produced by his cronies in Troyes. An address sent to the National Convention announced that "fanaticism, the inseparable companion of despotism no longer exists in Troyes. Priests, formerly so common inside the walls, no longer have any influence." Troyes' terrorists thanked the "Revolutionary representatives of a free people" for having dispatched Rousselin "to return their liberty." They made their gratitude tangible by sending cash "gifts" to supplement the product of "revolutionary taxes."[4] Such support helped buoy Rousselin's standing but could not offset Danton's declining influence.

After a month-long illness, Danton had received legislative permission to go home to Arcis to recover in October 1793. That fall, the capital experienced a struggle between those who wanted to accelerate and those who wanted to restrain the Terror. Danton missed it all while recuperating. Upon his return, he no longer hid his view that the Terror should be moderated, a position that was unpopular with those focused on maintaining the war effort at fever pitch. Rousselin understood the dangers of this position and searched with even greater urgency for new patrons and new networks.

Between December 1793 and March 1794, several key figures reached the conclusion that the clash between factions was dangerous for the Republic.[5] Robespierre focused on the corruption of "moderates" who wished to rein in the Terror. He also emphasized the threat posed by radical Revolutionaries who wanted "another 31 May" to purge anyone who jeopardized the Revolution or the war effort. Robespierre described the two groups' vices as "moderatism which is to moderation what impotence is to chastity; [and] excess, which is to vigor what dropsy [swelling] is to health."[6] Ongoing fighting between factions prevented consolidation of the Republic and convinced influential decision-makers to decide that both groups must be eliminated. The Committees of Public Safety and General Security also determined to check the independence of Paris's popular movement. During a crisis of this depth, governing was harder than rising to power.

In the winter of 1793–94, momentum built for further purges of the Revolution's leadership. Camille Desmoulins' decision to publish an inflammatory newspaper, *Le Vieux Cordelier*, played an important part. Rousselin's former boss criticized the extremists who congregated in the Cordeliers

ROBESPIERRE.

FIGURE 3.1 Maximilien Robespierre. The Miriam and Ira D. Wallach Division of Art, Prints and Photographs: Print Collection, The New York Public Library. "Robespierre" New York Public Library Digital Collections.

Club for abandoning the principles of the group's founders. As an influential member of the Cordeliers from 1790 to 1792, Desmoulins's thrust drew blood. So too did public accusations of treason exchanged by a number of Danton's friends and the radicals. Meanwhile, food shortages energized Paris' popular movement. That both the political elite and the people of Paris shared a deep-seated fear of plots to overthrow the Republic further destabilized the situation.

THE RADICALS REFERRED to as the Hébertists, for Jacques-René Hébert, provoked their doom. Hébert, publisher of the influential newspaper *Père Duchesne*, claimed to speak for the sans-culottes and held important positions in the Paris Commune. At the Cordeliers Club, on 4 March 1794, influential radicals demanded an insurrection. They placed a veil over the plaque in their meeting hall inscribed with the Rights of Man "until the people shall have recovered their sacred rights . . . by the destruction of the [moderate] faction."[7] Hébert sealed his fate when he said that Robespierre was "misled" for defending the "traitorous" Desmoulins.

The radicals were accused of planning an insurrection. Given the lack of concrete preparations, this charge seems unfounded. However, the Committees of Public Safety and General Security, along with their allies in the Convention, were not going to let facts get in the way of what they saw as a necessary action. As a known terrorist and an outspoken champion of the influence of the sans-culottes, Rousselin was seen as an adherent of those who "like a bird of bad omen spoke only about ... riots and pillaging."[8] The radicals were arrested on 13 March on broad, largely trumped up charges. President of the Convention Jean-Lambert Tallien claimed that those who demanded an insurrection were actually monarchists in sans-culotte clothing. The people "will see that these men, despite their trousers and clogs, are nothing but aristocrats." Earlier that same day, the Convention officially redefined the term "traitors" to include "corruptors of public opinion."[9]

In the *Journal of Public Safety*, Rousselin wrote: "These debased beings prepare for the fall of the Republic by degrading it. . . . Believing that patriotism was not the order of the day, they expected to describe Robespierre as a *moderate* and be applauded. They risked using the term and were unmasked by the People who recognize their true friends."[10] This same charge was leveled against every faction. Desmoulins further inflamed the situation in the rumored seventh issue of *Le Vieux Cordelier* part of which circulated in manuscript by challenging the authority of the two great committees and the need for the Terror. With a keen understanding of the political moment, Rousselin recognized the danger of moderation. He quickly and publicly parted ways with that position. Although his actions in Provins and Troyes augured the actions demanded by the current Cordeliers, Rousselin instead sought the protection of Robespierre and the Committee of Public Safety.

Rousselin's job compiling the reports of Paris' police spies enabled him to pass along the information that justified the arrest of the Hébertists. "In the cafés and on street-corners," Rousselin wrote, their supporters were described as "traitors and imbeciles" who should be eliminated. "Hébert and his clique" sought to make "the People die of hunger."[11] As for those charged with "the diabolical conspiracy uncovered by the Committee of Public Safety . . . the day of their judgment comes too slowly for the liking of citizens who wish to see them go to the scaffold to the last traitor." One sans-culotte commented, "the Committees of Public Safety and General Security: there is my jury. They have never been wrong."[12] Public opinion in Paris supported the two great committees.

In his haste to express a popular view, Rousselin went too far too fast. He took a leading role in purging radicals from the Cordeliers Club on behalf of the Committee of Public Safety. At the Jacobin Club, Rousselin said that the accused "term a 'faction' anything that is not part of their plot; 'traitor' anyone who threatens to denounce them." But, he stated, the situation was well in hand because the accused "do not have as much courage as they have audacity." He pressed for the Jacobins to print his speech and distribute it to the membership.

For many Jacobins, led by Robespierre, Rousselin overreached. They were not sure whether he was merely an opportunist or just seeking his own aggrandizement. The Incorruptible demanded that certain "inaccuracies" in Rousselin's interpretation of events be corrected before publication was considered. Robespierre did not seem to want this ambitious, well-known acolyte of Danton to have the last word.[13]

The "trial" of the Hébertists was a sham. When the Revolutionary Tribunal's notorious prosecutor, Antoine-Quentin Fouquier-Tinville, told the Committee of Public Safety that there was no evidence against the accused, he was told to "amalgamate."[14] In other words, evidence against certain people in this diverse group of defendants was applied to all. This strategy constituted a particularly ruthless form of guilt by association. It was used against many, perhaps even most, leading Revolutionaries who came before the Tribunal in 1794. A major goal of the indictment was to warn the popular movement of the dangers of defying the great committees. After a three-day trial in which the defense was not allowed to call witnesses, the radicals were convicted. They went to the guillotine on 24 March. This purge might be understood as the first step in another reaction because the more extreme group lost, rather than a continuation of the methods and means developed over the previous eighteen months of Terror.

THE RADICALS' FALL meant something for the Revolution's experiment in direct democracy. But exactly what remained uncertain. There was no question, however, as to who was next in line for the guillotine. By mid-March, the two great committees had already decided to bring down "the Indulgents," a disparate group loosely associated with Danton. This move would insulate the accusers from both the charge of moderation and the corruption of some of these figures. "All the factions ought to perish by the same blow," declared Robespierre on 15 March.[15] In the campaign to inculcate Republican virtue, Robespierre began to think that Danton was part of the problem. Although he resisted the idea for months, Robespierre dropped a number of hints that neither their friendship nor their shared experiences sufficed to protect the great orator.[16] Rousselin understood the deadly consequences of Danton's isolation long before his mentor. Fear provoked his impulsive actions against the Cordeliers.

Rousselin recognized that the push toward eliminating challenges to government came from more than one source. In the vulnerability of his patrons, he saw his own exposure to charges of corruption. Public opinion in the capital associated Robespierre's vision of a Republic based on virtue, articulated in early February, with the attack on the Indulgents. To fulfill his reputation as the Incorruptible, Robespierre wanted to ensure that "if the government forgets the interests of the people, or if it lapses into the hands of corrupt individuals, according to the natural course of things, the light of recognized principles will illuminate their treachery, so that every new faction will discover death in the mere thought of crime."[17] On 19 March, member of the Committee of Public Safety, Jean-Marie Collot d'Herbois, warned: "The faction that we have laid low is not the only one that exists. Opposing factions wish to profit from their fall to advance themselves" but "the moderates" should not "imagine that we have given them victory."[18]

Several sympathetic observers warned the moderates of the storm on the horizon. Tallien and Antoine-Claire Thibaudeau claimed to have told Danton that the committees would soon move against him. Robert Lindet, another member of the Committee of Public Safety, also alerted Danton of the danger. After a dinner party on either 21 or 22 March, Vilate d'Aubigny, a clerk in the war department who also served on the jury for the Revolutionary Tribunal, supposedly told Rousselin, "We must have the heads of Danton, Camille Desmoulins, and [Pierre] Philippeaux within eight days." Rousselin immediately passed the information along. Danton's response shifted swiftly from "they would not dare" to "why would they want me to die?" Roussselin suggested leaving France, citing examples of other proscribed deputies. Danton rejected the idea. He asked, "To leave? Isn't that to emigrate? Can you take your country with you on the soles of your shoes?" Desmoulins expressed similar views. As a final gambit, Rousselin urged Danton either to become more active in his own defense or to consider seizing power with the help of sympathetic generals. Danton responded, it "would require even more blood. Enough of that has been shed. I would prefer to be guillotined than to guillotine others." He concluded, "My life is not worth living. I am tired of humanity."[19] World-weary and resigned to his fate, Danton did little to defend himself until it was too late.

Despite their legal immunity from prosecution as members of the legislature, Danton, Desmoulins, and two other members of the Convention were arrested during the night of 30–31 March 1794. Only Louis Legendre defended them in the Convention. But his objections were brushed aside by Robespierre and Barère. Louis-Antoine Saint-Just, for the Committee of Public Safety, read a lengthy indictment. He emphasized the Indulgents' "criminal hypocrisy" before censuring them for being royalists bent on "destroying the Republic and undermining liberty" on behalf of foreign powers. He charged "those I denounce have never been patriots. Rather, they are more adroit and secretive aristocrats than those at Coblenz [where the émigrés gathered]." Saint-Just asserted that the Committee of Public Safety had now "abolished the factions," which would inaugurate a halcyon age.[20]

Rousselin needed to distance himself from "the villains and false patriots" who had been his patrons. The day of the Indulgents's arrest, he convinced the revolutionary committee of the Unity section to endorse an address he wrote to the Committees of Public Safety and General Security. It was then hurriedly approved by the section's assembly. A delegation of "all the [section's] citizens *en masse*" presented it to the National Convention. Rousselin affirmed that the two great committees were the "faithful executors of Revolutionary government" and defenders of "a free people." The petition approved the arrest of Danton, Desmoulins, and the other "Indulgents." Rousselin and other section leaders feared the consequences of their ties to both the recently destroyed factions and hoped to ingratiate themselves with the great committees.[21]

As with the Hébertists, the Revolutionary Tribunal's prosecution of a diverse group of Indulgents constituted a show trial. It began on 3 April. Danton's standing and popularity made it politically impossible to deny him a hearing. Echoing the coup against the Girondins, the trial was preceded by the removal of Danton's, Desmoulins', and the other deputies' parliamentary immunity. Danton's defense on 4 April vindicated his entire career "in the People's cause" with a "clear conscience." He challenged accusers who "slandered" him to "dare to attack me to my face" before asserting that he had "vital evidence to reveal; I demand an undisturbed hearing. The Nation's safety makes that imperative." Listeners close to the courtroom passed his words back into the waiting crowd demonstrating his oratorical mastery. To justify silencing his defense, the Committee of Public Safety quickly fashioned a rumor that Danton and his fellow defendants were preparing to lead thousands of prisoners to assassinate the members of the great committees and then overthrow the government. The National Convention muzzled the defendants on 5 April, preventing Danton from appealing to the crowd. After

Marc-Guillaume Vadier and Jean-Baptiste Amar, influential members of the Committee of General Security, threatened the jury, a guilty verdict was reached in ten minutes. Fifteen Indulgents went to the guillotine that very afternoon. Desmoulins predicted that "the monsters who murder me will not long survive me," perhaps referring to his cousin Fouquier-Tinville or his schoolmate and close friend Robespierre. As he mounted the steps for his appointment with the revolutionary barber, Danton's final words were: "Don't forget to show my head to the people: it's worth seeing."[22]

Six months later, Rousselin described his patrons' last moments. An "unnumerable crowd" lined the streets where the carts bearing Danton and Camille traveled on their way to the Place de la Révolution. Barère and Billaud-Varennes had taken the precaution of stationing hundreds of police, both mounted and on foot, along with National Guard units and battalions of artillerymen. They had been on alert for two days to forestall an eruption of popular violence. Rousselin asserted that "these silent soldiers, blindly executing the orders of their tyrannical superiors, seemed less to be obeying the orders of the Committee of Public Safety than forming an honor guard around Danton." Proud as a hero, he carried himself with "the dignity of innocence." As the dénouement approached, "A profound and gloomy silence, a mournful and somber sadness reigned among the People. They were stupefied and astonished to see their best friends treated like conspirators. Eyes fixed to the ground, everyone feared to look at their neighbor. On the sly, consoling glances mixed with tears were aimed at the victims." To drive the point home, Rousselin observed that "terror and force in the name of law compromised the vitality of the regrets that escaped despite the [threat of] violence." Once they returned home, "they wept as an expression of a private affection because their sadness was so sincere." That summer, Danton's lingering popularity and the disillusionment of much of the Parisian population would have important consequences.[23] Saint-Just's claim that factionalism was dead ended neither denunciations nor the Terror. A Jacobin who had supported the Mountain noted, "Death hovers over everyone's head"; "None of us can be certain of avoiding it, since it strikes anywhere and everywhere."[24]

Rousselin's position grew ever more tenuous: his efforts to shore up his networks and find new patrons were unsuccessful. He had overreached with the Jacobins and become estranged from Robespierre and the Committee of Public Safety. His well-known ties to Danton and Desmoulins almost automatically made him suspect, especially as continuing fallout from the trials led to the execution of Desmoulins's wife Lucile on 13 April. The same day, several prominent activists from the Unity section were executed for corruption. The Convention had already disbanded the Revolutionary Army on 27 March. The ministries were eliminated just two weeks later, with the great committees absorbing their functions. Rousselin grew ever more isolated from the centers of power. Increasingly, the Terror was driven by the Revolution's political leadership, not by popular action.

These developments were exacerbated by news from southern Champagne. The Revolutionary Committee of the department of the Aube jailed more and more prominent activists in the sections, with special emphasis on former priests. To make matters worse, these officials could not gather enough grain to meet the department's quota. In fact, so little grain left the Aube that the Committee of Public Safety required daily reports on the progress of requisitions. They promised close "surveillance" of "administrators who had failed in their duty."[25] With Danton gone and many Revolutionary institutions associated with the popular movement on the defensive, Rousselin was vulnerable. Demoralized and desperate, he knew that his own denunciation was only a matter of time.

The shifting political climate of the spring of 1794 left Rousselin's actions in Troyes open to censure. Danton's death, the Committee of Public Safety's criticism of administration in the Aube, and the attack on institutions like the Revolutionary Army encouraged the political elite of southern Champagne to act. They sought to liberate hundreds of suspects and to escape the control of the Revolutionary Committee while taking revenge on their tormentors. Rousselin tried a preemptive strike before charges could be filed against him.

In a long, impassioned speech at the Jacobin Club, Rousselin went on the offensive against Troyes' sections. In the name of "the indivisibility of the Republic," Rousselin contrasted the sections' endorsement of federalism and civil war in provincial cities with the patriotism and emphasis on the "unity of the people" advocated in Paris. He condemned the composition of the membership of "falsely named popular societies." The participation of three specific groups undermined the sections' legitimacy, said Rousselin. First, lawyers "play too great a role. Sans-culottes listen to them speak against the People without understanding their perfidy." Lawyers' "bad faith" was exacerbated by merchants' "insatiable greed." Their "search for sordid or illicit profits is too deeply ingrained" for them to display "Republican virtues." Finally, Rousselin argued that the admission of women—which he had supported until the Convention moved to outlaw female societies in the fall of 1793— transformed "fraternal societies" into "hermaphroditic societies." After disparaging the inclusion of women in the business of the sections, Rousselin remarked: "A club composed solely of women is no less dangerous than the immoral meeting of the two sexes in an arena where debates can offend modesty." As a result, the sections were rife with "scandalous intrigues" where "only the wicked prosper." Because of his own marginalization, Rousselin's broadside was largely ignored.[26]

Rousselin was not alone in his desperation. On 24–25 May, two assassination attempts roiled the Jacobins. Henri Admirat, an employee of the national lottery, waited long hours for Robespierre on 24 May , but when he did not appear, Admirat took two shots at Collot d'Herbois instead, wounding Geffroy, a locksmith, who tried to help. The next day, sixteen-year-old Cécile Renault, armed with two small knives, tried to enter the house where Robespierre boarded "to see what a tyrant looked like."[27] That afternoon, both members of the Committee of Public Safety received enthusiastic applause in the Jacobins. Legendre asked whether deputies should have bodyguards, an idea that received a strongly negative reaction. Rousselin then proposed that Geffroy be given "civic honors" at the Festival of the Supreme Being to be held on 8 June. This seemingly innocuous proposition infuriated Robespierre and Georges Couthon, his closest ally on the Committee of Public Safety.

According to Robespierre, honors given to deputies or "to those who defend them are only an adroit trap invented by partisans of tyranny." Bodyguards would "isolate" the deputies from the people and earn them "disfavor while attracting envy and slander." Robespierre claimed to be "astonished that someone who appeared only rarely at the Jacobins" persisted in making "insidious motions." He then accused Rousselin of trying to distract attention from Danton before his fall. Robespierre charged the young man with making his suggestion about Geffroy on behalf of Dantonist ex-minister Paré (who had been in prison since 1 April). Gesturing wildly in his wheelchair, Couthon announced that Rousselin had been denounced to the Committee of General Security for having spent 80,000 to 100,000 livres on mission, for having peddled Paré's works, and for "other facts." After a brief debate, Rousselin was purged from the Jacobin Club as "the executor of Danton's will." The Committee of General Security ordered his incarceration in the desperately overcrowded La Force prison, while more information was gathered for a trial. His papers and possessions were sealed. The expected blow had landed, but from an unexpected direction. The suddenness of this shift in fortunes demonstrated why the Revolutionaries so feared denunciation.[28]

The expected storm from the east blew in soon afterward. Antoine Garnier, deputy of the Aube, wrote home on 26 May: "Justice caught up to Rousselin, the guilty one, who caused so much trouble." Garner reported that Rousselin had been arrested, thanks to Robespierre and Couthon: "Sing hymns of joy! The punishment of such brigands is a victory that avenges humanity and fortifies virtue!"[29] A few days later, writing from prison in Troyes, Augustin Guélon published an eight-page printed accusation against Rousselin. Guélon was a cloth merchant who had supported the Revolution from the beginning. Elected lieutenant colonel of the city's National Guard and a founding member of the local Jacobin Club, Guélon served with distinction in several administrative posts. He was imprisoned by Bô on 29 December 1793 for "questioning the [civil] commissioner in his section and for doing the same in the popular society, accompanied by threats."[30]

Guélon pulled no punches. He denounced Rousselin for "conspiring against the unity and indivisibility of the Republic to annihilate the sovereignty of the French people through arbitrary arrests, squandering public money, demeaning legitimate authorities, preaching atheism, and engaging in secret relations with Danton." He also accused Rousselin of exceeding his powers. Guélon railed against Rousselin's "seduction" of the battalion of the Revolutionary Army through distribution of massive quantities of wine and his use of "tyrannical means of collecting the revolutionary tax." He "tried to cause a famine" by claiming that aristocrats in Troyes had hoarded huge stocks of grain which led the Subsistence Committee to requisition too much. By removing "proven patriots and good administrators" from office, Rousselin "completely disorganized the city of Troyes." He caused "the most horrible anarchy by filling posts with men whose immorality, defiance of revolutionary laws, rapacious greed, and atrocious despotism, served Danton's faction so well." Guélon demanded a full financial accounting and asked Parisian authorities to investigate these charges.[31]

Another Troyen named Robert, a former Oratorian priest, sent his own denunciation to Robespierre, who oversaw police matters on behalf of the Committee of Public Safety. Robert accused Troyes' Revolutionary Committee and Rousselin for "illegal exercise" of "despotic authority." The Incorruptible presented the denunciations to the Committee of Public Safety on 5 June.[32] The next day, at Garnier's suggestion, Robert and Guélon were brought to Paris to present their charges in person. In the meantime, Rousselin's call for help from his supporters in the Aube bore fruit, as the popular society and the district both certified his "good conduct in his mission" and challenged the veracity of Guélon's pamphlet.[33]

At the Jacobin Club on 14 June, Robert depicted Rousselin as the head of "the faction" of "the perfidious Danton." He claimed that "oppression of the patriots of that city is the order of the day" and asked for protection. The Club named two commissioners to escort the Troyens to the Committee of Public Safety. Couthon weighed in to warn of the ongoing threat of factions, foreign plots, and division in the National Convention. He asserted:

The Republic has placed all its confidence in the Convention. It merits that confidence and has never ceased to merit it, but there are still some malcontents who seek to create disastrous divisions among the representatives of the people which appear to the Committees of Public Safety and General Security like the horrible traits of a Sulla or a Nero [notorious despots]. They deliberate in secret and form lists of those to be proscribed to which they add citizens to inspire their fears and lead them astray.

The time is coming when these traitors and villains will be unmasked and punished. Happily their numbers are small. Perhaps there are only four or six.

Rumors are spreading that in a few days, the committees will arrest 18 members of the Convention and that they have already been named. Those who make this noise are accomplices of Hébert and Danton. They fear punishment for their criminal behavior and join with people of known purity in the hope that, hiding behind them, they can escape justice.[34]

In the aftermath of the passage of the law of 22 Prairial (10 June 1794), also proposed by Couthon but supported by both committees, such a statement was no empty threat.

The controversial Law of 22 Prairial inaugurated the so-called Great Terror by widening the authority of the Revolutionary Tribunal in political cases and requiring citizens to denounce suspects immediately. Trials were limited to three days of testimony. The Tribunal was not allowed to summon witnesses, nor could defendants call any. Decisions were based solely on the official accusation and the testimony of the accused. The only possible verdicts were acquittal or death.

Months before, Rousselin had recognized that his networks would not protect him. A noted terrorist with close ties to Danton, he had been involved in a dispute with Robespierre that had led to his arrest. The execution of sixty people linked to Cécile Renault, Robespierre's attacker, on 17 June surely struck fear into the hearts of those like Rousselin who might be considered a "malcontent" by Couthon.

The Committee of Public Safety gathered information about Rousselin's actions in the Aube. On 16 June, the group asked deputy Nicolas Maure, who was on mission nearby, about those detained by Bô. When Maure's response did not satisfy, an experienced police spy, Pierre-Polycarpe Pottofeux, was dispatched. His ostensible assignment was to ferret out a counterfeiting ring, but his real charge was to investigate the situation in Troyes. The locals did not trust him or his questions, but were overjoyed when the Committee of Public Safety began to liberate suspects incarcerated by Rousselin and/or Bô.

Another denunciation of Rousselin from Troyes received by the Bureau of General Police described him as a dechristianizer who "always professed atheism and immorality."[35] On 18 July, Robespierre ordered the release of 320 suspects from the Aube. The next day the Committee appointed Maure as representative on mission to the Aube, charging him with purifying local administrators and regenerating public spirit. The Committee of General Security ordered the arrest of twelve of Rousselin's closest collaborators on 26 June and four more on 10 July. All were brought to Paris to stand trial at his side. Meanwhile, René-François Dumas, president of the Revolutionary Tribunal and Robespierre's close ally, attempted to have Rousselin brought before the court even though no warrant had yet been issued. Dumas's effort to circumvent even the appearance of legality was thwarted by Gabriel-Jérôme Sénart, secretary-general of the Committee of General Security, even though he "found only proofs" of Rousselin's guilt in the accompanying documents.[36] Rousselin appeared to be on the verge of becoming one of the Terror's next victims, primarily for being an *ultra*-terrorist.

At the Jacobin Club, Augustin Guélon made a second assault on Rousselin on 14 July. Citing the law of 22 Prairial, Guélon wondered why the twenty-eight charges he had leveled at Rousselin had been ignored. The bulk of this speech condemned the former "sans-culotte mayor" of Troyes, François Gachez, who he linked not only to Rousselin, but also to Joseph Fouché, the ultra-terrorist "butcher of Lyon." This was a different version of guilt by association. Gachez's politics infuriated Guélon. But "corruption" angered him even more: "I denounce his villainous and dirty life, his immorality, his shameful excesses with two 'public women,' *in the temple of reason* [the former cathedral] . . . and for passing days and nights in debauchery with Rousselin and his consorts."[37] Again Couthon intervened. He labeled Rousselin's actions as "an outgrowth of the system developed by the Héberts and Dantons," whom he called "villains who sought to exasperate the People through atheism and food shortages." Guélon was invited to attend the next day's meeting of the Committee of Public Safety, after which, Couthon added, "without doubt, the result of all the information gathered will be to send Rousselin and his accomplices to the Revolutionary Tribunal."[38] The Committee issued orders to that effect on 15 July.

Rousselin actively defended himself. In addition to soliciting expressions of support from Troyes, he distributed copies of the printed *Report* of his mission. A list of actions either approved by Bô or accepted by the National Convention was also circulated by his friends. Rousselin told people that he owed his job in the Ministry of the Interior to Paré's predecessor, who had rewarded him for serving on the Revolutionary Committee of the sections in the coup against the Girondins. Finally, he asked to be heard and then judged by the Aube's parliamentary delegation rather than the Revolutionary Tribunal.

At the same time, Rousselin described his denouncers as suspects or as the parents of men arrested as suspects. Behind the scenes, his allies disseminated a response to Guélon's charges. On 17 July at the Jacobin Club, an outraged Guélon objected to the "printed libel in which the facts he advanced were treated as slander." Guélon swore "on his head" that his facts were correct and demanded that the authors' "conduct be examined." His critics replied that Guélon was actually the slanderer. They suggested that, in the end, Guélon would be punished, not Rousselin. Another of Rousselin's friends observed, "it was not surprising that Guélon offered his head to guarantee his veracity; his family had experience in such tactics. His parents offered their heads to defend the tyrant [Louis XVI] and his family." This same speaker announced that he had sent the memoir which outlined Guélon's activities that provoked the uprising of Troyes' sections to the Committee of Public Safety, an exchange many newspapers reported. An essential rule of Revolutionary politics was that the best defense was a good offense: Attacking the Revolutionary credentials of one's own accuser in front of the Jacobins either in person or by proxy was standard practice.

Beyond these actions and the fact that he received many visitors in prison, little is known about how Rousselin felt during this period. However, his *Report*, written in anticipation of the possibility of denunciation, provides clues.[39] Rousselin believed that he had acted both reasonably and honestly in response to the Revolutionary crisis and that the accusations against him were unjust. In the battle against "fanaticism," he relied on "weapons of reason and persuasion." Rousselin described his Troyen opponents as bloodsucking "vampires. . . . The hands of these villains are more accustomed to taking than to giving." He lamented that "in the provinces nothing is said face to face, everything is done on the sly." When he arrived in Troyes, public officials were "servile and insignificant men" who "thought only of reelection" rather than the needs of the Republic. They "automatically delayed, focusing on the *text* when they ought to be struck by the *haste* needed to regenerate [the Republic]."

Perhaps because of his "extreme youth," Rousselin was a weathervane tilting whichever way the wind blew. In the Aube, he implemented the politics of the moment. Active in Paris' sections and working with a detachment of the Revolutionary army, he clearly believed that winning the support of the sans-culottes was the key to introducing Revolutionary government in Troyes. When he returned from Paris in December 1793 with 400,000 livres to support the unemployed and restart manufacturing, he was received with joy and "fraternal embraces of the greatest purity." He found "in these moments the most delicious reward of my life." That he was detained in his room by guards—a situation which he equated to prison—and had to be "rescued" by Bô was a fair price to pay for someone "charged with executing the national vengeance," who worked "only for the good of the People." That Rousselin shifted his goals and methods or sought new patrons and networks did not necessarily make him an opportunist. He was, after all, a man of his times.[40]

Rousselin had the courage of his convictions and was not focused solely on survival. But he had learned from Danton, his other mentors, and his own experience to pay close attention to the vagaries of public opinion. Rousselin stated that "as the representative of the National Convention, I made it a principle to go *as fast*, but *no faster*" than the People when pushing for change. He made clear "that perhaps I have vigorously followed my principles, but I have never been an *ultra*." In December, he reminded his accusers, a report of his most controversial actions had been reprinted in the *Bulletin of the Laws* with honorable mention by the Convention. As a result, he was confident that his actions enjoyed official approval at the time he made them.

By the time he wrote the *Report* in the early spring of 1794, Rousselin understood that the political climate had changed. Nonetheless, he rejected charges of impropriety or unorthodoxy. During the Terror, people were denounced for being out of step with the times. It was the result not of their actions, but of changing perceptions of those actions. Danton's path to the guillotine and Robespierre's role in the destruction of the factions must surely have reinforced this all-important lesson. As pressure against him escalated, there was little Rousselin could do other than to mobilize his political connections in hopes of shifting assessments of his actions in a more favorable direction.

Rousselin and sixteen "accomplices" went before the Revolutionary Tribunal on 20 July 1794. Rousselin had been imprisoned since 25 May. The intervening seven weeks were spent in denunciation, counterdenunciation, and fact-finding. Fouquier-Tinville's act of accusation charged the group with having "conspired against the unity and indivisibility of the Republic and the liberty and security of the French people by committing all kinds of vexatious actions" while holding positions of authority. The accusation conflated Rousselin with Danton by emphasizing the former's efforts to "corrupt morals, dissolve the national representation, subjugate legitimate authorities, and reestablish tyranny," which actually referred to the latter. The public prosecutor also asserted that "without the active vigilance of the Convention" certain departments like the Aube would be controlled by "the liberticide faction," because of the defendants' accumulation of posts. Fouquier-Tinville concluded that "Rousselin's objective was to serve Danton's faction through all sorts of crimes." His collaborators were portrayed as "interested solely in lining their pockets with generous salaries, pieces of silver plate, and other treasure taken from the Aube's churches along with the bribes they solicited from those seeking to avoid or escape denunciation." All the defendants were censured for having "exercised arbitrary authority."[41]

The appearance of witnesses signaled that this was a political trial, not a typical session of the Revolutionary Tribunal that no longer required such niceties. After the accusation was read, president of the Tribunal Dumas, summarized the law on perjury. Proclaiming that the most important thing for the jury to know was the morality and civic commitment of the accused, Dumas excused the witnesses, except for Alexandre-Edme David-Delisle, a radical member of the Convention from the Aube closely linked to Danton. David-Delisle declared that he knew the accused as excellent patriots and that they had been persecuted because of the spirit of federalism dominant in Troyes. This legislator asserted that Guélon's earlier endorsement of federalism made his accusations null and void.

Guélon tried to press the indictment. He asked to read his original denunciation and thirty-five other documents into the record. His request was denied flatly because the jury could read the papers during their deliberations. Dumas swiftly turned the proceedings against Guélon. Ignoring the signs that the political winds had changed direction, Guélon gamely repeated his demand that Rousselin produce certain documents. Fouquier-Tinville dutifully asked Rousselin for them, but when the young defendant responded that "they were sealed" in his lodgings, the matter was dropped. For the rest of the proceedings, Guélon was treated as the accused rather than the accuser. Garnier, also a deputy of the Aube, demanded to speak. He had been a key supporter of Guélon and the sections of Troyes, but on 20 July Garnier observed that two of the other three projected witnesses had not witnessed events, being out of town, while the third was closely allied to the defendants. Two delegates from Troyes' popular society were allowed to testify; they justified the defendants' actions and vilifyied Guélon who protested in vain. Dumas told Guélon that he did not have the floor and immediately ended all discussion with a short resume of the case before releasing the jury to consider a verdict.

The jury deliberated a mere five minutes, hardly enough even to read the full titles of the thirty-seven supporting documents. The jurors "acquitted and freed" the defendants.[42] At the request of Fouquier-Tinville, Guélon was then charged with "perjury" and "having conspired with enemies of the People to bring false denunciations against innocent patriots."[43] Guélon was allowed only a brief defense. When he demanded that the documents be read before he was judged, the jury somewhat surprisingly agreed. Meanwhile, Guélon was sent to the Conciergerie, one of Paris' most notorious prisons. His trial was scheduled for a week later, 9 Thermidor (27 July 1794).[44]

The verdict stunned even well-informed contemporaries. When representative on mission Nicolas Maure heard the news, he immediately wrote to the Committee of Public Safety. He noted "the definitive and genuine manner with which the Revolutionary Tribunal acquitted Rousselin and his co-defendants and ordered the arrest of Guélon" before inquiring if this verdict affected his orders.[45]

For the Revolutionary Tribunal to acquit a Dantonist accused of excessive zeal as a terrorist by Robespierre and Couthon in July 1794 was startling. His case demonstrated the limits of Robespierre's influence. When he found out about Rousselin's acquittal, a contemporary reported Robespierre's fury. Supposedly, Robespierre wondered, where "is my power when I cannot place the head of an accomplice of Danton under the sword of justice?"[46]

THE FALL OF the factions in the spring of 1794 did not stabilize Revolutionary government. The Hébertists were gone, but the sans-culottes remained, though they had lost most of their institutional power bases. With the popular movement in check, committed revolutionaries like Collot d'Herbois and Billaud-Varennes worried about their loss of influence once they no longer spoke for "the People." Execution of the Indulgents did not catch all of Danton's many friends and collaborators, nor did it purge everyone who thought that the Terror needed to be reined in, though few were willing to say so openly. Each grouping formed a loose network of likeminded, related, or allied people that ran both vertically and horizontally through the institutions of Revolutionary government. These complex networks experienced rapid fluctuations in membership and influence. Their mutability made political calculations temporary and dependent on external factors.

On the Committee of Public Safety, Robespierre had the strong support of Couthon and Saint-Just. Between late April and late June, he generally exercised the Committee's police oversight. Then Saint-Just resumed the task. Saint-Just also became increasingly involved in supervising the Republic's armies. The issue of control over the police deepened the wedge between Robespierre and the Committee of General Security, whose leading members thought the Incorruptible and his allies were trespassing on their responsibilities and usurping their power. The Committee of General Security also resented that Robespierre had packed the Revolutionary Tribunal with his friends and allies. Saint-Just's growing immersion in military affairs angered Lazare Carnot, who, along with Robert Lindet, Claude-Antoine Prieur de la Côte-d'Or, and André Jeanbon Saint André, directed the war effort. This powerful quartet was allied with army officers and representatives on mission whose tasks centered on military supply or who provided liaison with France's forces in the field. In previous administrative conflicts over "turf," Robespierre and his supporters had sounded a public alarm. With the support of the popular movement, they had been able to get their way in the name of Revolutionary unity, purity or national defense. With the destruction of the factions in the spring and the taming of the popular movement, Robespierre's group was isolated.[47]

There was also a growing sense that France no longer faced an extreme domestic and international crisis. By the late spring of 1794, the Federalist revolt had been defeated completely and the Vendée temporarily pacified. The Spanish invasion had been repulsed, and a string of military successes on the northern frontier in May culminated in victory at Fleurus on 26 June. This triumph protected France from invasion and opened up Belgium and later the Netherlands to French occupation. With France's armies on the offensive, many dedicated Republicans believed that it was time to scale back the Terror.

Robespierre's position in Revolutionary politics was also in flux, exacerbating potential conflict among the factions.[48] The spring's assassination attempts demonstrated concerns with his growing authority and the seeming lack of effective checks. Cécile Renault's reference to him as a "tyrant" highlighted this perception. Robespierre's vision of a Republic based on virtue (also articulated by Saint-Just) had genuine support among a significant segment of the Revolutionary political class. His status as "the Incorruptible" amidst the confusing welter of plots and corruption also lent him unmatched moral and political legitimacy. That status invited accusations that he wanted sole power. Robespierre was also blamed for the actions of certain Revolutionary institutions particularly the Committee of Public Safety and the Revolutionary Tribunal. Such allegations effectively undermined his popular support, especially when Robespierre could not or did not choose to defend himself.

Deteriorating health and judgment first opened and then widened a gap between Robespierre's potential and actual political influence. Beginning in early February, illness regularly forced Robespierre to miss meetings of the Convention, the Committee of Public Safety, and the Jacobins. His absence between 19 April and 7 May and again from 18 June to 26 July, contributed to his waning influence. In the first seven months of 1794, he gave sixteen speeches in the National Convention, a far cry from the 101 he delivered in 1793. Robespierre's long career and complex involvement in Revolutionary politics estranged him from many influential figures. Amar and Vadier of the Committee of General Security personally detested him. On the Committee of Public Safety, Collot d'Herbois, Billaud-Varennes and, increasingly, Carnot, found his sanctimony insufferable. Such animosity was dangerous since everyone knew each other and they spent much of the day and some of the night together conducting the business of the Revolution; personality conflicts were inevitable yet profoundly dangerous.

From spring into summer, the Committee of General Security, pushed by Amar and Vadier, ignored few opportunities to embarrass or oppose Robespierre. Vadier referred to this policy as "a state of legitimate defense."[49] On May 12th Catherine Théot, a demented old woman, was arrested as a public nuisance. She preached that Robespierre was one of two new messiahs and that, as the "Mother of God," she would soon give birth to a deity. Reporting to the Convention on 15 June, Vadier's discourse on "fanaticism" portrayed Théot as a tool of the English. The report came a week after the Festival of the Supreme Being which was associated closely with Robespierre in the public mind because, in his role as president of the Convention, he gave two speeches during the ceremony that outlined his hope for a regeneration of French public spirit. Such as association was unsafe even though the Festival itself was wildly popular—about 500,000 people attended—because it prompted heated criticism. Jacques Thuriot, who had close ties to Danton, complained, "It is not enough for him to be master. He has to be God."[50] The

Festival stoked fears that Robespierre meant to institute a republic of virtue sooner rather than later.

The Committee of General Security's report on Théot was a masterpiece of slander, innuendo, and forgery. It ridiculed religious "superstition" and linked Robespierre to a host of alleged misdeeds. As president of the Convention, Robespierre could not defend himself for procedural reasons, though he ensured that Théot would not be sent to the Revolutionary Tribunal. Some contemporaries thought that the acrimony of this debate led Robespierre to avoid meetings of the Committee of Public Safety.

Others thought that he stayed away because a joint meeting of the great committees on 29 June was a tipping point. Carnot accused Robespierre and Saint-Just of being "ridiculous dictators" and stormed out in a rage. Such open criticism of Robespierre makes the charge seem ludicrous, but it demonstrated that the Incorruptible was neither untouchable nor invulnerable.[51]

In the summer of 1794, the ultra-terrorists feared Robespierre. He had already recalled many of them in the spring. Robespierre was appalled by the actions of certain representatives on mission especially Jean-Baptiste Carrier, Fouché, Paul Barras, Louis-Marie-Stanislaus Fréron, Tallien, and Edmond-Louis Dubois-Crancé. The Law of 22 Prairial was a clear and present danger to these deputies, but many other deputies had cause to wonder if their activities had crossed some invisible, and potentially shifting, line.

The threat of a move against the ultra-terrorists by Robespierre and his faction loomed ever larger during the summer of 1794. In a halting series of long drawn out steps, Robespierre hinted at his plans. He slowly edged closer to naming names thereby triggering the next purge. Two days after the passage of the Law of 22 Prairial (on 10 June), Robespierre argued with François-Louis Bourdon (of the Oise) on the floor of the Convention. In the course of a debate about the existence of a conspiracy against the Mountain, Bourdon insisted that Robespierre "name them." Robespierre responded, "I will name then when I need to," but refused to be more specific.[52]

Tensions grew even as Robespierre largely abandoned his administrative activities. Claude Payan, Paris' national agent, investigated the Committee of General Security's conduct of the Théot affair. On 27 June, Payan suggested to Robespierre that purging this Committee and diminishing its power would smother dissent and protect the authority of the Committee of Public Safety. "You cannot choose better circumstances for striking at all the conspirators," he observed.[53] Although suggestive, it is unknown what effect this private letter might have had on his thinking.

On 1 July, Robespierre announced to the Convention that there was a vast conspiracy that he had only begun to uncover. A week later, he gave a speech at the Jacobins about the existence of new plots. Defending the need to denounce conspirators, he said: "I speak not to provoke harsh measures against the guilty. . . . My intention is to warn every citizen of these traps and to extinguish the new torch of discord they seek to light in the Convention." He acknowledged his opponents' efforts: "They [the conspirators] wish to corrupt the Convention through a system of Terror. Gatherings are taking place in which the only goal is to spread these disastrous ideas. They seek to persuade every member [of the Convention] that the Committee of Public Safety intends to proscribe them."[54] Yet still Robespierre hesitated.

Meanwhile, certain ultras and former Dantonists circulated different lists of those to be purged. Edmond Biré, a keen observer of the political landscape, noted that "the first of these lists had only 12 names, another indicated 18, and a third contained 30."[55] Just days before 9 Thermidor, Robespierre criticized his colleagues' lack of nerve when Garnier of the Aube reported that the circulation of a list with thirty names was causing "general alarm" in the Convention.[56] According to Biré, the list of twelve included Legendre, Bourdon, Fouché, Tallien, Dubois-Crancé, Fréron, and Barras along with another deputy from the Aube, Danton's friend Edme-Bonaventure Courtois. Among the eighteen were noted terrorists Claude Javogues and Garnier, as well as former Dantonists like Thuriot. The thirty added Vadier and two other members of the Committee of the General Security, as well as Billaud-Varenne and Collot d'Herbois from the Committee of Public Safety. Perhaps forty different individuals were named. Rousselin was not listed: he was already under indictment.

Contemporaries noted that these lists exceeded the number of Robespierre's intended targets. Biré remarked that "Robespierre left the Convention in doubt. He threatened everyone without daring to name anyone. The vague, mysterious hesitation that surrounded his plans spread anxiety everywhere giving his enemies time to spread the alarm, frightening a crowd of deputies who he never considered striking." Robespierre had enemies,

> perhaps six or seven of them, a dozen at most. With that list, he could have walked boldly to the tribune and made sure that the other deputies knew that they had nothing to fear. He could have made his formal demands [for their proscription] at that very minute. Audacious without doubt, perilous definitely, the coup would very probably have

succeeded. Both fearful and reassured, the Convention would have followed him.[57]

Thus, Robespierre's own tactics provided the strength of numbers and desperation that powered the coalition that rose against him.

The deliberate pace of the run-up to 26 July, when Robespierre finally took action, is curious. His uncertain health surely played a part. But there can be no doubt that Robespierre personally detested Revolutionary violence. His sister Charlotte observed a meeting with Fouché where Robespierre rebuked the recently recalled representative on mission. She remembered Robespierre saying that "Nothing could justify the cruelties which he was guilty of. Lyon was in revolt against the National Convention, but that was not a reason for firing grapeshot at a group of disarmed enemies."[58] Robespierre's move to expel Fouché from the Jacobin Club on 14 July was taken as a sign that he intended to condemn the ultra-terrorists. How many were in his sights was hotly debated, but the number was certainly not as large as fear made it. Members of the great committees and former representatives on mission dreaded Terror in the name of virtue as personified by Robespierre.

Robespierre's speech to the Convention on 26 July, repeated at the Jacobins later that day, consisted of nearly two hours of vaguely menacing, overblown rhetoric. He defended himself against charges of "dictatorship," decried the widespread scapegoating of his actions, and railed vaguely against new plots. Only three deputies were identified as needing to be purged, all for corruption, though Robespierre made it seem like many, many more were suspect. The fuzziness of Robespierre's charges allowed those most in danger of being purged to mobilize far more deputies than might otherwise have been the case. Fear of being the next victims of the Terror drove the coup against Robespierre and his faction, not genuine concern that he might become a dictator. That was merely a convenient charge to level against him.

In this overheated cauldron of intrigue, image and reputation were as important as reality. Successful appeals to public opinion were phrased in terms of representing the general will. Just as reputations could be made or destroyed in a heartbeat, public image was changeable. Networks worked the same way: they emerged, collapsed, were rebuilt, merged and divided as conditions evolved. Stability was in short supply in Paris in the summer of 1794.

What Robespierre might do worried many different groups. Ultra-terrorists Fouché, Carrier, Tallien, Bô, Garnier, Barras, Fréron, and Dubois-Crancé took the lead. They received strong support from those tied to the Hébertists, such as Billaud-Varennes, Collot d'Herbois, Amar, Vadier, and

Armand-Joseph Guffroy, who also sat on the Committee of General Security. Financial whiz Pierre-Joseph Cambon, Laurent Lecointre, and Barère took action because of public censure by Robespierre. Former Dantonists like Legendre, Courtois, Thuriot, and Bourdon de l'Oise suspected that they would not escape the coming purge. The Committee of Public Safety's military "technocrats," Carnot, Lindet, Prieur de la Côte-d'Or, and Jeanbon Saint André, stood aside and let Robespierre and his faction become the Terror's next victims.

On 27 July 1794 (9 Thermidor, Year II), Robespierre, Couthon, and Saint-Just were arrested. Deputies Augustin Robespierre and Philippe-Joseph-François Le Bas, along with some of their allies on the Revolutionary Tribunal and in the municipal government or National Guard of Paris, were also apprehended. The ineptitude of the move, their subsequent escape, and the haphazard resort to force reveals that there was no single, well-orchestrated plot directed by a central group of conspirators. The coup brought together different groups and their networks, all of whom were motivated by the uncertainty of their own positions and their fears for the future. That these groups agreed on little else was a problem for another day. Twenty-two members of the Robespierrist "faction" were guillotined on 28 July. A few months later, Rousselin could not help remarking that no one wept when Robespierre was guillotined. Rousselin described "the procession of abominable men, covered in blood, mud, and bruises that presented the most hideous and disgusting spectacle. Numerous people accompanied them howling and yelling with a furious and frenzied joy." It was "so different from Danton's execution."[59]

After Danton's death, Montagnard Nicolas Ruault wrote that the Revolution "devours its own children; it kills its brothers; it gnaws at its intestines; it has become the cruelest of monsters."[60] Rousselin's association with Danton tied him to Legendre and Courtois. The latter deputy was charged with inventorying Robespierre's papers after 9 Thermidor, a vital position that signals his prominence in the coup.

From his position in the ministry, Rousselin kept his friends and acquaintances abreast of police surveillance. He defended them and their reputations in the pages of the *Journal of the Republic*. Legendre, who had worked together with Rousselin in the Jacobins on 25 May and was concerned about his own survival, was appalled by Rousselin's expulsion and dispatch to the Committee of General Security. The speed of Rousselin's fall from grace was, in some ways, just as troubling to contemporaries. Courtois worried about the venom directed at Danton's ghost by Robespierre and Couthon, a sign that they were unnerved by the lingering presence of the great orator's

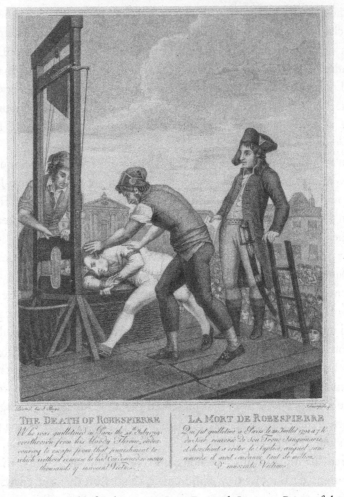

THE DEATH OF ROBESPIERRE | LA MORT DE ROBESPIERRE

FIGURE 3.2 The Death of Robespierre. Getty Research Institute, Prints of the French Revolution, 1774–ca. 1840.

friends and allies. The clear antagonism to Rousselin's "Dantonism" motivated this group to convince other members of the Convention of the dangers of continuing the Terror. Fittingly, as the deputies shouted down Robespierre's attempt to rally support in the Convention on 27 July Antoine Garnier shouted, "Danton's blood is choking you!"

In the minds of many deputies, Garnier de l'Aube was connected to Danton. But he was also a well-known terrorist who oversaw the bloody repression of federalism in the department of the Jura. In the summer of 1794, he attempted to escape both of these identities by relentlessly attacking

Rousselin for terrorism. Yet when David-Delisle exculpated Rousselin and his co-defendants before the Revolutionary Tribunal, Garnier did little. Inclusion on some lists of those to be proscribed motivated Garnier to become one of the most active conspirators against Robespierre. Rousselin's acquittal was a sign of Robespierre's waning power, as well as a demonstration of the coalescing of his enemies. Garnier was rewarded not only by surviving, but also with election to the Committee of General Security in November 1794.

Rousselin had close ties to several ultra-terrorists, most notably Barras and Fouché who received a great deal of positive, almost fawning coverage in the *Journal of Public Safety*. Rousselin also helped Fouché hide once it became clear that Robespierre and Couthon wanted to purge the "butcher of Lyon." It was no coincidence that Fouché was expelled from the Jacobins— even though he was the president—on the same day that Rousselin was sent to the Revolutionary Tribunal. Barras had been on the fringes of Danton's circle. He knew Rousselin well and appreciated his abilities. Rousselin aided both men in identifying and making contact with the like-minded, while lobbying others, like Barère, to act. Fouché was perhaps the most energetic conspirator against Robespierre. Barras was entrusted with commanding the Convention's military forces on 9 Thermidor. The most convincing evidence of these deputies' esteem is that both Fouché and Barras later employed Rousselin in sensitive positions.

THE TROYENS' ACTIONS, and their limits, are also important parts of the story. Despite the concerted efforts of the National Convention and the Committee of Public Safety to rein in and centralize the Terror, outside Paris, the system was in trouble. The inability of Troyes' Revolutionary Committee to fulfill military supply quotas was a major concern. In the late spring of 1794, provincial victims of the Terror became increasingly willing to confront their tormentors. Deputies who had been terrorists themselves suddenly agreed to support them. The political consensus that gave birth to the Terror was breaking down. Provincial restiveness was a key component of the threat to the faction headed by Robespierre that wished to continue the Terror, at least temporarily.

Many Troyens refused to accept Rousselin's acquittal, even as the institutions of the Terror were slowly dismantled. Their doggedness demonstrated that the Terror was neither forgotten nor forgiven. The Troyens' determination to punish Rousselin represented the terrorists' greatest fear: that they would be held accountable for their actions by their surviving victims.

Rousselin played no part in the events of 9 Thermidor despite being acquitted by the Revolutionary Tribunal a week before. Only two days after being released by the Revolutionary Tribunal, Amar ordered his arrest on behalf of the Committee of General Security. Amar was perfectly willing to defy Robespierre but he disdained Rousselin's terrorism and his "moderation." Thus, Rousselin went from the exaltation of exoneration to the agony of imprisonment, a victim of Amar's vendetta against the surviving Dantonists. In jail, Rousselin welcomed numerous visitors and passed many messages through them to others. But when the coup of 9 Thermidor began, he was locked up in the Conciergerie.

This is where Legendre found him. Unlocking Rousselin's cell, Legendre gave him "a swift kick in the pants." "What are you doing in there, you damned rascal? Get out, quickly!" cried the former butcher, using the authority delegated by the Convention to liberate political prisoners.[61] Guélon, Rousselin's accuser, was detained nearby. His perjury trial had been scheduled for that very day. Only a clerical error delaying the trial kept him from the guillotine. Although he must have been glad to avoid facing the Tribunal, it had to have been galling to watch Rousselin go scot free. Guélon was not released for another eight days.

Free once more, Rousselin seems to have returned to his section. Unity had fiercely objected to his second incarceration. On 9 Thermidor, like most of Paris' sections, Unity strongly supported the National Convention against Robespierre and his faction. Rousselin kept out of the public eye for his own safety and avoided the Jacobin Club even after Legendre reopened it on 29 July. Rousselin could not count on another 9 Thermidor to liberate him if Amar, or another enemy, went after him again. He was afraid for the future, and for the first time in years, there was very little he could do about it.

Rousselin used his new-found freedom to visit friends, both old and new who remained in prison. Interestingly, these friends included foreign nationals suspected of being spies. Before his acquittal on 20 July, Rousselin had been incarcerated in the Talaru mansion, a lovely, if decrepit, old building on the Right Bank where prisoners paid for their own upkeep in private rooms for a phenomenal 18 livres a day, double the daily wage of a skilled laborer in Paris. At the same time, inmates had to pay the Commune to guard their home. Where Rousselin got the money to pay the city so lavishly for several weeks of these accommodations is a mystery. It is also unclear how he supported himself after 9 Thermidor. He did not resume work either at the ministry or the newspaper (which closed in early September). One of his few public actions during this period was to demand the recovery of "two pistols" and then "a knife with an ivory handle and scissors" that had been seized when he was arrested.[62] Perhaps he needed to sell or pawn them.

Or maybe the Troyens' charges of graft had merit and he used their wealth to pay for his upkeep.

A hint at his activities comes from an undated letter written sometime that fall in which he asserted that he devoted "my obscure faculties against the remains of tyranny." How? He claimed that it was agents of Robespierre who sent him to the Talaru. As an "outraged plebian" he complained about "the scandalous privileges enjoyed by rich nobles." Rousselin denounced them, but they were never tried. The rest of the letter implied that he was keeping tabs on these potential enemies of the Republic for the police. In fact, he asked to recover his written denunciation so as not to lose his cover as a police spy.[63] For someone with his broad circle of acquaintances and close ties to the machinery of police supervision, the transition from collating reports to making them seems natural. He had few other potential sources of income. Although he was a true believer in Revolutionary methods when he brought the Terror to Provins and Troyes, his experiences in 1794 undercut that faith. Rousselin was less an opportunist than a survivor. Except for his stint in prison, Rousselin's lifestyle did not suggest that he benefited financially from his work as a missionary of the Republic. Police spy, however, was a role that Rousselin would play intermittently for the next twenty years.

The Terror did not end with Robespierre's fall. His faction was removed—bloodily—from its institutions as the victors blamed the excesses of the Terror on those purged on 9 Thermidor. The Revolutionary Tribunal was suspended on 29 July. On 1 August, the law of 22 Prairial was revoked and Fouquier-Tinville arrested. Neither these measures, nor the subsequent outpouring of scapegoating, concluded the Terror. On the recommendation of a member of the Committee of General Security, the Convention established a temporary commission to replace the suspended court. A close colleague of Garnier's suggested that the commission be termed the "Provisional Revolutionary Tribunal." On behalf of the Committee of Public Safety, Barère defended the need for a Tribunal to be active in "destroying the enemies of liberty and purging the soil of liberty": "The training of the group needs to be revised with that wisdom that perfects without weakening and that recomposes without destroying . . . in the name of justice and the Revolution."[64] The names and the targets changed, but the practice of Terror continued almost unchanged. Months later, deputy Jean-Baptiste-Michel Saladin reported that in the 45 days before 9 Thermidor, the era of the Great Terror, the number of victims was 577 while in the 45 days after this supposedly decisive change, he counted 1,286 victims. Rather than a turning point in the Terror, 9 Thermidor marked only the doom of another faction.

Although political networks centered on Paris intersected with those that were provincial in aim and origin, that overlap was imperfect. After 9 Thermidor, networks in the capital and in the provinces waited anxiously for the other shoe to drop. Who would be next? What would happen now that the Incorruptible was gone from the scene?

Shifts in political tone took quite some time to become apparent in the provinces. After their acquittal, Rousselin's co-defendants resumed their administrative positions. Representative on mission Maure prevented them from taking revenge on their denouncers. His report to the Committee of Public Safety on 11 August repeated the slanders of critics of the former civil commissioner. Maure referred to Rousselin as a "lightweight and inconsequential young man" who "always made jokes and sarcastic remarks as he gave favors" and "surrounded himself with men greedy for position." Four days later, Maure provided a more measured evaluation. Rousselin was "inconsistent" in his actions and permitted the "excesses, zeal, and inaccuracies" of his supporters while surrounding himself with a guard. Maure asserted that a portion of the money he oversaw either "profited him or was spent on some extraordinary expenses" (Rousselin claimed the latter). He concluded that "Rousselin is hated by the People, the sectionnaires, and the aristocracy" of Troyes. But Maure acknowledged that this "aristocracy had played an active, though secret, part in all recent events. Presently, the aristocracy applauds the sectionnaires and supports them. What is appalling is that they are dragging the People along with them."

Maure also described the locals who had been denounced for supporting Rousselin as having "reputations for integrity," except for Gachez. These "true Republicans" were ambitious and "their patriotism burned too hot," but they were "good sans-culottes." Yet he fired the inner circle of Rousselin's closest supporters even though they were not imprisoned or sanctioned, while leaving most of Rousselin's/Bô's appointees in place.[65]

At the same time, Maure, who in other times and other places was an effective missionary of the Republic, continued to liberate Troyens imprisoned by Rousselin or Bô.[66] He released so many that, in late September, he had to defend himself on the floor of the Convention against charges of "royalism" because he freed twenty-six priests and eleven wives of émigrés. Courtois and Garnier also earned political capital in Troyes by using their influence with the great committees to sponsor the release of many prominent lawyers, merchants, and landowners. Other suspects, however, remained incarcerated until 1796. In the department of the Aube, the official Terror ended soon after the fall of Robespierre, though the Incorruptible himself had begun the process with his attack on radicals like Rousselin and his cronies. For this fractious department, however, dealing with the consequences of the Terror emerged as the central task of Revolutionary politics across the remainder of the decade.

In late summer and fall, the pendulum swung as people described as "terrorists," "sans-culottes," and "Jacobins" were targeted by their former victims. French military success and widespread disgust for the methods of the Terror combined to propel this shift toward the politics of vengeance. The Convention shuttered Paris' Jacobin Club definitively on 11 November. Appalled by Jean-Baptiste Carrier's excesses in Nantes, the deputies willingly sacrificed him to save themselves by voting to remove his parliamentary immunity. He was guillotined soon after on 16 December. Former minister Dominique-Joseph Garat wrote, "The Terror no longer existed in law, but it persisted in spirit."[67] After 9 Thermidor, the Terror and the practice of denunciation took on new, only slightly less violent, forms.

Alexandre Rousselin became a victim of this political shift. He was exposed to renewed denunciation from Troyes, especially after Maure's negative report on his mission. Even though the Terror was far less destructive of life and property in this department than in most places, the Aube's elite remained fixated on vengeance. Recognizing their singlemindedness, Rousselin spent the fall searching unsuccessfully for new patrons. On 11 December 1794, the Committee of General Security ordered him arrested for the third time. Warned by friends, Rousselin went into hiding. When the police visited his apartment, they found a woman living there who claimed that Rousselin "left for Melun fifteen days ago without leaving any other address."[68] Rousselin was finally caught, but his allies in the coalition against Robespierre continued to work on his behalf. The order liberating him on 27 January 1795 was signed by Legendre, Guffroy, and Garnier.

Swiftly, Rousselin was denounced once more. Infuriated by his re-release, Troyes' popular society wrote the National Convention four days later. The Troyens described him as an "imitator of Carrier" who should be "equally liable to face national justice." They sent "a copy of his tyrannical 'populicide' action . . . which had already been denounced by the city's 6th section a year earlier." Perhaps unwittingly echoing Rousselin's evocation of Marat, they called on the deputies to "announce your indignation throughout France because publicity is the safeguard of the people." The Troyens focused on Rousselin's petition for "the immediate construction of a guillotine" and his denunciations of the rich for hoarding. They demanded that these acts should be "judged in first and last resort by the provisional criminal tribunal."[69] The Troyens were emboldened by the arrival of yet another representative on mission, Jean-Bernard Albert, on 31 January 1795. He was charged with invigorating public administration and restoring calm after a series of food riots. Albert promptly conducted a thorough purge of the Aube's administrators, the seventh since the declaration of the Republic in September 1792, returning more moderate republicans to office. These elites were committed to the idea that Rousselin had to suffer for his actions in Troyes.

THE WINTER OF 1794–95 witnessed profound changes in Rousselin's family situation. After nearly twenty years of separation, his parents François and Nicole took advantage of the possibility of divorce offered by Revolutionary legal changes in December 1794. The sundering of this union allowed Laurent Corbeau to wed Nicole in January 1795. Sadly, their marriage lasted only eighteen months before Nicole died. Nicole's divorce and remarriage had little impact on the twenty-one-year-old Alexandre Rousselin's life in the short term, but the consequences of his mother's remarriage eventually transformed his life.

The first eight months of 1795 witnessed an accelerating attack on perpetrators of the Terror known as the Thermidorean Reaction. The National Convention freed the surviving Girondins and restored them to their posts. Although the economy was in freefall after the Maximum was terminated as a tool of the Terror in December 1794, treaties ended hostilities with Prussia, the Netherlands, and Spain in April, May, and July respectively. The Convention decided that a new constitution had to be written to replace the democratic 1793 version that had been suspended "until the peace."

On 10 April 1795, the deputies ordered that all "terrorists or supporters of Robespierre" be disarmed. This measure gave new impetus to what became known as the "White Terror" directed against the leaders of Revolutionary government. In the south of France, "bands of Jesus" formed to attack ex-terrorists.[70] They massacred incarcerated Jacobins in Lyon on 24 April. Ongoing violence by gangs of the capital's "gilded youth" targeting sans-culottes and Jacobins contributed to widespread lawlessness and the thirst for vengeance. In response, Paris' sans-culottes rioted on multiple occasions. They sought food and the application of the Constitution of 1793. On 20 May, militants invaded the Convention to present their demands to the deputies. The army put down these "insurrections." Such a political climate bolstered the Troyens' efforts to strike back at someone who had levied a "revolutionary tax" to benefit "poor sans-culottes."

Rousselin performed the same scapegoating function for the Aubois that Robespierre did for France as a whole. Albert's report on 19 March mocked

Rousselin's youth and lack of experience and accused him of trying to provoke a revolt in the department by sending too much grain to Paris while the troops dependent on food from southern Champagne starved. Albert blamed all of Bô's actions on Rousselin. He claimed that it was to prevent the occurrence of a "second Rousselin" that all "sans-culottes" and "artisans with no aptitude for administration" had to be purged from office.[71] Five days later, the municipality of Troyes proclaimed that the city "had no need of an *uncivil commissioner*, a *Rousselin*, nor the permanent presence of a guillotine to force it to open its coffers." The People know "their true friends."[72] Taking advantage of the call to disarm "terrorists," on 1 May 1795, Troyes' popular society again denounced Rousselin to the Convention for the "ferocity" of his acts and for the "crimes" he "committed while serving as a commissioner of executive power."[73] Soon afterward, Rousselin was jailed for the fourth time.

Initially, he was confined in the Port-Libre prison, which was in the midst of a conflict between rich inmates and former sans-culottes. After a month, he was transferred to Quatre-Nations (in his home section), where influential former Jacobins were incarcerated. The Committee of General Security did not abandon him. Rousselin's allies in Troyes had been jailed in April and then freed on 4 July. The Troyens were infuriated and grew even angrier when Rousselin was liberated on 13 July 1795 after about three months in prison. Once again Rousselin could not insulate himself from their vengeance. Four days later, "notwithstanding any other release order,"[74] Rousselin was arrested a fifth time and sent to Plessis prison, considered "the roughest prison in Paris."[75] Both in Paris and in Troyes, the movement to punish terrorists borrowed many methods from its victims to overcome the influence of Rousselin's remaining friends, allies and patrons.

That Alexandre Rousselin survived the denunciation of Robespierre and Couthon and his trial by the Revolutionary Tribunal was described by a contemporary as "a miracle."[76] In 1794, the fear that drove the Terror was felt not only by the enemies of France, but also by former terrorists themselves. As a system of government, the Terror broke down that summer under renewed challenges from the provinces and ongoing factionalism. The system may have been on the verge of collapse, but its tactics long outlived the annihilation of Robespierre and his faction on 27–28 July. The victims changed, but the methods stayed the same.

Both Robespierre's fall and Rousselin's ability to survive can be attributed to the mobilization of diverse networks of neighbors, friends, allies, and supporters. This mobilization can also be understood as a series of plots; in some ways, the Revolutionaries' anxiety about plots was based in the reality of faction-fighting. Changeable groups united by experience, ideology, place of residence, and mutual fear coalesced to bring down the Incorruptible. After the collapse of his primary networks in the spring of 1794, Rousselin was able to strengthen certain ties and build others that saved him from the guillotine in July. Over the course of 1794–95, the evolution of Revolutionary politics undermined some but not all of those associations as Robespierre was increasingly scapegoated as a "man who would be king" and simultaneously as the instigator of a heightened Terror. The oscillation of these networks explains why Rousselin repeatedly suffered and then escaped the vengeance of the Aubois. His experience anticipated the see-saw politics that characterized the rest of the Revolutionary decade.

The Revolutionary emphasis on the idea of the general will meant that the People always knew who their "true friends" were. But the ability to speak on their behalf was unstable. Claiming that mantle was a vital element of factional conflict in 1792–1794. Most people were denounced not for what they had done but for being out of step with the political moment. Such condemnations meant different things at different points, even at the height of the Terror. The need to steer a steady course in the center of the current represented an important continuity in Revolutionary political culture. Alexandre Rousselin learned this lesson well, and more importantly, he learned how to tack and maneuver amidst a constantly shifting political landscape full of opportunities and perils. His efforts to escape the White Terror reveal that when ideology no longer motivated political action, networks provided a means of rehabilitating the reputation of even well-known terrorists.

4

Rehabilitation: Political, Literary, and Social, 1795–1815

*Are you a liar or have you been lied to? Are you the agent
of faction that persecutes anyone who honorably leads an
army? Or are you simply the dupe of some rogues?*

—GENERAL LAZARE HOCHE TO DEPUTY JEAN-NICOLAS
DUFRESNE-SAINT-LÉON, 13 August 1797

*In matters of the heart, nothing is true except
the improbable.*

—ANNE LOUISE GERMAINE DE STAËL TO JULIETTE
RÉCAMIER, 5 October 1810

*What then is, generally speaking, the truth of history?
A fable agreed upon.*

—NAPOLEON BONAPARTE TO THE COMTE DE LAS
CASAS, 20 November 1816

ALEXANDRE ROUSSELIN SURVIVED both the Terror and the White
Terror with his core beliefs in the promise of the Republic and in the need
for popular participation in politics intact. His experiences convinced him,
however, that different methods were needed to protect and preserve the
Republic. At heart a patriot, Rousselin still intended a career in public service. But first he had to get out of jail and remake his reputation. With few
exceptions, terrorists were no longer welcome in Revolutionary administration. Beginning soon after he returned from Troyes in early 1794, Rousselin
spent much of the next two decades rehabilitating his reputation. His trajectory mirrored that of hundreds, if not thousands, of former missionaries
of the republic who wanted a new start in French society after 9 Thermidor.

The Making of a Terrorist. Jeff Horn, Oxford University Press (2021). © Oxford University Press.
DOI: 10.1093/oso/9780197529928.001.0001

Deputy Jean-Lambert Tallien coined the term "terrorist" the same day that Maximilien Robespierre went to the guillotine.[1] On 19 August, Tallien linked the system of Terror and despotism: "Terror is the weapon of tyranny." Politics drove Robespierre and Georges Couthon to censure Rousselin's terrorism and send him to the Revolutionary Tribunal just as his ties to Danton led Jean-Baptiste Amar to order his imprisonment even after his acquittal. Over the long term, the enmity of the Aubois—driven fundamentally by a desire for vengeance—proved an equal threat to Rousselin's life and freedom. He escaped the guillotine and was liberated twice by the Committee of General Security, but fresh accusations kept returning him to prison. Denunciation for graft and the exercise of arbitrary authority overcame the support provided by Rousselin's network of protectors. His freedom was assured only after an abortive, purportedly "royalist" uprising of 5 October 1795 led the National Convention to proclaim an amnesty releasing prisoners whose "acts related purely to the Revolution" on 25 October.[2] Although the Troyens made a strong case that Rousselin's acts went beyond what was strictly necessary, he was freed in early November 1795, this time for good. He had no job, no clear prospects, and had been branded a "Terrorist." He was twenty-two years old.

The period after 9 Thermidor is often glossed over in accounts of the French Revolution. Beyond the war effort, the heroes seem less heroic, the villains less villainous. The meaning of events of the day was hard to grasp, but they cannot be ignored in the trajectory of a single life. The five years from July 1794 to November 1799 shaped societal memories of the Terror and provided its survivors with a wealth of lessons for governing France that Alexandre Rousselin and his contemporaries struggled for years to understand and apply.[3]

The National Convention which took office in September 1792 ruled France until November 1795. Its members voted to kill Louis XVI and resorted to a systematic use of Terror. In 1793–94, the Convention also delegated tremendous authority to the Committee of Public Safety and then recovered it. Robespierre and his faction were guillotined in July 1794 ostensibly to end the Terror. But ending the Terror and keeping the war effort at fever pitch while maintaining the economy proved impossible.[4] The Convention acted slowly across the fall of 1794 touching off a host of recriminations. Almost immediately, many victims stepped up their efforts to seek bloody vengeance on perpetrators of the Terror, like Rousselin. These efforts, known as the White Terror, presaged the fluctuating or see-saw politics that typified the era until 1799.

The deputies to the National Convention recognized that the Terror alienated almost all politically active Frenchmen from the government, especially in the provinces. Foreign invasion, civil war against the Federalists and in the Vendée, with an economy in free-fall justified the Terror, but those justifications no longer applied and were no longer accepted. Public opinion had turned against the methods of the Terror even if the cause was just. For the next five years, the Revolutionaries searched for ways to build (or rebuild) a republican consensus. Their labors were hampered by the strains of ongoing foreign war compounded by devastating inflation and economic dislocation that followed the dismantling of the wage and price controls known as Maximums. A political culture in which denunciation and vengeance had become all too pervasive also obstructed the deputies' efforts. Widespread banditry and frequent challenges to the social order were signs of the French state's inability to pacify the people or win their trust.

To maintain a moderate republic, the National Convention discarded the democratic Constitution of 1793. The successor Constitution of 1795 aimed to prevent dictatorship by establishing firm checks and balances. The new structure was based on a five-man executive known as the Directory and a two-house legislature elected through a limited, though still broadly based, suffrage. Both the voting restrictions and the fact that the deputies mandated that two-thirds of the new legislature must come from the Convention reflected their recognition that the fragile consensus in favor of the measures taken in 1793–94 had wholly collapsed. The new government faced challenges both from those opposed to the republic, often termed royalists, and from those who wanted a more democratic solution. The Directory undermined its own credibility by resorting repeatedly to violence, thereby keeping the legacy of the hated Terror alive.[5] The state faced several coup attempts, some more serious than others. More significantly, the Directory annulled national election results in 1796, 1798, and 1799 that rejected the political perspective of a majority of the sitting deputies.[6] By the end of the decade, the regime was perched on a precipice. The only real question was which way it would fall.

Like many others, Rousselin believed in the promise of 1789. He also recognized the force of circumstances that had led to the Terror. Republicans searched in vain for means of fulfilling their principles under a deeply unpopular and highly ineffective government. That task was complicated by the unwillingness of that government to trust them enough to let them defend their political views. Under the Directory, republicans compromised, experimented, and advocated. Their innovative efforts forged the regime that took power in 1799, the legacy of the French Revolution, and ultimately the emergence of liberalism. Alexandre Rousselin played an important part in this struggle.

To justify his freedom, much less earn rehabilitation, Rousselin needed to separate perceptions of his actions from the arbitrariness associated with the system of Terror. Instead, he emphasized a different part of his experience by portraying himself as a Dantonist who had braved Robespierre's animosity. Thanks to the great orator's belated efforts to curb the system of Terror, Danton's mantle could safely be claimed. At the same time, scapegoating Robespierre was a routine feature of politics after 27 July 1794. That he was often mistaken for a militant member and sometime president of the jury of the Revolutionary Tribunal, surnamed "Osselin," known for trying to send the surviving Girondin deputies to the guillotine also endangered Rousselin's position.

Early in 1796, just a few weeks after being released, the situation came to a head. He had to respond to the clamor of complaint about the freedom of the "bloody handed Rousselin." A prominent journalist confused him with Osselin while compiling information about surviving Jacobins. The compilation identified Rousselin as a member of the jury of the Revolutionary Tribunal. In a public letter, Rousselin observed that, "far from being a judge, he had been judged by the Revolutionary Tribunal." He rebuked the journalist for being a poor speller and ignoring the facts, thereby "depriving" him of the status of having been a victim of the Terror, which "is so important to my story."[7] The letter stressed that he was a target, not a perpetrator, of Terror. Shifting perspective was central to his efforts to achieve redemption. This task was made easier by the publication of Louis-Marie Prudhomme's *General and Impartial History of the Errors, Mistakes and Crimes Committed during the French Revolution*, which emphasized Robespierre's angry response to Rousselin's acquittal. The lack of corroboration of Robespierre's reaction or of many other purported "facts" advanced by Prudhomme did not inhibit the great popularity of this sensationalistic attack on the Jacobins. Rousselin's reputation recovered enough for him to consider resuming government work.

Once again, his friends and networks came to his aid. This time assistance came from Jules-François Paré and Paul Barras, both linked to the Dantonists. With the latter's support, the former hired Rousselin to be secretary-general of the department of the Seine, which included Paris. To entrust Rousselin with this sensitive position early in 1796 shows Paré's confidence, the lack of attention paid to bureaucrats, and the dearth of qualified alternatives.[8] After only a few months, Paré was forced to resign as the government's commissioner for the Seine, after being suspected of complicity in Gracchus Babeuf's

"Conspiracy of Equals" to overthrow the Directory.[9] Rousselin left too as a fresh spate of new denunciations accused him of being a Jacobin who "looked down his nose at legitimate complaints with haughtiness and insolence. You had to be a supporter of Babeuf to be greeted with courtesy by Mister Rousselin," claimed the *Le Courrier républicain* of 27 May 1796.[10] At this sensitive juncture, he could not afford to be associated with plots against the government, especially those with no chance of success. To rebuild his reputation, Rousselin needed to avoid dangerous affiliations.

BARRAS
Membre du Directoire Exécutif
Né à Foxemphoux près Barjole Département du Var le 31 Juin 1755

FIGURE 4.1 Barras, Membre du Directoire Exécutif. Bibliothèque nationale de France. Recueil. Collection de Vinck. Un siècle d'histoire de France par l'estampe, 1770–1870. Vol. 49 (pièces 6584–6796), Directoire, Consulat et Empire, 6586].

Barras found Rousselin a soft landing place. As one of the five executive directors of the Republic, Barras oversaw all French troops inside the country. He sent Rousselin to work in military supply for General Lazare Hoche who commanded French forces in the west. This assignment came just as Hoche defeated the remnants of the Vendée uprising and the émigré royalist rebels supported by the British. Hoche was then charged with preparing for an invasion of Ireland, in order to support the rebellion led by the United Irishmen. Since this task was largely a matter of logistics, Rousselin's organizational and administrative skills were useful. However, Rousselin's true value to Hoche was as a confidential secretary whose political acumen and close ties to Barras and other important political figures were essential to gathering the men and munitions needed for a sea-borne invasion of 15,000 soldiers and forty-three ships. Hoche compared liberating Ireland from English domination to freeing the French people from the yoke of the old régime.[11] Hoche's expedition left in mid-December 1796, but storms scattered the fleet and prevented the bulk of the troops from landing. Some of the ships, including Hoche's, limped home in January 1797.

Although this mission failed, Hoche still enjoyed the Directors' support. He begged for another chance to liberate the Irish from the English. Instead he received an important command critical to the survival of the Republic. When he took charge of the Army of the Sambre and Meuse deployed on the eastern frontier in late January, Rousselin went with him. This force desperately needed food and the means to transport it. Hoche planned to resume the offensive and take pressure off France's overextended positions in Italy and Switzerland. From the Vendée, he had experience in both organizing large-scale foraging and requisitioning supplies from a resentful population. He had to reorganize and revitalize the civilian administration, tasks also well-familiar to Rousselin from his missions to Provins and Troyes. Hoche cracked down on corruption and all "those who regard the public treasury as certain prey" while imposing strict military discipline.[12]

Invigorated and adequately fed, the Army of the Sambre and Meuse defeated an Austrian force at Neuwied in mid-April 1797. It then swiftly occupied much of the west bank of the Rhine River, a victory that cemented Austria's willingness to make peace with France later that year. In part because of health problems and in part realizing the impossibility of another naval expedition to the British Isles, Hoche, with Rousselin again in tow, returned to Paris in July. There, Hoche accepted Barras' nomination as Minister of War amidst harsh press criticism because of the general's ties to the Jacobins. Barras hoped that Hoche would furnish the troops needed to enforce a coup d'état against both moderates and royalists. Thanks to the angry reaction of two directors, Hoche learned that Barras had lied to him about a number of issues. He found himself ineligible to serve in that post because he was one year shy of the age requirement of thirty. Publicly, Hoche was furious at Barras' betrayal. Subsequent events, however, suggest that their estrangement was a political tactic aimed at hiding their plans. A week later, Hoche left to resume command of the Army of the Sambre and Meuse. He demonstrated his firm attachment to the Republic by staging a widely publicized festival in honor of the events of 10 August 1792 when the monarchy was overthrown.

Rousselin was torn. He could accompany an increasingly ill Hoche to an army camp on the eastern frontier just as peace was being negotiated. Or he could stay at the heart of political intrigue in his native Paris as Barras' confidential secretary. He chose Paris and Barras.

This decision seems to have been influenced by the start of a long-term affair with Julie Talma, seventeen years his senior. Julie was married to the greatest French actor of the day, François-Joseph, a close friend of Napoleon Bonaparte. In the early years of the Revolution, she had hosted a salon that attracted many of the Girondins, along with Camille Desmoulins and Georges-Jacques Danton, where they first met. They corresponded frequently while he was with the army and began a physical relationship upon his return to Paris. Despite his apparent jealousy over her brief liaisons with others, the affair lasted off and on for two years. Julie Talma's contacts and support were of vital importance to Rousselin's career.

As one of Barras' two confidential secretaries, Rousselin was enmeshed in high-level political machinations. The fate of the regime hung in the balance because "royalists" dominated the spring 1797 legislative elections. Plots and counterplots, libels and denunciations, threats and attempted assassinations marked the summer of 1797: Rousselin felt right at home. Barras certainly needed him. An admittedly biased rival wrote of Barras: "If his youth had been as studious as it was debauched, it would have made him a man of worth. Instead, he is incapable of applying himself to study or to business. But, on the other hand, he has a great aptitude for intrigue. At that he is tireless."[13] On 3 September, Barras sent Rousselin to visit former General Jean-Charles Pichegru, president of the lower house of the legislature, the Council of 500. Pichegru was Hoche's mortal enemy. He had successfully denounced Rousselin's former boss in 1794, leading to a trial and a death sentence. Yet the deputy agreed to the meeting because of his friendship with Lieutenant-Colonel Laurent Corbeau, Rousselin's foster father.

No doubt enjoying what was coming and knowing that they had an impressive collection of evidence concerning Pichegru's treasonous flirtation with royalism, Rousselin assured Pichegru of Barras' esteem and desire for an accord. Rousselin convinced Pichegru not to act before a meeting of the two leaders scheduled for the following day. That night, in violation of the Constitution, some troops from Hoche's Army of the Sambre and Meuse and more from Bonaparte's Army of Italy entered Paris. They enforced a coup d'état by three of the directors—led by Barras—against two more moderate members of the executive including Lazare Carnot. As a result of this coup, known by the date on the Revolutionary calendar of 18 Fructidor (4 September 1797), a number of ministers were replaced and almost two-hundred deputies were unseated, including Pichegru, who was sent to a prison in the Caribbean. In his memoirs, Barras paralleled his actions with those of Danton and depicted 18 Fructidor as "another 31st of May."[14] Like the Mountain in 1793, the instigators of the coup seemed to be in firm control of France's government, but their unwillingness to follow constitutional procedures did not bode well for the long-term stability of the Republic. Ironically, Barras later came into possession of Pichegru's memoirs, which he gave to Rousselin, who withheld publication of an account critical of both Hoche and Barras.

Two weeks later, on 19 September, Hoche died of a sudden illness. After an autopsy, Rousselin claimed that he had been poisoned, but would not say by whom. Rousselin arrived in time for Hoche's funeral, which he later described in florid detail. Although he professed to be the general's "agent," he was probably sent by Barras on behalf of the Directory to seize Hoche's papers. Rousselin was charged with writing the dead general's biography, but his actual job was keeping sensitive correspondence about 18 Fructidor from the public eye. Hoche's widow was incapacitated by grief and would be unable to keep certain letters private, declared Rousselin. To jumpstart his literary career, he wrote a quick, highly romanticized, patriotic biography.

WHILE CONDUCTING RESEARCH for this biography, Rousselin returned to the army near the end of 1797. He joined the staffs first of General Louis-Nicolas-Hyacinthe Chérin, Hoche's former chief of staff and the commander of the Directory's guard detachment on 18 Fructidor, and then, in November 1798, that of Jean-Baptiste Bernadotte while Chérin was on sick leave. Both were stationed in the western part of the German lands. Although Rousselin nominally worked in military supply, he actually served as the confidential secretary for these two ambitious, politically engaged generals. After Bernadotte quit his command because he did not agree with its strategic objectives, Rousselin returned to work for Chérin, then stationed with the Army of the Danube in Switzerland. When Bernadotte was recalled to Paris in June 1799, he asked Rousselin to go with him, giving him a full-blooded stallion as a mark of his esteem.

Named Minister of War on 2 July, Bernadotte made Rousselin secretary-general. France's struggle against the Second Coalition of Great Britain, Austria, Russia, the Ottoman Empire, Naples, and Portugal needed Rousselin's talents. In a personnel evaluation, Bernadotte wrote that he trusted Rousselin with sensitive tasks because the latter "enjoyed the deference of an intimate who made decisions based on a proven character." Rousselin's "honest head and heart" and "strongly critical political instincts" were lauded by Bernadotte, who used him to communicate with the revived Jacobin movement.[15] He relied "on his young secretary whose pen was as lively as his personality was positive." Barras depicted Bernadotte embracing Rousselin and saying, "My friend, you have more political fortitude than I do. You are more than a pen, more than a brain: you are my loins, you are my guts!"[16]

Bernadotte devoted himself to improving the deteriorating military situation. Bonaparte's forces were in the Near East engaged with the Ottoman Empire. Meanwhile, French occupation of northern and central Italy had been overturned, and Switzerland had been lost. In Belgium, the Netherlands, and along the Rhine, France's position was weak leaving the Republic exposed to invasion from the north and east. Supplies were hard to come by and the money to pay for men and material was even more scarce.

According to Barras, Bernadotte rose at 3 a.m. each day, picked up Rousselin, and they arrived together at the ministry by 4 a.m. Bernadotte insisted that "nothing should remain for more than twenty-four hours undisposed of, or at all events, unconsidered and unanswered." Rousselin was responsible for ensuring the execution of these orders despite the tremendous volume of paperwork entailed in running such a far-flung military establishment. Along with a coterie of Bernadotte's army aides-de-camp, Rousselin worked long hours under tight deadlines and close supervision. The minister reported daily to the Directors, either in person or more formally in writing. After a fifteen- or sixteen-hour stint at the office, the group dined at Bernadotte's home, only to repeat this exhausting routine the next day.[17]

Bernadotte turned things around quickly. In his own words, mobilizing the frontier departments threatened with invasion and reenergizing the war effort through "moral means" helped to "electrify the soldiers who had been worn down by fatigue and their needs."[18] More than 90,000 conscripts were armed, equipped, and clad. Forty-thousand horses were levied to remount the cavalry. Thanks to the Ministry's labors and Bernadotte's inspired strategic direction, the lines stabilized. France's military position was restored.

Meanwhile, the Republic lurched toward another political crisis. Bernadotte had troubled relations with the Directors, despite clear evidence of his administrative and military competence. The Jacobin resurgence in the elections of 1798 led the government to purge the newly elected deputies on 11 May. Another political upheaval on 18 June 1799 left Barras and would-be kingmaker and new Director Emmanuel-Joseph Sieyès as the dominant figures in French politics. It was Barras who wanted Bernadotte as Minister of War, in part because of his well-known Jacobinism. Sieyès, however, disliked Bernadotte and considered his success a hurdle to putting a more amenable general in charge, while he himself held power behind the scenes.

Bernadotte's views on Bonaparte surely played some role in his dismissal. News of defeat in the initial battles against the Second Coalition led Barras to propose recalling Bonaparte from Egypt. At a meeting of the directors in September, Bernadotte told Sieyès: "You know his taste for dictatorship and in our present circumstances, would we not be offering it to him if we sent ships to bring him here?"[19] Perhaps even more provocative was Bernadotte's harsh response to (his brother-in-law) Joseph Bonaparte's inquiry about bringing back Napoleon. Testing the waters, Joseph asserted that "as he [Napoleon] has conquered Egypt, his work is done, and nothing remains for him to do out there." Bernadotte rejected the idea that Egypt had been subjugated, "Besides, your brother has no right to quit the army. He knows the military laws, and I do not think he will expose himself to punishment under them. He is too well aware of the consequences of such a proceeding."[20] Sieyès' plan to overthrow the government and put a compliant general in charge would unravel if military discipline was levied against Bonaparte.

The animosity between Sieyès and Bernadotte came to a head in mid-September 1799. The denouement seems to have been part of the most recent turn against the Jacobins. It was precipitated on 13 September by Jean-Baptiste Jourdan's demand in the Council of 500 to proclaim that "the fatherland is in danger." Such a public invocation of the justification for the Terror led the directors, especially Sieyès, to seek to replace Bernadotte with a safer, less popular, less Jacobin, less capable minister. At Sieyès' urging, Barras had a long, late-night conversation with Bernadotte about the political situation. To save the Republic, internal dissension had to be avoided. Bernadotte should resign, said Barras. The minister promised to consider the matter.

The next morning, to his great surprise, Bernadotte received a letter from Sieyès on behalf of the directors accepting his resignation. Dejectedly, he began to compose such a letter. Rousselin arrived and told him that General Armand-Samuel Marescot had appeared at the Ministry to take over. Bernadotte related his conversation with Barras. According to Barras, Rousselin demanded: "Have you really tendered or merely promised your resignation? In the former case, you are outflanked; you lose in a single moment all the dignity and glory you have won through your military victories, your political behavior, and your administrative talents." He observed that the general was "In a position which will determine the honor of the rest of your life" and counseled Bernadotte to refuse to resign as "unworthy of you."

Rousselin quickly composed a revised letter that Bernadotte sent. It read: "I received, citizen President, your decision of yesterday and the civil letter accompanying it. You accept a resignation which I have not tendered!" Bernadotte wrote, "If he had perhaps spoken about returning to the troops in the field, it was on finding himself powerless to ameliorate the cruel situation of his brothers-in-arms, when seeing with deep pain the insufficiency of means placed at the disposal of the War Department." He continued, "Such are the facts and it has been incumbent on me to set forth the facts, to the honor of truth, over which we have no control, citizen Director. It belongs to our contemporaries, to history which awaits us." Bernadotte concluded with a request to be placed on military half-pay.[21]

The publicity given to this letter embarrassed the three directors who had sought to get rid of Bernadotte: Sieyès; Barras; and Roger Ducos. The other two directors, Louis-Jérôme Gohier and Jean-François-Auguste Moulins, both more friendly to the Jacobins, tried to mitigate the damage by making a joint official visit to Bernadotte's home to thank him for his outstanding service. Sieyès lost the point with public opinion, but he got what he really wanted. Bernadotte was no longer minister of war and the Jacobins remained on the run, allowing the directors to defeat Jourdan's proposal to declare a national emergency. Rousselin and most of the other Jacobins holding important positions in the ministries left with Bernadotte.

Napoleon Bonaparte's landing at Fréjus on 8 October and his swift arrival in Paris encouraged Sieyès to reach out to him about fronting a coup d'état.[22] Bonaparte's wife Joséphine obtained the help of Joseph's wife and her sister, the former Desirée Clary, to set up a meeting. Since Desirée had once been engaged to Napoleon, but had married Bernadotte, she was the perfect intermediary. The two generals discussed the situation in Egypt and the need for a new government in France. Bonaparte resented Bernadotte for thinking

FIGURE 4.2 Napoleon Bonaparte. The Miriam and Ira D. Wallach Division of Art, Prints and Photographs: Print Collection, The New York Public Library. "Napoleon" New York Public Library Digital Collections.

himself his equal, while Bernadotte feared that his rival was preparing to seize power. After this initial meeting, Bernadotte sent Rousselin to report his suspicions to Barras.

Lucien and Joseph Bonaparte were assigned to convince Bernadotte to meet again with Napoleon. Rousselin accompanied Bernadotte and raised the question of the Jacobins. In the course of what became a heated argument, Bernadotte asserted, "Your brothers are among its [the revived Jacobin club's] principal founders." Given that fact, he did not understand how the Jacobins could be "blamed for the turmoil you complain about."[23] Bonaparte laid his cards on the table: "Well General, I will tell you plainly—I should prefer to live wild in the woods than in a state of society, which affords no security." Fearing for the future, Bernadotte responded: "My God, General, what security would you have?"[24] At this point, Joséphine Bonaparte, who was on good terms with Rousselin, asked him several questions on a neutral topic in order to change the subject and calm tempers.

In the days leading up to the coup d'état of 9 November 1799 (18 Brumaire) establishing the Consulate with Napoleon as First Consul, Bernadotte publicly proclaimed his opposition to Bonaparte's "pretensions." He also declared that he was "resolved to oppose it by every means in his power."[25] At the same time, however, he met repeatedly with the Corsican general. To forestall any action on the former minister's part, Joseph Fouché, as Minister of Police, and Barras were delegated, in the former's words, to "divert Bernadotte from helping" "former and new terrorists" because "the most fervent patriots eagerly solicited Bernadotte to mount his horse and declare himself in favor of a tumult that would be both civil and military." Fouché reported that "without doubt ambition consumed him, but that it was a useful and noble ambition: he truly loved liberty." Together he and Barras were able to "mollify" Bernadotte.[26]

With Bonaparte in charge, Rousselin was again out of favor since he had openly shared his mentor's opposition to the coup. Bernadotte was sent to command the Army of the West and later was implicated in a trivial plot against the First Consul. Unlike his other mentors, Bernadotte left Rousselin in the lurch. Rousselin followed Bernadotte west, but the general remained silent when Bonaparte refused to employ his protégé. Barras, however, remained in close contact and the two steadily grew closer, though he could do little because of his own depleted influence. In 1800 Rousselin did get a minor, temporary appointment on the Émigré Commission that helped to decide who should be added and who could be removed from that list, but this was his last administrative work on behalf of the Republic. Soon after 18 Brumaire, Rousselin was forced to shift his considerable energies in different directions. At age twenty-seven, his career as a Revolutionary bureaucrat was effectively over.

As the new century dawned, Rousselin's political prospects were poor.[27] His obvious patriotism and ties to the military could not overcome his close links to the Jacobins who had been the target of the coup of 18 Brumaire. Still frequently confused with the jury member of the Revolutionary Tribunal, Rousselin was accused of having packed the War Ministry with former terrorists "turning these offices into revolutionary committees." His critics were pleased by his resignation from the War Ministry: "May all Jacobins face justice which will rid France of these gnawing insects!"[28] With his chief "protectors" either disgraced or out of power, Rousselin had few means of repairing his reputation.

Despite this unsettled situation, Rousselin had managed to achieve some level of rehabilitation under the Directory. Although still associated with the Terror and dedicated to greater democracy, he no longer feared an attack from Troyes such as the ones that had seen him imprisoned several times in the mid-1790s. His hard work on behalf of the military showed his commitment to the Republic and earned him a degree of safety. Dissatisfaction with Bonaparte and his regime left Rousselin outside the corridors of power with no clear path back inside the charmed circle. Political rehabilitation during the Directory left Rousselin with few options under the Consulate.

WRITING FOR THE public is no simple act, especially during a Revolution. Considerations of intent, audience, and reception always influence writers, but for Alexandre Rousselin, such issues took on even greater importance. As a quasi-public figure, politics colored his actions and provided a distinctive hue to everything he published. Rousselin also wrote to make money: he never had much and during the Directory and Consulate he needed to support himself, especially when he was between administrative posts.

Rousselin wrote to rehabilitate himself by justifying his choices. These goals were certainly political, but, at the same time, they expressed what he had seen, done, and thought during the French Revolution. He claimed:

> Silver is not the money that pays a true Republican. In a country where the institutions of government protect the Republic, the goal of every good citizen ought to be to do nothing that does not support it against its enemies' attacks. That was my intention when I wrote the biography of one of its most zealous defenders. Sure knowledge of having fulfilled that intention is my sweetest reward.[29]

This statement summarized his political hopes and literary aspirations. His scribblings, many of them unpublished during his lifetime, provide a measure of the man and his times.

His first biographical subject was General Lazare Hoche. Commissioned by the Directory, preparation of this biography took Hoche's papers out of circulation to avoid official embarrassment in the aftermath of the coup of 18 Fructidor. Rousselin swiftly penned a biography that appeared a little over two months after the general's untimely death. The work is a straightforward narrative stressing Hoche's virtues in a style and manner intended to recall Plutarch, his favorite writer. Like Rousselin's first publication, a compilation of the letters of émigrés, the biography included a wide selection of Hoche's correspondence. The inclusion of hundreds of pages of letters, speeches, and military orders both justified having taken possession of his papers and bolstered Rousselin's pretentions of being an historian, rather than just a former aide lauding his popular and much lamented boss.

While serving on the staff of General Chérin, Hoche's former chief of staff, now part of the Army of Germany, Rousselin supplemented his official duties by traveling to battle sites and talking to Hoche's friends, rivals, enemies, and acquaintances to flesh out his rather slapdash account of the general's life. An expanded version, in two volumes, appeared in 1798 with a larger publishing house that had a better reputation. It made far more of a splash, both politically and financially. Sales were brisk, bringing Rousselin some much-needed income. Never one to let pass an opportunity for either self-promotion or rehabilitation, Rousselin sent his book to the Council of 500's Commissions of Public Instruction and Republican Institutions suggesting that it be endorsed by the legislature and sent to municipalities and military units to edify France's youth at public festivals or in schools. Hoche's example could inspire them to greater sacrifices on behalf of the Republic, he opined. Rousselin hoped to duplicate how the National Convention purchased newspapers and patriotic pamphlets in huge quantities at public expense and sent them to the armies in 1792–1794.

Rousselin's effort paid significant rewards, at least in terms of publicity. The Commissions strongly endorsed Rousselin's biography. This "hero," this "illustrious general," offered "a model" for the young, wrote the joint Commissions' reporter, Albert-Augustin-Antoine-Joseph Duhot. He asserted that it was the legislature's responsibility to support talented authors whose "works are of interest to society because they reveal so powerfully the glory of the Republic." Duhot enthused: "I pay tribute to you, Rousselin: You have served your country and offered to posterity the life of a Frenchman so distinguished by his illustrious military virtues." The work was timely because of "the spirit, at once patriotic and philosophical, which directs it . . . so necessary to combating unceasingly the fanatical ideas that people still espouse. The people must be shown constantly the advantages of liberty to ensure that they detest tyranny, cherish the Republic, and have the greatest veneration for its laws."

The Commissions recommended dissemination of *The Life of Lazare Hoche*, and the Council of 500 wrote to the Directory suggesting that the work "be distributed as prizes to young citizens as a national reward." The executive might also want to send copies to Hoche's family. Perpetually short of funds, there is no evidence that the central government purchased Rousselin's book beyond a few token copies given formally to the two houses of the legislature. Public recognition of the book's patriotic usefulness, however, surely contributed to Rousselin's rehabilitation. Closer identification with the military, and especially with a revered general like Hoche, insulated Rousselin from his terrorist past while supporting his literary and political ambitions. Slightly expanded third and fourth editions appeared in 1799 and 1800.[30]

Rousselin desperately wanted to be known as an historian. But as contemporaries noted, that did not stop him from taking certain liberties with his subject. The deviations from a strictly factual account reflected both his classical education as well as his schooling in Revolutionary politics. Rousselin described himself as a "patriot historian" whose duty it was to "remember constantly the sentiment which animated Pompey when he returned from the war in Spain." Obscure references to the campaigns of Roman generals aside, Rousselin wanted his work to be seen as "historical truth," not a partisan piece. For him, providing a flavor of the time while conveying political lessons was the purpose of historical writing.

To demonstrate his seriousness of purpose, Rousselin described his methodology at length.

> The information that I found in Paris was insufficient. Not only to treat my subject with sincerity, but also to give my conscience the security of the truth, it became necessary to confirm with the witness of my eyes the information that I have gathered. I needed to see the battlefields where Hoche faced action. I went to the armies he commanded. I visited hamlets that were initially frightened by his victories, but that he left contented. I wanted to capture the character of the man. Nothing was too minute that could provide an indication: his domestic habits, his words, even his gestures, sometimes unappreciated by the vulgar, often provide wisdom to the historian searching for causes. I questioned everyone's memories with curiosity. I lost myself, so to speak, in the life of Hoche, as I followed up on every trace of his character, even into the heart of his enemies.

In addition to these realistic touches modeled on Plutarch, *The Life of Lazare Hoche* was a romantic-tinged "narrative of the heart" that owed much to Rousseau's sentimentality. Rousselin practiced what he preached: he "paid tribute to Hoche by shedding tears upon his tomb." He could tell the truth because "the liberty of the Republic has given to virtue the right of thinking anything, saying anything, and writing anything."

In Rousselin's account, like many other military biographies written at this time, Hoche rose through the ranks on merit to become a general.

He was also depicted as a virtuous "child of the Revolution." Despite being wrongfully imprisoned during the Terror, Hoche never lost his faith in the Republic. Rehabilitated after 9 Thermidor, Hoche "carried in his heart the sentiments of the Revolution." He was devoted to the cause of justice and rejected the "accumulation of prejudices" stemming from "14 centuries of tyranny." Honest and straightforward, Hoche avoided the temptations of corruption while maintaining his troops' discipline and Revolutionary fervor. Having pacified the Vendée and earned victories on the northern and eastern frontiers, in Rousselin's overblown, yet heartfelt rhetoric, Hoche had earned "undying glory" as a stalwart defender of the Republic. Official recognition and popular success, as well as enduring use by scholars of the period, suggest that Rousselin's biographical approach struck a chord with diverse audiences.[31]

Rousselin followed up *The Life of Lazare Hoche* with a brief *Notice on Chérin* after this general succumbed to battle wounds on June 8, 1799 while serving heroically in Switzerland. Appearing a mere week after Chérin died, Rousselin sought to capitalize on the vogue for military subjects during the war crisis caused by the attack of the Second Coalition. It appeared as an eight-page pamphlet to be sold on the streets and by booksellers under the imprimatur of the Council of 500. It was also appended to the fourth edition of *The Life of Lazare Hoche*. Rousselin did not detail Chérin's distinguished military career, but instead sought to capture the man based on their extensive interactions. Referring to Chérin's relationship with Hoche, Rousselin recounted that "in his heart, friendship came just after love of country. Rather, he demonstrated that these two sentiments form a whole." "His gentleness was the basis of the character and public-spiritedness" of this "military philosopher," wrote Rousselin. Chérin had "given to the fatherland his deep and undying affection" and devoted his energies to preserving and extending "the liberty of free peoples."

Rousselin painted an evocative picture of Chérin's final moments. "Let us, however, avoid thinking that Chérin's last sigh was despairing. On the edge of death, he raised himself from his bed of pain and, having gathered his strength, he turned toward France and with his last breath pronounced the name of Sieyès as he expired." This account was so obviously an attempt to ingratiate himself with the key figure in Bernadotte's dismissal that Rousselin provided a footnote citing a source. Rousselin lobbied for Chérin to be buried next to Hoche in the mausoleum of the Army of the Sambre and Meuse at Coblenz. Recognition of his biographies continued Rousselin's rehabilitation but failed to win him favor with the leaders of the coup of 18 Brumaire.[32]

The following year, Rousselin published another short "notice" of a recently deceased general: Jean-Antoine Marbot died during the siege of Genoa in April 1800. This work was more explicitly political. In the fall of 1799, Marbot had been a deputy in the Council of Elders as well as the military commander of Paris. Concern about how he would react to a coup d'état led to his reassignment to Italy under the command of General André Massena. "Less great than Hoche or [Barthélemy-Catherine] Joubert as a warrior, his loss is no less regrettable because of his virtues, his character and his devotion to liberty," opined Rousselin. He criticized those "reactionary representatives of the people" who, after the fall of Robespierre, had sought to "destroy public spirit, the creator of victories, by discharging Marbot as a terrorist." Clearly empathizing with him, Rousselin observed that when the general returned home, "his fellow citizens soon took their vengeance by naming Marbot to the Council of Elders." The *Notice* emphasized Marbot's rejection of all attempts to "corrupt" him. Rousselin cited testimony that "the death of our friend did not have a natural cause," but, as with Hoche, he did not name names. The work concluded with a plea "to renew the hatred of some corrupt men, but also to return to the path of morality and liberty those who do not have an implacable aversion to them." The implication was obvious: those directing the coup of 18 Brumaire could not be redeemed as republicans as he had been.[33]

As a biographer, Rousselin was attracted to heroic, virtuous, Jacobin generals who died "for the fatherland." He knew his subjects personally. Aspects of their life stories mirrored his own. Contemporaries disrespected Chérin for being "only an administrator." Hoche and Marbot were jailed for political reasons associated with their Jacobinism. In a biography of General Jean-Étienne Championnet published posthumously, Rousselin explained that he chose his subjects for their patriotic devotion and republican principles.[34]

Writing about military subjects meant writing about republican virtue, dedication to hard work in the face of overwhelming odds, anti-clericalism, and social equality, the issues that had fired his imagination and directed his actions for years. These biographies expressed Rousselin's vision of the Republic's role in propagating the essence of the Revolution itself. At the same time, Rousselin seemed to crave the reflected glory of association with these "martyrs of the Revolution." It is no accident that the first word of Rousselin's biography of Hoche is "I."

As always, Rousselin had political goals. His admiration for Hoche highlighted his rejection of the grasping clique that seized power on 9 November 1799. He stepped up that critique in the Chérin work, in which he openly contrasted this general's high morals and unflinching heroism with that of "Buonaparte" and his supporters. In *Marbot*, Rousselin made his position on the coup crystal clear.[35] By choosing these latter two generals, Rousselin also solidified his bond with Bernadotte who had also been their friend and mentor. The three biographies of "Jacobin" generals portrayed these defenders of the Republic as honest men who rejected the arbitrariness, corruption, and political involvement by the military for which Rousselin faulted Bonaparte.

Notice on Marbot was Rousselin's last biography to appear during his lifetime. While he penned others, some did not see the light of day until after his death and others have never been published in any form. He did not explain the hiatus in writing or why he did not publish his other biographies. Nonetheless, the published works earned Rousselin a measure of rehabilitation and a reputation as a patriotic, devotedly republican biographer.

Rousselin never abandoned his literary pretentions. But as the Consulate solidified, public criticism of the First Consul became increasingly risky. So Rousselin confined his efforts to a more select, more explicitly intellectual circle. Under the Empire, keeping out of trouble emerged as an even higher priority. Looking back, he asserted, "I was the object of an unceasing persecution. I can thus repeat, not without some pride, that I was never exempted from the rigors brought against the defenders of liberty."[36] For this staunch republican, the Jacobin legacy became as much of a burden as the "terrorist" label had been a decade earlier. Despite "persecution," Rousselin continued to champion the Republic as the chief legacy of the Revolution. In resisting Napoleon Bonaparte's ever tighter grip on power not just in France, but across the continent, Rousselin's weapon of choice was the pen not the sword.

As censorship, both formal and informal, was imposed, Rousselin aimed at a "high culture" audience. He wrote many epigrams, which depended on cleverness and following a strict form. A few found admirers. His most famous epigram, from 1799, skewered the French Republic's corrupt agent in Switzerland, Jean-Jacques Rapinat, making a chicken-egg jibe based on the similarity of his last name and "rapine." Rousselin's lyric poetry enjoyed some success. It attracted the interest of two well-known composers who made him their librettist. In 1806 he and André Guétry began a correspondence that culminated in the libretto for a sentimental opera, *The Joys of Getting Along: It is Indeed Sweet* in 1809 that, although completed, does not seem to have been performed. This association led to collaboration with Étienne Méhul, the first composer to be called a "Romantic." Rousselin authored the libretto for "Charles Martel or the Parisienne" in 1814. These literary endeavors were clearly diversions from the political engagement so near and dear to Rousselin's heart. However, his tenuous status and the growing un-willingness of the Napoleonic regime to allow dissent led Rousselin to refrain from writing about politics for a broader public.

With his classical education, strong and precise command of language, patriotism, and capacity for hard work, writing biography came easily to Rousselin. It was also a natural choice for rehabilitating his reputation. Although he had been able to return to public service under the Directory, his postings tended to be short, if intense. Still associated with the Terror, Rousselin was known as an extreme Jacobin even after his definitive release from prison at the end of 1795. Staff positions with Jacobin generals like Hoche, Chérin, and Bernadotte provided both political cover and a means of continuing to serve France.

The political and financial success of *The Life of Lazare Hoche* contributed to a shift in Rousselin's public persona. Although his political affiliations con-tinued to bedevil him, he was also perceived as a patriotic man of letters associ-ated with the glory of the French army and its commanders. Around the turn of the century, twenty-seven-year-old Rousselin realized that Bonaparte's growing grip on power left no opportunity to advocate for the ideals that meant so much to him. For a variety of reasons, Bonaparte was antagonistic. As Rousselin had learned years before, sometimes it was necessary to follow prevailing winds in hope of finding a safe harbor. These winds blew far longer and far stronger than Rousselin hoped, but he managed to navigate successfully in large measure be-cause he maintained ties with old mentors and recruited new friends.

HOCHE'S DEATH BROUGHT Rousselin fresh problems, but possessing his papers allowed him to befriend others with access to different networks and opportunities. Perhaps the most famous of these friends was Marie-Josèphe-Rose Tascher de La Pagerie, more commonly known as Rose de Beauharnais before she married Napoleon Bonaparte. Taking advantage of Julie Talma's connections, Rousselin's charm, wit, ability, and political stance helped him enter the circle of some of the era's leading intellectuals. These ties had their drawbacks: they kept him in Napoleon's crosshairs and ensured that he was excluded from a meaningful public life until the fall of the Empire.

Born on the French colony of Martinique in 1763, Rose had married vi-comte Alexandre de Beauharnais at age sixteen. They had two children, but their marriage was so stormy that a court ordered them to separate. General Beauharnais was arrested on 2 March 1794 for having lost the city of Mainz and was guillotined on 23 July. Rose was jailed in April and sent to the Carmes prison in Paris, where she encountered Hoche. Rumors of a liaison between the two spread quickly despite the fact that Hoche had recently taken a young bride. Some of Rose's letters certainly seem to suggest intimacy. She was released on 28 July and he soon afterward. Whatever the truth of their relationship, when Hoche returned to the army, he took Rose's son Eugène, who he "thought of as his son," with him.[37] The young widow soon became the mistress of Paul Barras. A year later, Barras introduced her to Napoleon and encouraged their relationship. Napoleon was smitten with her looks, sophistication, and money, but did not like her name, calling her Joséphine instead. Despite the fact that she was six years his senior, they married in March 1796. Bonaparte left soon after for command in Italy.

The Life of Lazare Hoche mentioned the general's friendship with Joséphine and hinted at the depths of their relationship. Joséphine feared that incriminating letters might surface that could endanger her marriage. She sent one of Napoleon's aides-de-camp, Joseph Sulkowski, to Rousselin to request the return of her correspondence with Hoche. Rousselin later claimed that "the principles that provide an education in honor directed my conduct" and gave the letters to Sulkowski, beginning a close friendship with him. According to Rousselin, "Madame Bonaparte appreciated this exchange which seemed so simple to me and since then, she has shown me kindness and evidence of a true esteem."[38]

Joséphine asked for Rousselin's help with various matters in 1798–99 when Napoleon was in the Near East. These requests concerned military appointments for her son and acquaintances. They went to Barras, to Director Louis-Jérôme Gohier, and to Rousselin. As secretary-general of the War Ministry, it was a simple matter for him to help. That led to a dinner invitation, which begat a personal correspondence that terminated abruptly with Bonaparte's unexpected return from Egypt. Famously jealous, the general did not appreciate having Hoche's former secretary, closely tied to both Barras and Bernadotte, connected to his wife. This combination of political affiliation with his rivals, along with suspicion regarding his wife's possible infidelity, ensured that Napoleon would remain "interested" in Rousselin long after consolidating his hold on power.

Despite Napoleon's discouragement, Rousselin kept in contact with Joséphine. Even with the First Consul and then Emperor so often away on campaign, this interaction did not go unnoticed. Napoleon's response was to appoint Rousselin vice-consul in Damietta, Egypt, in 1804. This post would get Rousselin out the way, prevent him from intriguing with others who were discontented with the regime, and might even get him killed. Rousselin did not cooperate. Using the British blockade and ill health as excuses, he never went to Egypt. Instead, he hid in Provence among Barras' relations. Foreign Minister Charles Maurice de Talleyrand-Périgord protected him and even ensured that he drew his salary despite not performing his duties. Rousselin also spent a significant amount of time in Geneva with exiled friends. Meanwhile, he and Joséphine continued to correspond.

In December 1809, Napoleon divorced Joséphine because she could not bear him any children. She retired to her chateau, Malmaison, and asked Rousselin to visit. He did so, "discreetly" but frequently, supposedly to discuss the publication of certain manuscripts. Police Minister Joseph Fouché, who employed Rousselin as a spy even though he was a "Jacobin," reported to Napoleon that these "intimate meetings" were "unsuitable." The note's clear implication was that the two had sex. Fouché also observed that, "In the eyes of many, Rousselin is an intriguer who keeps bad company. He once talked to the Prince de Ponto-Corvo [Bernadotte's Imperial title] and today, he speaks to the [former] Empress."[39] Both Barras and Rousselin later emphasized Joséphine's promiscuity—including their own sexual liaisons with her— and stressed the political importance of her sexuality to Napoleon's initial successes. Some of Rousselin's closest friends thought he had had an affair with her that began years before, perhaps as early as 1804.

Whatever the truth of the matter, Napoleon ordered Rousselin not to visit Joséphine and suggested, none too subtly, that he report to Damietta. Instead, Rousselin resigned, reminding the Emperor of his service to his ex-wife, adding "I have gotten no profit from the interest of the Empress Joséphine in the rulings of Your Majesty."[40] The Emperor refused to accept the resignation and ordered Rousselin to leave immediately for Egypt. Regular meetings with Talleyrand, Fouché, Bernadotte, and Minister of War General Henri Clarke, the duc de Feltre, provided enough protection for Rousselin to avoid retribution for disobeying Napoleon.

Rousselin visited Lyon, where he successfully eluded the watchers of the foreign and police ministries and went to Provence. In May 1811, his resignation was finally accepted though the uproar ensured that he never saw Joséphine again before her death in 1814. Ordered to live at least 100 miles away from Paris, he spent eighteen months in Normandy. Citing another bout of ill health, Rousselin received permission to visit the healing waters at Aix-les-Bains in October 1812. Once again, he ended up in Geneva with other exiles, including his close friends, great intellectuals and writers, Henri-Benjamin Constant de Rebecque, known as Benjamin Constant, and Anne-Louise-Germaine de Staël-Holstein or Madame de Staël.

Julie Talma introduced Rousselin to the celebrated couple in the winter of 1798–99. Constant began writing to Rousselin at the War Ministry asking to get a soldier discharged because he was the "sole support of two infirm old men."[41] This request sparked a friendship that also involved Talma and de Staël. Both personal and political, the link between the two men lasted more than thirty years, though they were closest during the Napoleonic era when they and their ideals were farthest from favor.

Constant was born in Switzerland in 1767 and educated in the Netherlands, Scotland, and various German lands. Greatly influenced by the work of Jean-Jacques Rousseau, he had a court appointment with the Duke of Brunswick when the French Revolution broke out. Inspired, he left his job, divorced his wife, and moved to France in 1793. Constant met the rich, famous, intelligent, provocative, and very-much-married de Staël in 1794. They began a tempestuous love affair that produced two children. Their intellectual collaboration lasted more than a decade. Constant published political tracts rejecting both the Terror and the Reaction in favor of constitutional republicanism on the British model. Appointed to the Tribunate, one of the legislature's three houses in 1800, Constant was pushed to resign in 1802 because of his increasingly open critique of the Consulate.[42]

De Staël was born in 1766, the daughter of Swiss financier Jacques Necker who served as Director of Royal Finances under Louis XVI and then chief minister in 1789–90. In association with her mother, she ran the most famous salon in Paris, honing her conversational skills and developing literary ambitions. Marriage to Swedish diplomat Baron Erik Magnus Staël von Holstein in 1786 enabled her to publish under her own name. Plays, a variety of works of fiction, and a treatise paying homage to Rousseau all appeared before 1789. She relocated to Geneva after the September Massacres. De Staël revived her salon in Paris during the Directory and wrote several well-received, critical works on literature and politics. As a result of her affair with Constant, she separated from her husband and moved frequently between Geneva and Paris. For both political and personal reasons, de Staël and Bonaparte developed a deep mutual dislike. She was exiled from Paris in 1804 for criticizing the First Consul. De Staël and Constant ended their love affair in 1806, though not their close intellectual collaboration. De Staël continued to antagonize the Emperor leading to her expulsion from France in 1810. She was under constant police surveillance but traveled widely, remarried, and continued to write, as one of the most influential women alive.

Rousselin's relationship with Constant and de Staël was based on conviviality, shared interests, and mutual assistance. As secretary-general, Rousselin wielded considerable clout, but even on the Émigré Commission and later as a police spy, he was well-placed to keep the couple and their friends apprised of developments behind the scenes. He was a "fixer" who knew how to get things done. Rousselin also discussed their works in progress. His connections in the publishing world helped get de Staël's work into print in a timely fashion. For Rousselin, Constant and de Staël provided entrée into a literary world that validated his desire to be—and to be recognized as—an intellectual. The group referred to him as "the historian" or as "Plutarch" when they wrote in code to escape the censors. Appreciation for his work and for his "just spirit and excellent heart" stoked Rousselin's ego and ambition.[43]

Their correspondence makes clear that the group simply enjoyed each other's company. In 1800, Talma wrote de Staël that "Rousselin is the only person you still flirt with." Rousselin was the raconteur of the group, known for his "unbelievable stories." He also had a wide set of acquaintances who provided valuable information. He helped the others buy property, find publishers, and negotiate contracts. Part of the world of actors and artists, Talma possessed a gracious temperament and solicitude that kept the group together. Constant brought passion and intellectual rigor to any discussion, while de Staël was one of the greatest conversationalists of the age. By 1802, Constant signed letters to Rousselin, "Farewell my dear friend, our friendship is *for life*," while exhorting him to respond swiftly to his letter and to "believe in my unshakeable friendship." Given their embrace of Romanticism, it is unsurprising that the correspondence embodies the language of affection. The friends often met for dinner, generally as part of a larger gathering, but sometimes more intimately. De Staël complained of Rousselin's "long and sad absence" in 1803 but assured him that "nothing has changed in my heart." When "you do not write" it felt like "we are separated by an ocean," wrote Constant.[44] Such endearments joined to frequent correspondence and regular social gatherings suggest the depth of their bond.

The group was deeply engaged in the study of the past. Both Constant and de Staël used historical evidence to illustrate points about contemporary events and to suggest the proper form of governments. The history of the ancient world, especially the republics of Greece and Rome, shaped their understandings of past, present, and future. Historical topics were also at the heart of much current theater. They were all suspected by the government and attempted to evade mail censorship and police surveillance whenever possible. Devising stratagems to get a few hours of freedom from police eyes, using double envelopes for letters sent to intermediaries, and establishing code phrases were frequent topics of conversation.

Finally, all were critics of Bonaparte and his regime. Their conversations featured negative appraisals of the administration. Alternatives, both faintly realistic and purely theoretical, were discussed and evaluated. A wide variety of "secrets," some more classified than others, were shared. Others whose devotion to the regime was also (if not equally) suspect were attracted to their salon. Several of Rousselin's former mentors such as former minister and Senator Dominique-Joseph Garat, Bernadotte, and Fouché, attended regularly. Since they did not trust the heavily censored accounts of events in the newspapers, these encounters were also important means of keeping abreast of what was really going on. None of them could abide "the silence." The core group presented "useful suggestions" to those still in power and used friendship to cope with their exclusion from decision-making. They also shared first the possibility and then the reality of exile.[45]

The gang broke up, as Talma died in 1805, and Constant and de Staël ended their sexual relationship the following year. All were exiled from Paris and/or from France for much of the Empire. This was also the period when Rousselin started a family and was frequently on the run to avoid going to Egypt. He remained friendly with both de Staël and Constant, though he saw more of the latter than the former. As the Empire ossified, their hopes of achieving change dimmed. In 1810, Constant reported to Rousselin, "Paris is deserted. The few people who wander this desert seem to take no pleasure there. Nothing is being published. Literature languishes. . . . Some work by habit, but without goal. Yet there are more writers than readers. This suggests that you should not regret your absence from us." Constant asserted that Rousselin might be gone but was not forgotten among their circle of friends and asked him to write when he could. But the connection between Constant and Rousselin was not as warm as the relationship that had united the four of them.[46]

During the Napoleonic era, some of Rousselin's friends were more infamous than famous. He became acquainted with Colonel Claude-François de Malet, during his service on the staffs of Chérin and Bernadotte. At the War Ministry in 1799, he advanced the career of this dedicated Jacobin, who was also acclaimed a "terrorist" of 1793–94. General Jean Étienne Vachier, usually referred to as Championnet, in command of the Army of the Alpes, needed staff officers, and Rousselin assigned Malet to this faithful republican. Malet impressed Championnet enough to earn a provisional promotion to brigadier-general and the post of chief-of-staff. After Championnet's death in 1800, Malet fought under General Massena until the peace of 1802. Malet vehemently and publicly opposed the

FIGURE 4.3 Claude-François de Malet. Ernest Hamel, *Histoire des deux conspirations du général Malet*, new ed. (Paris: Librairie de la société des gens des lettres, 1873), frontspiece.

proclamation of the Empire in 1804 but managed to get appointed governor of Pavia in the Kingdom of Italy. Suspended in 1807 for having run illegal gambling operations, Malet was recalled to Paris. Only six weeks later, he was imprisoned for belonging to the "Philadelphes," a quasi-Masonic group of republicans who opposed Napoleon. While Napoleon was in Spain, the plotters intended to appeal to the Senate to overthrow the Emperor. The police easily got wind of the operation long before anything actually happened. Malet was imprisoned.

On the night of October 22, 1812, Malet escaped from the sanitarium where he had been sent at his wife's request. Taking advantage of the Emperor's absence on campaign in Russia, Malet and a small group of co-conspirators, many of them royalists, attempted a coup d'état using forged documents claiming that Napoleon had been killed. Malet impersonated a general to take control of the Paris garrison on behalf of a "provisional government." He managed to convince a few National Guard officers of his story and freed two republican generals who joined the coup. The plotters arrested the minister of police and a few other police officials, but failed to suborn any military commanders, which led to the swift unraveling of the plot. Malet and his collaborators were arrested by the Imperial Guard, tried by a council of war, and shot on 29 October.[47]

Napoleon was outraged that the coup attempt got as far as it did. He was unnerved by the ineptitude of several key figures in his government. News of his death should have seen his infant son immediately proclaimed as Napoleon II. The Malet conspiracy encouraged the Emperor to abandon the Grand Army then retreating from Moscow and hurry back to Paris.

Other than helping Malet in 1799 and being accused of being a member of the Philadelphes, there is no direct evidence of Rousselin's involvement in the attempted coup. However, Rousselin later wrote a highly positive, even laudatory account of Malet that is heavily weighted toward the Philadelphes of 1808. It cites a significant number of original documents that Rousselin had collected and preserved. In this version, General Malet was a "hero" devoted to the Revolution and to restoring the Republic. Rousselin linked the two intrigues and claimed that several senators were involved in the plots, especially in 1808. Napoleon had hijacked the "great nation," he wrote. The Emperor's "ambitions" and "Machiavellian politics" had made "slaves" of the French, leading "numerous," dedicated patriots to join the "society of virtue" or Philadelphes. This group was "a society within society, a real Republic, living and powerful. It was found within the other republic which weakened every day and had become only a name." Once the coup failed, Malet decided not to name his fellow conspirators, preferring "to be useful to the fatherland" through his silence. "General Malet had long since sacrificed his life." The conspiracy was "the sole obstacle that might stop absolutism." According to Rousselin, the government silenced Malet to avoid having to reveal the extent of the conspiracy and thus of opposition to the Empire. During the Restoration, Rousselin helped Malet's widow get a pension from Louis XVIII, claiming that she merited support because her husband had "died for humanity and liberty" on "the field of honor."[48]

The problem with Rousselin's depiction is that the Philadelphes almost certainly never existed. Historians are convinced that this conspiracy was created out of whole cloth by ranking members of the Imperial administration to distract the Emperor and undermine his confidence. The actual "conspiracy" of 1808 brought together a diverse, ragtag bunch with some ties to the Jacobins that posed no threat to the regime. Nor did they espouse the purportedly lofty goals of the Philadelphes. So why did Rousselin devote so much attention to the group?

The Philadelphes were likely the type of conspiracy that Rousselin wished had existed and that he had participated in. As an informer/spy for the police among intellectuals, former Jacobins, and the nobility, he listened to and reported on the clandestine complaints of many who—like himself—were discontented with the Empire. He recognized the gap between this gossip and an effective, much less potentially successful conspiracy. A "real Republic" led by a "hero" willing to "sacrifice his life" reflected Rousselin's hope for the future. Since 1794, he had ascertained that relatively few French espoused the same Republican and Revolutionary ideals; nor did he believe that a hero like Cincinnatus who reformed Roman society and then gave up power would appear to save France from itself. As Rousselin grew older and further removed from the crisis of 1793–94, his Revolutionary principles were increasingly subordinated to a more moderate set of views linked to the notion of a moderate republic. Rousselin's fictionalized account of Malet and the Philadelphes represented an idealized version of how a Revolutionary democrat became a liberal, at least in retrospect.

WHEN ROUSSELIN NEEDED a hiding place to avoid going to Egypt in 1804, one of his longtime mentors put his network of friends and relations in the south of France at his disposal.

Paul Barras was born Paul-François-Jean Nicolas, vicomte de Barras. To keep his personal correspondence away from Napoleon, who had some justified concerns about its contents, Barras had given it to Rousselin for safekeeping in 1801. At Barras' request, a cousin, marquise Marie-Françoise-Joséphine de Trémolet de Montpezat, the daughter of a duke, welcomed Rousselin into her home. They had met in Paris during the Directory, at a time when her daughter, Marie-Gaspardine-Justine-Clémentine de Montpezat (born in 1774), was rumored to be looking for a husband among the gilded youth. The marquise was a dedicated royalist who was in contact with Louis XVIII and was swept up in a wave of arrests after a failed royalist assassination plot of 1804. She was soon freed but remained under surveillance until 1814. A contemporary account claimed that Rousselin had become "secretly attached to the party of the king" and that in 1803, he had been "the intermediary between the principal heads of the opposition and the agents of His Majesty."[49] No evidence for this involvement exists. Moreover, it would have been difficult to fulfill this role while under police scrutiny, but Rousselin did correspond with both mother and daughter.

Alexandre and Clémentine soon began a physical relationship. Some sources assert that they were secretly married in 1800, others in 1804, but their legal marriage occurred in 1807.[50] Their son, Marie-Philibert-Hortensius, was born in December 1805. How was an impoverished intellectual with few prospects and a dubious past as a terrorist able to marry a beautiful, accomplished granddaughter of a duke? Was it simply to legitimize their son, as Benjamin Constant asserted? Louise-Marie-Victoire de Chastenay claimed that the two were "married in secret," "for love," and that Clémentine's "destiny" was "storybook."[51] Barras remarked of his cousin's choice: "She preferred the man who owed everything to his intellect, and who promised to develop great faculties, to what are commonly called the most brilliant matches. The choice of her heart has been justified by a reciprocal attachment; personally, I have felt satisfied with and flattered at an alliance honorable in its purity."[52] Barras' emphasis that the marriage was "honorable in its purity" is suggestive. However and whenever their legal union began, Rousselin had a noble bride and a son to provide for—as well as many new, profoundly royalist relations— which helps to explain his ongoing unwillingness to go to Egypt as well as his recruitment as an informer by Fouché. By all accounts, this union was a happy one and Rousselin was a fond father to Hortensius.

The next change in Rousselin's family circumstances was very different. When Napoleon created the imperial nobility, his widowed stepfather, Antoine-Pierre-Laurent Corbeau de Saint-Albin, had no heir.[53] The retired lieutenant-colonel attested that, "his father and mother, grandfather and grandmother were dead and that he had never had a legitimate child." He attested that "I served as a father to Alexandre Rousselin, son of Madame de Corbeau, my wife."[54] Corbeau de Saint-Albin filled out the paperwork in December 1812, which was registered by a justice of the peace in January 1813. At a stroke, Alexandre-Charles-Omer Rousselin became Alexandre-Charles-Rousselin Corbeau de Saint-Albin.

"Near the end of a long and painful illness," Corbeau de Saint-Albin entreated the police "to allow him to see his son again before his death." But Alexandre was under detention in Lyon for visiting Geneva and, in any case, he was barred from Paris. Referring to his long military service and acquaintance with the Emperor, Corbeau asked for an exception, "an insignificant favor," to allow Alexandre to come to the capital "solely to ease the last moments of a father, who on his deathbed wants only the consolation of seeing his son again." This touching appeal seems to have worked. Though Alexandre had to submit to "close surveillance," he was granted permission to come to his father's deathbed on 13 October 1813. This grace came a little too late. Comte Laurent died on 6 October 1813, leaving his title to his new-made son. The generosity of a devoted foster father changed the trajectory of his adopted son's life.[55]

Alexandre signed his surname as Rousselin until the Restoration. From 1814, it became "de Saint-Albin." Hortensius endorsed a gloss on his father's life which described the new reality: "Alexandre-Charles-Rousselin Corbeau de Saint-Albin was the son of artillery colonel Antoine-Pierre-Laurent de Corbeau, the son of marquis Antoine de Corbeau de Saint-Albin."[56] This version of Rousselin's background was repeated in almost every contemporary biographical dictionary and nearly all the historical references to his actions during the Revolution. Alexandre perpetuated this account of his background in his unpublished biographical sketch of General Jean-Baptiste Kléber's meeting with his adoptive father:

> This artillery colonel was the comte Corbeau de Saint-Albin, a commendable man who is owed particular public recognition. Is the justice that we give him suspect of partiality because we are tied to this virtuous citizen by the tender sentiments of close kinship? What so-called law of history could be applied to omit important facts because they honor the memory of a father? M. de Saint-Albin enjoyed a simple and pure life joined to a very enlightened spirit capable of noble and elevated views.[57]

His mother was never mentioned, and his actual father, François Rousselin was consigned to the dustbin of history.[58] Alexandre and his well-connected noble family did an excellent job propagating the idea that he was the child of Laurent and grandson of the marquis. An aristocratic ancestry helped the family to join the ranks of the nobility as comtes de Saint-Albin. In the first decades of the nineteenth century, deciding what to forget and what to remember were vital to dealing successfully with the Revolutionary legacy.

THESE SAME ISSUES of remembering and forgetting in the name of creating a new reputation shaped Rousselin de Saint-Albin's response to the Restoration of the Bourbon dynasty in April 1814. Despite recent acquisition of an old régime title and marriage into a royalist family, he did not greet the return of Louis XVIII with open arms. Even though he had been in de facto exile for most of the Empire, Rousselin de Saint-Albin worked diligently to undermine the monarchy and facilitate Napoleon's return.

Explaining this seeming change of heart is not clear-cut. Ideology was certainly one element: the House of Bourbon was unlikely to endorse the republican values that he held dear. The legacy of the Terror was perhaps more important. Those members of the National Convention who voted for the death of Louis XVI expected to be put on trial themselves. That list included many of Rousselin de Saint-Albin's patrons, including Paul Barras, Lazare Carnot, and Joseph Fouché. Although he had not served in the legislature, Rousselin de Saint-Albin had worked for regicides Camille Desmoulins and Georges Danton. His own violent rhetoric that the king must die had also been widely publicized. Given the threats promulgated by the duc d'Artois (the future Charles X) and his supporters, Rousselin de Saint-Albin might have worried about his own safety as well as that of his mentors. Whatever the reasons, in association with regicide deputy Antoine-Claire Thibaudeau, another former radical Jacobin who suffered disgrace and exile under the Empire, Rousselin de Saint-Albin, partly at Fouché's bidding, used his contacts to set the stage for Bonaparte's return.

Rousselin de Saint-Albin sought to stimulate French patriotism by composing "France Delivered or the Lyonnais: A National Song" in response to allied occupation in 1814. The overly erudite lyrics stemmed from his recent experience as a librettist. He lamented the "trespass of the fatherland's frontier." "All citizens are soldiers," he wrote, and "Napoleon, king of a faithful people" cannot be "confined." The song concluded: "Let us all rally for the final battles. Sweet peace, the daughter of victory, is conquered on the noble field of glory." The song was well-received and demonstrated the patriotic and military themes used by the Emperor's supporters to undermine Louis XVIII. Rousselin de Saint-Albin helped win back the hearts and minds of the French people for Napoleon Bonaparte.[59]

This task was not as difficult as it might have been. Louis XVIII had been placed on the throne by France's enemies. Being ruled by a man who literally returned in the baggage train of a foreign army did not sit well with a political elite used to the glory of decades of military victory. The loss of both territory and the income from extensive holdings outside France, along with the decision to discharge veterans and place most officers on half-pay, a common practice in peace-time, also alienated many. His brother's threats to take revenge on the Revolutionaries along with economic dislocation following so many years of war also damaged Louis XVIII's standing and support. When Napoleon escaped the island of Elba off the coast of Tuscany and set foot on French soil on 1 March 1815, many French welcomed him home.

Rousselin de Saint-Albin was more skeptical. On 20 March when Napoleon entered Paris and proclaimed the revival of the Empire, Rousselin de Saint-Albin observed that the Empire was "neither a national instrument nor a military instrument" because Napoleon had "abused everyone too much."[60] For the first time in almost fifteen years, however, Rousselin de Saint-Albin took public action. He recalled, "some publicists and I, we decided, in the middle of the general despair, that we should not despair for the future." They "noticed that the party of the opposition was not represented in the country." The group decided to create a newspaper that responded "to the needs of the Nation." On 1 May 1815, "we planted the flag" of *L'Independant*, which became *Le Constitutionnel* later that year.[61]

Recognizing that the Empire could not be run on the same narrow basis as before, Napoleon endorsed a veneer of liberalism. How deeply the Emperor felt that commitment is hotly debated.[62] For Rousselin de Saint-Albin, however, Napoleon's request that Benjamin Constant draft a new constitution likely decided the matter. The Additional Act to the Constitutions of the Empire was approved, like the previous Napoleonic charters, by plebiscite based on a wide suffrage. This was a very different blueprint for society than previous Napoleonic constitutions. It included explicit protections for freedom of worship, equality before the law, and security of property, while mandating a greater role for elections in determining the composition of the political class. The Additional Act also guaranteed that "every citizen has the right to print and publish his thoughts in signed form, without any prior censorship, subject to legal responsibility, after publication, by jury trial, even when there may be occasion for the application of only a correctional penalty." Although hardly Revolutionary, much less democratic, thanks to Constant, the Additional Act was liberal in aiming to "strengthen public liberty."[63]

To convince the French people that he had learned his lesson and returned to his roots, Napoleon asked Carnot to serve as Minister of the Interior. It was not for Carnot's personal qualities or beliefs that Napoleon made this offer. Someone (likely Fouché) told Rousselin de Saint-Albin that Napoleon "judged that this action provided 500,000 men with a stroke of the pen . . . those who made up the thinking and active class."[64] Carnot, who had opposed Bonaparte's growing despotism during the Consulate, had returned to public office after the disastrous Russian campaign. Rousselin de Saint-Albin described Carnot's decision to support Napoleon in 1815—and thus his own—as a combination of duty and the actions of an "honest man" who knew his "purpose," which was "the pursuit of justice."[65] On Fouché's advice, Carnot made Rousselin de Saint-Albin secretary-general with special responsibility for reforming public instruction. Rousselin de Saint-Albin was picked because of his journalistic experience. He, along with Carnot and Fouché wanted to revive *La Feuille villageois*, a weekly educational journal founded in 1790 that informed the rural population of current events, administrative developments, and scientific advances, especially in agriculture.

As secretary-general, Rousselin de Saint-Albin opened the minister's correspondence and received his orders, ensuring that everything was dealt with appropriately and in timely fashion. Carnot told him, "Monsieur, each morning, you will tell me the truth, and all the truths."[66] Carnot liked a lively discussion before making a decision. "The division chiefs were always assembled and each time he gave [the debate] all his attention."[67] Each issue was resolved in turn, with no digressions, following the rules he had set forth. This administrative style worked, at least in the short term, but was uncongenial to many of his subordinates. Rousselin de Saint-Albin focused on writing two reports on mutual instruction in elementary education that were published in the official newspaper to wide acclaim. Mutual instruction (by students) could overcome the practical difficulties of establishing enough elementary schools and finding and paying for sufficient teachers to educate the entire population. According to Barras, "Bonaparte was clever and politic enough to appropriate the principles, for the purpose of pluming himself on them in the eyes of the nation." Rousselin de Saint-Albin worked with noted philanthropists and educational advocates Charles-Philibert de Lasteyrieand and Alexandre-Louis-Joseph de Laborde in "setting in motion this great and useful engine throughout the whole of France."[68]

One-hundred days passed quickly. Rousselin de Saint-Albin had experienced similarly brief but intensive and productive periods of administrative work before. He focused on the newspaper once the House of Bourbon returned after Napoleon's defeat at Waterloo on 18 June 1815. The newspaper gave him political influence, established his reputation as a pundit, and made him wealthy and respected. In 1815, the paper was a fledging enterprise with a dubious future because of the politics of its editors as well as the troubled economic environment. Nevertheless, he worked in the press once more.

Rehabilitation is rarely complete. After being definitively released from prison in 1795, Alexandre Rousselin made a place for himself in French society. He did so by getting others to forget his actions during the Terror, or at least to see them in a different light. Working in military supply or, more precisely, as the confidential secretary to generals, and writing patriotic biographies enabled Rousselin to recover enough influence to once again be an eyewitness to and even a minor participant in affairs.

Loyalty to a particular vision of the Republic left Rousselin de Saint-Albin outside the corridors of power. While on the outs, he developed close friendships with influential intellectuals, thanks to his lover. He also had a son, married, and became a noble. Refusing to accept Napoleon's growing power, he spent much of the next decade on the run or in exile, even though he maintained some links with the government by serving as an informer and police spy.

When Napoleon was pushed from power, Rousselin de Saint-Albin forgot these slights and remembered that, in his youth, Bonaparte had been a Jacobin. The new comte's devotion to the republic's ideals outweighed his opposition to the Empire. The networks he established during the Consulate and the Empire did not eclipse, much less supplant, his earlier ties. Thus, his seeming volte-face in 1814–15 can be seen as political and even ideological continuity, rather than mere opportunism.

When he was released from prison for the last time, a career in public service was Rousselin's ambition. Being deputy consul in Damietta did not fulfill this urge. Although he served briefly during the Hundred Days, after 1800, he developed a new set of priorities. With the founding of *L'Independant*, he became a newspaperman and adopted the identity of Saint-Albin, a liberal noble, hoping to abandon forever the reputation of Rousselin the terrorist.

5

Liberalism and the Press, 1816–1838

> *First ask yourselves, Gentlemen, what an Englishman, a Frenchman, and a citizen of the United States of America understand today by the word "liberty." For each of them it is the right to be subjected only to the laws, and to be neither arrested, detained, put to death or maltreated in any way by the arbitrary will of one or more individuals. It is the right of everyone to express their opinion, choose a profession and practice it, to dispose of property, and even to abuse it; to come and go without permission, and without having to account for their motives or undertakings. It is everyone's right to associate with other individuals, either to discuss their interests, or to profess the religion which they and their associates prefer, or even simply to occupy their days or hours in a way which is most compatible with their inclinations or whims. Finally it is everyone's right to exercise some influence on the administration of the government, either by electing all or particular officials, or through representations, petitions, demands to which the authorities are more or less compelled to pay heed.*
>
> —BENJAMIN CONSTANT, 1819

HOW DID A Revolutionary who used Terror to save the Republic become a liberal constitutionalist? What political compromises was Alexandre Rousselin de Saint-Albin willing to make on behalf of his country, his ideals, and his family? Where did he draw the line? Did his opportunism trump his idealism? What, if anything, was he still willing to fight for? The answers to those questions shaped the rest of Rousselin de Saint-Albin's life.

The transformation of an impoverished intellectual and sometime public servant into a rich and powerful press baron was nothing short of astonishing,

The Making of a Terrorist. Jeff Horn, Oxford University Press (2021). © Oxford University Press.
DOI: 10.1093/oso/9780197529928.001.0001

even after he inherited his foster father's noble title. Under the revived Bourbon monarchy, surviving Revolutionaries had a choice. They could either adapt to the drastically altered political and social milieu that emerged after Napoleon's banishment to Saint-Helena or go into exile. Some former deputies who had voted for the death of Louis XVI had no choice: they were forced to emigrate. For other republican activists and for those who had supported the Hundred Days, dealing with the Second Restoration of the Bourbon monarchy was neither simple nor straightforward. Advocating for a republic or even seeking to protect the rights guaranteed by Napoleon Bonaparte could provoke official persecution. Such positions were also, at least temporarily, outside the mainstream of political discussion. What was a Revolutionary, a republican, to do?

Rousselin de Saint-Albin's ability to navigate this transition demonstrates yet again how adept he was at taking advantage of opportunities, even as he remained faithful to certain of his former principles.[1] The desire for wealth and family played their parts in his conversion to a liberal, but so did education, political experience, and networks. Despite the reappearance of many pre-1789 political and social forms, Rousselin de Saint-Albin's successes and failures illuminate how much French society had changed during the Revolutionary era.[2]

With public service out of the question, journalism was an attractive career choice for Rousselin de Saint-Albin in 1815. He had experience in the field, having worked on the *Journal of Public Safety* in 1793–94 and having tried to start a political and literary weekly under the Directory. Where Rousselin de Saint-Albin's financial investment in the paper came from is a mystery, but he may have inherited enough money from his foster father to give him a stake. Typically, he wagered on his own success.

L'Independent first appeared on the afternoon of 1 May 1815 during the Hundred Days. Espousing a liberal Bonapartism, it was founded by fifteen investors, each of whom put up 500 francs, with a promise to commit up to 3,000 francs if needed.[3] In addition to Rousselin de Saint-Albin, this group of Parisians contained several noted republicans, including Antoine Jay, a member of the legislature and historian who was later elected to the Académie française; Marc-Antoine Jullien, who like Rousselin, had served as a civil commissioner of the Committee of Public Safety and was perceived as a terrorist; and Jean-Denis, comte de Lanjuinais, a former member of the National Convention and current president of the Chamber of Peers. Other prominent investors included François Gémond, a former member of the jury that condemned Queen Marie-Antoinette to death; journalist and tax official

Alexandre Chevassut; and Armand-Louis-Jean Fain, a prosperous printer. The paper was an immediate success. Within a month, it had over three thousand subscribers.

At the time, newspapers were not allowed to be sold individually and were available only to subscribers. How many people had access to a copy, either because they shared the costs of a subscription or saw it second-hand, perhaps in a reading room or coffeehouse, is unknown, but total readership was many multiples of circulation. Only four pages long and about half the size of a present-day US newspaper, no advertisements distracted readers from current events, in-depth political coverage, and literary or theater criticism. Given the considerable expense of subscription, rising from 56 francs in 1815 to 72 francs in 1816 to 80 francs in 1827, as well as the rather rarified content, most newspaper readers were, not surprisingly, well-off. They had the education and leisure time to appreciate the rhetorical flourishes, classical allusions, and subtle or even hidden political messages of the heavily censored press. At the same time, the paper depended on prurient middle-class interest in murders, suicides, and gossip to attract new readers. A German-speaking visitor to Paris was astonished to observe that "everybody reads—the cab-driver while waiting for his client, the fruit dealer in the market, the porter in his hallway. In the Palais Royal a thousand persons sit about in the morning reading newspapers."[4] Although the press' audience was growing in the capital, newspaper reading was not yet for the masses. In the first third of the nineteenth century, the intended audience of the daily press was the expanding middle classes, along with elites.[5]

Articles were generally unsigned though occasionally an editorial might bear an author's initials. This structure and the high-brow content placed the onus on the ability and taste of the editor or editors. It also made it difficult to determine who wrote what piece and how editorial decisions were made. Although contemporaries reported that Rousselin de Saint-Albin was an active editor and wrote many articles, we cannot be sure exactly which pieces were his or how his contribution ebbed and flowed over the twenty-three years he was involved with the paper. Since he defended *Le Constitutionnel*'s pieces written by others as he did his own, its positions and actions will be analyzed as his.

Given its Bonapartist ownership, predictably, *L'Independant* did not long survive the Battle of Waterloo. An article published on 6 August 1815 defended General Charles Angélique François Huchet, comte de la Bédoyère, who defected to the Emperor in March and served as his aide-de-camp. He was captured trying to visit his wife before fleeing the country forever. The piece caused the suppression of the paper. Huchet was tried by a military court and executed, but Rousselin de Saint-Albin's newspaper rose from the ashes by purchasing the name of the *Les Nouvelles du soir*. Another censure soon followed, forcing another name change to *Le Courrier*, which lasted from 26 August to 23 October.

As *Le Constitutionnel*, the newspaper resumed publication on 29 October and ran daily through 23 July 1817. It was quashed anew for an article about a painting that appeared on 16 July. The reviewer raved about the artist's use of blue, white, and red flowers known as "forget me nots" to call attention to the virtues of a beautiful child. The censor decided that the flowers represented the tricolored flag of the Revolutionary era and that the child was Napoleon's son and heir, the duc de Reichstadt. He also concluded that the artist's depiction of flowers in relation to the child urged readers not to forget either political ideal or the link between them. For such oblique actions, an overly imaginative censor, whose primary job was as a medical doctor, suppressed the paper a fourth time.

It returned swiftly as the *Le Journal du commerce, de politique et de littérature*. This fourth censure, when things were going so well financially, seems to have bitten deeply. The editors adopted a less confrontational political stance, at least temporarily. Even the title suggested the growing importance of money. The owners were able and willing to spend 50,000 francs to purchase the name of a paper that had been in operation (in diverse forms) since 1794. As part of the deal, two ownership shares (out of fifteen) were given to former legislator Jean-Charles Bailleul and his journalist brother Antoine. Three new faces joined Jay and Rousselin de Saint-Albin on the editorial team: a young, energetic republican journalist from Bordeaux, Évariste Dumoulin; Charles-Guillaume Étienne, recently the chief editor of a rival paper; and Pierre-François Tissot, formerly head of the Collège de France who later joined Jay in the Académie française. All three were accomplished poets as well as experienced journalists. Despite frequent affirmations of support for the government, their sympathy for the opposition, especially liberal Bonapartists, was evident.

Rousselin de Saint-Albin mobilized his wide and diverse networks of friends to lobby key government ministers to allow the newspaper to change its name back to *Le Constitutionnel*. He told the duc de Richelieu, "That title is more appropriate than any other and we demand it of you as a means of defending the Charter and our constitutional institutions." Adopting the motto "defender of the laws" (*defensor legume*) and switching to a morning edition, the reborn *Le Constitutionnel* began publication on 2 May 1819. After receiving compliments for accomplishing this task, Rousselin de Saint-Albin told everyone, "My friends, with this name, we will seize our fortune and the flag of the world."[6] His rhetoric may have been overblown, but the paper remained in operation until the First World War.

At its rebirth, *Le Constitutionnel* enjoyed an impressive 11,500 subscribers, making it the second largest daily newspaper in France and in the world at the time. The political conflicts of the 1820s attracted many new subscribers. It was the only French paper that could afford the huge investment needed to install the faster and more precise steam-powered printing presses developed in England. By 1825, *Le Constitutionnel* had more than 16,000 subscribers, surpassing *Le Journal des débats*. The largest British papers of the time, *The Times* of London and the *Morning Herald*, each had about 10,000 subscribers. The following year, *Le Constitutionnel* hit 20,000 subscribers. An important reason for the paper's rapid growth was the habit of the government and its supporters of buying enough stock in opposition newspapers to take editorial control and then shifting their politics. This tactic benefited papers like *Le Constitutionnel* that kept their stock closely held among the editors and their allies.

Le Constitutionnel generated impressive wealth for its stockholders. In 1819, profits came to 90,000 francs, then doubled in 1821. In 1826, gross receipts came to a bit more than 1.3 million francs. The stamp tax on newspapers was the single largest expense at 450,000 francs, far more than the 400,000 francs spent on editorial and administrative expenses. Delivery cost 100,000 francs. That left an annual profit of 375,000 francs or 25,000 francs for each of the fifteen shares. Profits peaked in 1828 at 32,000 francs per share though the number of subscribers continued to climb until 1830 when they surpassed 23,000. Rousselin de Saint-Albin owned two shares, giving him an annual income equivalent to a very large landowner, or an extremely successful merchant, manufacturer, banker, or lawyer. This level of profitability made the shares valuable property even though the number of subscribers fell steadily after 1830. When Rousselin de Saint-Albin sold his shares in 1838, he realized more than 270,000 francs. This fortune, and the influence that his journalistic activities provided, transformed his life.

The addition of new editors was both the cause and effect of this success. The most prominent newcomer was a lawyer named Adolphe Thiers, who acquired a share and began playing an editorial role in 1821. He contributed numerous articles on politics and the arts.[7] Another talented addition was Louis-Augustin-François Cauchois-Lemaire. This dedicated Bonapartist journalist returned from exile in 1819 and immediately began to write for the paper. After the Revolution of 1830, he acquired a share and served briefly as *Le Constitutionnel*'s chief editor. Rousselin de Saint-Albin was part of a brilliant team with diverse ideas, political positions, and experience that sought to play an oppositional role in the elite politics of the Restoration.

Rousselin de Saint-Albin's professional success, which included induction into the Legion of Honor, was balanced by personal heartbreak.[8] Clémentine de Montpezat died young in 1816, after nine years of marriage. Their son Hortensius was ten. Perhaps in reaction, Rousselin de Saint-Albin threw himself into his editorial work with great dedication. He was thirty-three years old.

LE CONSTITUTIONNEL'S POLITICS were always a work in progress. Although many of its editors and chief writers were dedicated republicans, that stance was unacceptable to the censors. The same was true of the liberal Bonapartism of the Hundred Days. Prevented from advocating for their true goals or addressing a genuinely popular audience, shaping public opinion during the Restoration required deft application of the art of the possible.[9]

Criticizing the pretensions of the Bourbon state and the Roman Catholic Church recalled the Enlightenment. But the French Revolution had removed much of the radical meaning from the same actions undertaken before 1789. In many ways, the royal administration and its censors fought battles that had already been lost. The Restoration government could only force its critics to veil their antagonism, while confining political debate to a tiny fraction of the population. The Bourbon state could compete solely in such a limited political arena. Lingering social tensions unresolved or even heightened by the shocks of the French Revolution and Napoleonic era were exacerbated by France's need to adapt to second-class political and economic status after 1815. Many former Revolutionaries understood the dangers of changing too much too fast. They did not want to unleash a new Terror, much less direct it themselves. This recognition of a genuine need for limits justified their embrace of liberalism.

Having seen their paper shut down five separate times, the editors of *Le Constitutionnel* assumed a moderate, relatively nonconfrontational political stance. Such a posture frustrated Rousselin de Saint-Albin, but he recognized its necessity. According to Léon Thiessé, another lawyer turned journalist, closely aligned with editor Charles-Guillaume Étienne, "The opposition of *Le Constitutionnel* was intended to warn, not to overthrow [the government]. It was an opposition in good faith such that one can conceive under a representative government and of which, one can say, it is a necessary cog."[10] *Le Constitutionnel* became an increasingly important political player. Within the fourth estate, its job, indeed its responsibility, was to publicize and rein in the excesses of the powerful.

In 1819, the owners—Rousselin de Saint-Albin prominent among them—adopted a set of editorial principles for *Le Constitutionnel*. They pledged not to publish "anything contrary to the Charter and to remain within the limits traced by the laws on the liberty of the press." These limits included maintaining "inviolable respect for the king and for the legislative chambers" and "absolute silence regarding private affairs." Astonishingly for a group educated in and devoted to history, they were willing to ignore the events of the previous generation. They expressed their "unanimous support for the wise intentions to forget the past contained in the Charter." For *Le Constitutionnel*, "if the editors adopt a dissident opinion, from that moment, the paper will be no more than the paper of a party." Clearly, these editorial principles were not those of true opposition. Equally clearly, accepting limits was necessary because of the Restoration's hyper-vigilant and hyper-sensitive press censorship.

The same document hinted at the owners' principles. The owners asserted their readiness to "censure those acts [of the king and the chambers] that deserve it" and "to uphold consideration for people's [rights]" while maintaining "a just and impartial spirit to discover the interest of all and of each." They also vowed to hear "the grievances of anyone who is oppressed without distinction of persons and opinions and to support all friends of liberty." In the name of political independence, the paper accepted "formal exclusion of any contact or the appearance of any contact with the ministers." With regard to diplomacy, *Le Constitutionnel* promised not to express "hostility to the heads of foreign governments," but would "support the efforts of neighboring peoples to obtain their liberty." These clues suggest some of the ways the paper tried to impact public opinion.[11]

High-level politics were personal during the Restoration. *Le Constitutionnel* strongly supported Rousselin de Saint-Albin's close friend Benjamin Constant, the spokesman of French liberalism who was perceived as a defender of the legacy of the French Revolution. Returning from self-imposed exile after the Hundred Days, he was elected to the Chamber of Deputies, the lower house of the legislature in 1817. Constant articulated many of the ideas that shaped the parliamentary group known initially as Independents and later as Liberals. Contemporaries knew that the two friends were in close contact. Breaking with the typical Enlightenment emphasis on the political ideals of the Greeks and Romans, Constant focused on England as an appropriate model for a large-scale contemporary society undergoing economic transformation. According to Constant, in the past, small, relatively homogeneous societies could support republics with high degrees of political participation only because slavery provided the necessary leisure to allow citizens to be deeply involved in the affairs of government. States with large populations where most people needed to work (ignoring the revival of slavery under Napoleon and its persistence in the colonies until 1848) had to limit the direct participation of the masses. Instead, a people could be judged to enjoy liberty if they were protected by the rule of law and undue state interference. The masses and the nation would be represented by elected deputies whose responsibility was to create worthy institutions to regulate social, political, and economic activity. In a speech delivered in 1819, Constant asserted that:

> Institutions must achieve the moral education of the citizens. By respecting their individual rights, securing their independence, refraining from troubling their work, they must nevertheless consecrate their influence over public affairs, call them to contribute by their votes to the exercise of power, grant them a right of control and supervision by expressing their opinions; and, by forming them through practice for these elevated functions, give them both the desire and the right to discharge these.[12]

Those peoples, those nations, that did not possess that liberty, deserved the assistance of those that did. As a result, Constant and many other liberals strongly supported the "liberal" revolts that occurred in Portugal, Spain, and Greece in the 1820s. Constant's distinction between ancient and modern liberty was closely linked to an analysis of why the social upheavals of the French Revolution led to despotism. This understanding of contemporary politics enabled former Revolutionaries like Alexandre Rousselin de Saint-Albin to make the switch from republican to liberal.

There were some boundaries that the classically educated editors of *Le Constitutionnel* were not willing to cross.[13] The paper was among the strongest defenders of classical literature against the burgeoning Romantic movement. Because the censors focused on so-called political articles, the editors could unleash their disdain for a genre they saw as impractical and pandering to mass taste. They criticized Romanticism for focusing on emotions rather than seeking to elevate minds and for ignoring important issues of the day. Most liberals thought that literature, like the writing of history, was supposed to be relevant. Romanticism's flights of fancy rubbed these artists of the possible the wrong way. *Le Constitutionnel* asserted that the goal of "the Romantic school in separating itself from the literary traditions of antiquity to achieve new effects allowed its practitioners to outrage taste, insult reason, and either descend to a most disgusting triviality or lose itself in the unlimited regions of the absurd."[14] Although the editors of *Le Constitutionnel* either scorned or ignored Romanticism, Rousselin de Saint-Albin himself adopted many of Romanticism's stylistic and thematic elements and his biographical and historical writing could easily be characterized as belonging to the movement.

The Charter guaranteed equality before the law and "personal liberty. . . . No-one shall be prosecuted or arrested except in cases provided for by law and in the form which it prescribes." Although Roman Catholicism was recognized as the state religion, the Charter established freedom of conscience and religious expression. At the same time, "investigation into opinions and votes given prior to the Restoration is forbidden." The manner of conscription, the limits of press freedom, and definitions of the "crimes of high treason and attacks upon the security of the state" were all established by law. *Le Constitutionnel* sought to ensure that the monarch and his ministers did not go beyond their self-imposed bounds.[15]

On 23 February 1820, *Le Constitutionnel* published an appeal to establish "a national subscription to support citizens who are or will be victims of the exceptional measure on [limiting] individual liberty" passed after the assassination of the duc de Berry, the king's nephew, second in line for the throne, who did not yet have any children, which left the House of Bourbon without an heir. The government prosecuted the paper for this article, but the aim of the piece, according to Antoine Jay, was to limit the government's illegal and "arbitrary actions." The well-publicized trial called attention to the consequences if the government exceeded the limits set by the Charter.[16] Rousselin de Saint-Albin faced constant police surveillance because he hosted gatherings critical of the Bourbons, especially the "miracle birth" of a new heir, the duc de Bordeaux, a full seven months after this father's assassination.

The editors worried that the central government's right to name almost all local officials, as well as both the judges and the juries, could easily become the foundation for despotism. In 1818, France joined the so-called "Holy Alliance" of Russia, Prussia, and Austria established three years earlier, which pledged their sovereigns to take as "their sole guide the precepts of that Holy Religion."[17] On 2 December 1822, *Le Constitutionnel* worried that these "precepts" were being used as an excuse "to paralyze if not radically destroy all liberal institutions and to establish others that would create an absolute monarchy, subordinating the middle classes to a powerful clergy and a privileged aristocracy." The minister of the interior fumed that the paper seemed to have access to "secret" diplomatic documents regarding plans to further limit press freedom. The minister described *Le Constitutionnel*'s stand as an expression of "hatred and contempt toward the royal government."[18] He recommended that the king "censor the issue" and asserted that the government had sufficient evidence to "ensure condemnation" if *Le Constitutionnel* was tried for violation of the press laws. King Louis XVIII flinched.

Minister of the Interior Jacques-Joseph, comte de Corbière became increasingly outraged by the paper's stance during a period when Rousselin de Saint-Albin was known to have been particularly active, perhaps because of his own experiences with the consequences of the central government appointing local officials. In July 1823, Corbière wrote, "each day, the paper contradicts its title because of the systematic opposition that it invariably pursues. In effect, *Le Constitutionnel*'s opposition is anti-constitutional because it is anti-monarchial and has no objective but to disrupt the government." The minister objected that the paper revived "with more or less art or audacity the former maxims of Revolutionary anarchy by aggravating long-standing divisions between social classes and by slandering the government's intentions."[19] Overt criticism of the government, reflecting Rousselin de Saint-Albin's combative style, made the paper "unrecognizable" in comparison to its initial stance which even one of its main contributors, Léon Thiessé, described as "weak." He observed that *Le Constitutionnel* "has always had the reputation of *saying much less than it thought*" and was appreciated for what it hinted at, but did not publish, as much as for what it did. But now, wrote Thiessé, "it does what it can."[20]

Le Constitutionnel expressed its principles most openly when it came to religious issues. Like Rousselin de Saint-Albin, the paper was deeply anti-clerical. It ran a popular daily column detailing the worst examples of clerics' behavior. Editor Antoine Jay drew a potentially dangerous parallel: "The Revolution has no greater guilt for the crimes that soiled it than the Catholic religion does for the crimes of the Saint-Bartholemew's Day massacre."[21] *Le Constitutionnel* wasted no opportunity to point out the threat posed by the revival of clerical power—and the pretentions that went with it—to the liberties protected by the Charter.

Although relatively tame by the standards of the overblown journalistic rhetoric from the Revolutionary decade, much less that of the popular press that emerged later in the century, *Le Constitutionnel* of the early 1820s effectively opposed both church and state. An 1825 government report testified, "There is not a corner of the realm where it has not reached. . . .What café, what reading room in Paris or in all of France, does not have a copy of *Le Constitutionnel*? . . . Even in the cabarets of many villages, it is the newspaper not only of the middle class, but of the lowest classes."[22] Thanks to its popularity, the paper could take chances. It flirted with the constantly shifting boundary between what was permissible and what was not. The paper and the liberal press in general often ran afoul of the censorship. This battle, waged over coverage of politics and religious matters, enabled *Le Constitutionnel* to make the leap from bestselling paper to iconic representative of liberal ideas.

Success also marked Rousselin de Saint-Albin's personal life. In 1821, at age forty-seven, he married the twenty-one-year-old Amélie Sophie Eléonore Marc, the daughter of a prominent doctor. They had two children: a son, Louis-Philippe de Corbeau de Saint-Albin (1822) and a daughter, Hortense-Joséphine (1824). The duc d'Orléans and his wife Marie-Amélie were the godparents and namesake for Alexandre's second son, suggesting his shifting loyalties.

The joys of family and growing prominence did not distract Rousselin de Saint-Albin from his goal of selling newspapers by advocating for greater ability to voice opinions critical of the government. The Charter established the broad outline of the press' rights under the restored Bourbon monarchy: "Frenchmen have the right to publish and print their opinions, as long as they conform to the laws for repressing abuses of this liberty."[23] Thus, laws sanctioned only by the king (the legislature's role was solely consultative) limited the liberty of the press. Those limits, however, ebbed and flowed. After 1815, the liberty of the press was a moving target that thoroughly confused attempts to make accurate judgments about what was permissible. Rousselin de Saint-Albin was both victim and beneficiary of the uncertainties of the press environment during the Restoration.

Initially, the Restoration government allowed a broadly based freedom of the press. To stifle criticism of the new regime, however, censorship was resumed in October 1814. Publications of fewer than twenty pages, which meant almost all newspapers and journals, had to have prior approval by government officials. The ultra-royalist legislature elected in 1815 enhanced those restrictions in November. Police censors were empowered to block the appearance of publications that committed libel, defamed institutions, might disturb the peace, endangered the Charter, or disrupted public morals. This press regime lasted until 1819 when the laws were relaxed somewhat. The courts took over press oversight. Newspapers were liable for crimes or serious misdemeanors that they could be considered to have provoked. Newspaper publishers also had to post considerable sums (10,000 francs for a Parisian daily paper) as "caution money" to ensure that they could and would pay off any fines or penalties.

The assassination of the duc de Berry in February 1820 was followed by a serious curtailment of press freedom. Many political papers closed. A new press law mandated that political articles from Paris-based papers be reviewed by a committee of twelve censors. In the provinces, three censors per department oversaw the press. Papers that violated the rules and were taken to trial could be suspended immediately. Those found guilty could be closed for up to six months on the first and second offenses and closed forever for a third violation.

Additional constraints were passed early in March 1822. The government could impose censorship by decree when the legislature was not in session. New papers required government approval. Jurisdiction over the press was taken away from easily swayed juries and given to hard-headed royal magistrates. Protection of Roman Catholicism, the state religion, and the monarchy was heightened now that "disloyalty" to these institutions could be prosecuted. More ominously, the new law made "tendency" a crime. Tendency was defined as "the attitude of a journal or periodical as portrayed by a succession of articles . . . tending to disturb the peace or to undermine proper respect for the state religion or for other legally recognized religions, or for the king's authority, or for the stability of constitutional institutions, etc."[24] A liberal noble, the duc de Broglie described the bill as "the most monstrous and dangerous measure it would have been possible to imagine."[25] This press law curbed criticism of the new regime, especially after *Le Courrier*, a new liberal paper, was suspended in April 1823 for its coverage of the French invasion of Spain which sought to rescue a corrupt monarchy from a liberal revolt. The state responded to criticism by buying a controlling interest in opposition newspapers. The Restoration government was determined to hamstring the press.

Paradoxically, the accession of the more conservative Charles X to the throne in 1824 restored press freedom. The growing influence of the opposition in the legislature and ever more vituperative criticism by papers like *Le Constitutionnel* spawned renewed efforts to muzzle them, but the new King did not want to resume the heavy-handed censorship so detested by public opinion. "It is time to bring an end to these woeful scandals and to protect the liberty of the press from the perils of its own excesses," he believed.[26] Opposition journalists were emboldened when the Chamber of Peers rejected a government proposal to re-establish a more draconian press law in early 1827. The administration's decision to dissolve the Chamber of Deputies in 1827 was followed rapidly by the reestablishment of censorship. In Paris and the provinces, government-appointed censors could remove material, jail or fine journalists and publishers, and even close down publications.

DURING THE RESTORATION, *Le Constitutionnel* fought a fifteen-year battle over censorship. The paper lost most of the early battles, as its repeated suppression demonstrates. Once established definitively and with a rapidly growing readership, *Le Constitutionnel* relied on different tactics. At times, the paper left large blank spaces in articles to illustrate that passages had been censored. By occasionally altering the layout, the editors emphasized certain words that they hoped would escape the censors' notice. The paper also published pieces that had been suppressed separately as pamphlets, often with the title "Censorship Rejects." One by one, these tactics were forbidden by the courts. The only safe "political" topic was verbatim accounts of debates in the Chamber of Deputies. To provide material, liberal deputies interjected their political views into debates on seemingly unconnected topics. These highly erudite speeches sprinkled with classical allusions were clearly meant to be read more than heard. Each paper picked and chose among those speeches, printing those that supported their distinctive political perspective to attract additional readers and the deputies more supporters. This symbiosis characterized liberal politics under the Bourbons.

To criticize the government, editors also publicized reports from the provinces. On 15 August 1822, *Le Constitutionnel* recounted an incident where the police stopped a stagecoach in Saint-Quentin and arrested a citizen for not having a passport that permitted him to travel. This individual did not think he needed "a passport to journey inside the city where he resided." The paper opined that such stops occurred "daily" and that the magistrate released offenders only after they made a "payment to the police." The article also mentioned that, two weeks earlier, "an unfortunate peasant" had been jailed for "having the indiscretion to tell the judge that the procedure seemed a little arbitrary to him."[27] The department's head magistrate said that "there had clearly been abuse taking place," but that "*Le Constitutionnel* had misrepresented the facts to exaggerate them." He remarked on the "drawbacks" of prosecuting the paper because "there were genuine irregularities in the measures taken" by his subordinates.[28] Exposing graft and corruption was a potentially dangerous tactic, but when the perpetrators were lowly provincial officials, the paper seems to have escaped prosecution far more often than not.

The opposition press sought to escape censorship and prosecution for libel by reprinting articles or materials gleaned from foreign papers, a tactic championed by Rousselin de Saint-Albin. In April 1822, the prefect in Strasbourg

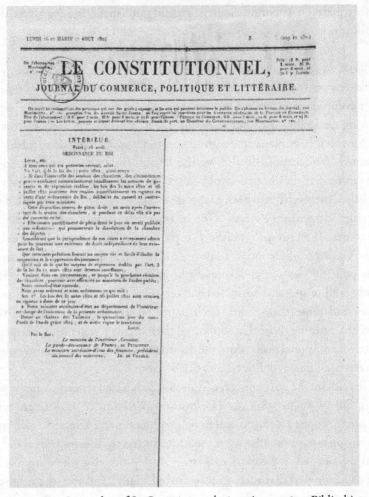

FIGURE 5.1   Fig. Censorship of *Le Constitutionnel*, 16–17 August 1824. Bibliothèque nationale de France, ark:/12148/bpt6kc.

reported that rumors were spreading that "a seditious song was inserted in the second edition" but that "research here has so far been fruitless." The song had appeared in the London *Morning Chronicle* on 12 April. Around the country, other prefects attested to hearing the same rumor but had the same lack of success in finding evidence to substantiate it.[29] In this instance, *Le Constitutionnel* had not reproduced any articles from abroad, but in numerous other cases, the paper did, observing only that the willingness of the foreign press to criticize the French state or the Roman Catholic Church openly was worthy of comment.

Opposition papers like *Le Constitutionnel* provoked police paranoia. In 1825, the two prefects in charge of Alsace on the eastern border reported that they had been "warned that *Le Constitutionnel* was being smuggled through Strasbourg and other points along the frontier. Four-hundred copies each were reaching a bookseller named Cotta in Stuttgart as well as two others in Aachen. Customs officials were facilitating the deliveries," they complained.[30] Although books and periodicals certainly were smuggled into France, such volume was nearly impossible. In later reports, the prefects admitted that they had not fully investigated the police's overblown claims. The opposition press had clearly gotten under the skin of the French police.

Le Constitutionnel and its liberal allies could not always avoid the tight leash of French censorship. The 13 December 1819 issue was seized for "outraging public and religious morals" for a story on a group of Catholic missionaries in the village of Croi. The article insinuated that the girls of the town were having "affairs" with a missionary. At trial, noted Orléanist lawyer André-Marie-Jean-Jacques Dupin claimed that *Le Constitutionnel* was criticizing only these particular missionaries whose actions and results were a matter of widespread public scrutiny. The editors had acted "in good faith," he contended, based on "reliable reports from witnesses." "The faith was always respected . . . and if one accuses the missionnaires [of acting immorally], that accusation only followed divine precepts."[31] *Le Constitutionnel* editorialized that that Dupin's defense "demolished the accusation." The jury, "deliberating only long enough to write down the verdict," acquitted the paper's chief editor.[32]

Even the most oblique reference to Napoleon angered Bourbon officials. A few days after the previous verdict, in January 1820, Nicolas-François Bellart, Paris' chief prosecutor informed the minister of justice that *Le Constitutionnel* had published a letter on 21 January attributed to Armand-Augustin-Louis, marquis de Caulaincourt, formerly duc de Vicenza, and Bonaparte's closest aide. The chief prosecutor recognized that the letter was probably not genuine, but "whoever is the author, it is eminently criminal." The "intentional usage" of "the usurper's title of emperor" violated the press law of 1819: "The letter constituted an attack on the authority of the King. Its intention was to show that a sovereign cannot consent to be contained by previous limits without debasing himself." He ordered the seizure of the paper with the "culpable letter" and the prosecution of "the author and editors."[33]

The censors removed a remarkable 40,800 lines of text from *Le Constitutionnel* in the first seven months of 1820. They charged the chief editor with seeking to "incite civil war" for an article published on 23 February. Editors usually escaped with fines because juries refused to convict the paper for libel. In March, Thiessé noted both the government's frustration with the juries' decisions and its attempts to pressure these handpicked men for their "horrifying licentiousness" by refusing to punish the papers. Thiessé explained that "out of seven or eight accused, juries condemn only around four." He demanded, "What passionless citizen would not have acquitted *Le Constitutionnel* for its article on missionaries? It was undoubtedly in poor taste, but the article could be condemned only according to literary critique."[34]

The paper could not, however, win them all. In April, a jury condemned the chief editor to five years in prison plus a penalty of 12,000 francs on the charge of "inciting civil war," a judgment that might have been even more harsh had Rousselin de Saint-Albin been in the post. On appeal, the judgment was reduced to two years in prison and a penalty of 10,000 francs. The accused was not permitted to have a lawyer present. The Censorship Commission intervened and added one month in prison and a fine of 200 francs to the ruling against *Le Constitutionnel*'s editor.[35] The same editor was condemned on 30 January 1821 to eight months in prison and fined 4,000 francs "for provoking disobedience to the law."[36] His ongoing freedom and continued involvement with the paper suggests that the government did not enforce the ruling. Juries were generally reluctant to follow the government's direction "except on matters related to religion."[37] The chief liberal papers also had deep pockets, thanks to burgeoning circulation. The government did not implement its own judgments. As a result, prosecutors' dedicated efforts to apply censorship had only limited effect.

Censorship frequently struck the opposition press collectively. In addition to *Le Constitutionnel*, the courts seized *Le Pilot*, *Le Journal du commerce*, and the *Le Courrier française* editions of 7 September 1822 at the post office before they could be distributed. Just eight days later, the same papers were confiscated. They contained a letter from Benjamin Constant that "insulted a public official in the exercise of his functions and a witness for their deposition."[38] Constant's letter did include those insults. On five separate occasions, he called attention to a "lie" in the account of Monsieur Carrère, the subprefect at Saumur. Constant referred to other officials whose versions did not jibe with the government's explanation of why a banquet uniting critics of the regime was cancelled. The subprefect's distorted description "insulted women. Excessive baseness is naturally associated with excessive ferocity. This genre has been lost since 1793," wrote Constant.[39] The editors of the four chief liberal papers were sued for libel, but the jury of the assizes court acquitted them. On 14 October, the censors condemned *Le Constitutionnel* alone. The paper was suppressed for "provoking revolt, hatred and contempt for the royal government, and insulting public officials." A judge accused *Le Constitutionnel* on 2 December of containing "several passages that seemed to me to incite hatred of and insult to the royal government," which closely followed some of Rousselin de Saint-Albin's earlier statements. These four incidents of censorship by royal magistrates all referred explicitly to the press law passed earlier that year.[40]

The cat and mouse game between liberal newspaper editors and government officials continued in 1823. During the French invasion of Spain, *Le Constitutionnel* was censured in July for "an article that announced the passage through France of a large number of foreign soldiers." The censor claimed that it "incited contempt for the government."[41] A confidential report on "the liberal press" asserted that dozens of issues of *Le Constitutionnel* in the first six months of the year had violated the press laws, but that the government had not taken action on more than a small fraction of those cases because of the journal's "tremendous influence." With more than 16,000 subscribers and with each copy examined by an estimated thirty people, nearly a half-million people read this liberal beacon.[42] Only after Charles X came to the throne and decided to abandon his brief experiment with liberty of the press did the Bourbon state get serious about curbing *Le Constitutionnel* and the other opposition papers.

In July 1825, Nicolas-François Bellart, chief prosecutor of Paris, "denounced" *Le Constitutionnel* and *Le Courrier* "for being the culprit of a *tendency* to undermine the respect owed to the religion of the state," namely Roman Catholicism. He claimed that the opposition press had "changed. They no longer attack the monarchy." The editors, including Rousselin de Saint-Albin, "have taken a very different, disastrous path. Instead of leading to the destruction of the throne, it will lead to the destruction of society itself." According to Bellart, "Today, religion has become the target of their nefarious plots. It is in the name of god that these new apostles blaspheme god and everything holy. Those who profess to venerate the religion of Jesus Christ are often those who undermine its foundations." Bellart's assertion that although "they usually hide their intentions, objectives can be recognized in their work" underpinned the case.

Bellart reluctantly agreed that it was "permissible to argue against the canonization of an individual before it was pronounced or against a particular miracle." However, the editors of the two papers went far beyond that acceptable level of "decent," "respectable" discourse. Instead, imitating Voltaire, they "mocked certain canonizations and all miracles. By debating the facts, they splattered a general contempt on all canonizations, on all miracles, on all invocations of the saints." He decried "the general tone of mockery which demonstrates the intent to present all religious acts as a heap of childish superstitions. Religion itself is shown as a lie that seeks only to keep men in ignorance while extinguishing Enlightenment and propagating errors." By criticizing the existence of and practices inside convents and monasteries, *Le Constitutionnel* and *Le Courrier* were "constraining the rights of religious orders." It was "an anti-religious system," Bellart concluded. The editors practiced "atheism and materialism, the two great solvents of all social organization."[43]

Le Constitutionnel made its case to the court of public opinion before the trial began. The editors focused on one sentence from the indictment, namely the claim that, "there was never a word, a single word in favor of the virtues or benefits that arise from an enlightened piety." A fourteen-page pamphlet printed by Fain, one of the paper's owners, appeared almost immediately. Composed largely of harmless excerpts from the paper, the editors sought to demonstrate the falsity of the claim while skewering religious hypocrisies yet again. An article of 1 April commented on the mistake made by those "whose devotion is only a mask for ambition or greed" because "people should fulfill their Christian duties to please god not men."[44] *Le Constitutionnel*, seconded by other liberal papers, gave full vent to its hostility to censorship, the regime, and the actions of ultra-montaine clergy. Rather than intimidating the press, indictment for "tendency" simply united all those who feared being muzzled.

The formal trial began on 19 November 1825. Jacques-Nicolas de Broé, the solicitor-general, presented thirty-four articles from the first seven months of the year to demonstrate the paper's "criminal tendency." Some articles were more controversial than others. For example, on 2 May, the paper critiqued a booklet (contained in Rousselin de Saint-Albin's library) entitled *Self Examination, Rule of Conduct, Remedies against Sin, and Summary of the Faith* intended for missionaries: "We found, instead of religious and moral instruction, obscene expressions, lewd particulars, in fact a complete account of the most monstrous schemes of debauchery." Far less aggressive was a review of a production of Molière's play *Tartuffe* in the Norman town of Fécamp published on 20 May. The review, one of several included in the indictment, noted the large audience. It closed: "The Bretons, famed as they are for bluntness of character, cannot put up with the Tartuffes of today," a subtle reference to the monarchy.[45] De Broé, however, was not interested in "refuting all of *Le Constitutionnel*'s slanders. That task would take too long and would transform the process into a sort of inquiry rather than a trial. According to the law, the trial should focus on the *spirit* of the denounced articles."[46]

André-Marie-Jean-Jacques Dupin again led the defense of the paper and its editors/owners. After contesting the charge of undermining Roman

Catholicism as too vague, he sought to turn the government's accusation inside-out. He argued, "it is not pouring contempt on religious practice, when one shows that something *is not religious*, but stems from fanaticism and superstition which the faith expressly condemns." Nor could "exposing the conduct of some clergy" be considered "demonstrating contempt for religious [orders]": they were not exempt from society's laws, he thundered. Dupin pointed out that the accusation itself admitted that *Le Constitutionnel*'s articles about the Jesuits and other clergy "contained some truth" and that "genuine mistakes were made by some clergy." To explain "the irritation of the dishonestly devout" regarding the attention paid to *Tartuffe*, Dupin observed, "they see themselves." "Religious practice is not wounded as much by just criticism as it is by the vices and hypocrisy of those clergy who degrade it,"[47] he concluded.

The best defense is a good offense. The key issue, for *Le Constitutionnel* and its liberal readership, was the role of religious orders in France, a subject of particular interest to Rousselin de Saint-Albin. In his defense, Dupin examined "the intrusion" of Catholic orders, especially the Jesuits, but also the Trappists and the Brothers of Christian Doctrine into "state affairs without any authorization in law or administrative ordonnance." Their illegal actions while serving as missionaries overshadowed any impropriety by the paper's editors, claimed Dupin. Recalling the powerful resistance of old régime judges to the dictates of church and state, he insisted that "*Le Constitutionnel* cannot be accused of bad faith . . . because it related the facts with sincerity as they were presented to them, seeking only the truth." The same could not be said for the clergy in question. In what contemporaries described as a hectoring tone, Dupin asked:

> Do you believe that on 13 June 1824, a festival day of the Holy Trinity, our lord Jesus Christ, who according to the evangelist, can only appear at the right hand of Our Father, to judge the living and the dead *appeared as a natural person* in the parish church of Lyon while they sang? He appeared for *a full half-hour* and "his footprints appeared on the tabernacle where they still remain and where they appear every day a miracle occurs." So read a poster that the police allow to be printed, peddled, and sold!

Next, Dupin evoked the Jansenists' battles with throne and altar by discussing the practice of some clergy and certain orders to refuse sacraments to anyone whose actions or ideas they disapproved. Whatever its theological justification or political motivation, Dupin declared, such acts certainly were news. In conclusion, Dupin marshaled twenty-five articles from the period covered by the indictment that reported particularly laudable instances of clerical charity or other positive acts to combat the notion that the paper exhibited any anti-clerical "tendency." *Le Constitutionnel* swiftly published a twenty-seven-page pamphlet reprising his arguments to make sure that their audience understood who was actually telling tales.[48]

The trial concluded on 2 December with Rousselin de Saint-Albin in attendance looking after his and the paper's interests. The next day, the judges issued their ruling after a mere half-hour's deliberation. They decided that among the thirty-four articles, "several contain expressions or even sentences that are improper or reprehensible on important matters, but the spirit resulting from the set of articles does not undermine the respect owed to the state religion." The judges concluded that "there is no need to suspend [publication]. Nevertheless, the publishers and editors are ordered to be more circumspect." The paper did not have to pay the expenses of the trial.[49] Two days later *Le Courrier* was acquitted in an even more sweeping decision in favor of freedom of the press.

These great victories emboldened opponents of the regime across the political spectrum. News coverage and political opinion contributed by Rousselin de Saint-Albin and the other editors became ever more pointed in its criticism of the monarchy, its ministers, and the Roman Catholic Church. Charles X and his supporters lost faith in the willingness of the judicial branch to support the royal government. After the acquittals, the king is said to have remarked, "We have a quite foolish judiciary."[50] This attitude underlay the press bill of 1826 that was defeated in the legislature in March 1827. The press was stifled by renewed strict censorship in July. Overcoming Charles X's reluctance to revive the practice was concern about the effectiveness of the daily papers, most notably *Le Constitutionnel*, in previous elections and trepidation over what the opposition press might accomplish in 1827.

Almost immediately, the government headed by Jean-Baptiste de Villèle brought charges against *Le Constitutionnel* and *Le Courrier*. The editors of these two liberal papers were indicted for an article published on 20 May. They were accused of suggesting that the police or other state agents provoked student unrest when the national guard was disbanded at the Collège de France and the Medical School three days earlier. When students then protested a proposal to move the schools of medicine and law to the provinces, their restiveness allowed the ministry to respond with unnecessary and excessive force, wrote *Le Constitutionnel* on 21 May: "Cavalry charges occurred in the streets and in public places. The blood of citizens flowed under the swords of the police. . . . It is necessary to hasten the calming of emotions. Doubtlessly, to accomplish that goal, police agents acted—they claim preventatively—but we name provocatively."[51] This incident triggered an initial accusation that the papers had "slandered the constituted authorities." A few days later, Jean Cophignon, a police agent, brought a civil suit against the same editors, saying that the article defamed him.

At the June 1827 trial and subsequent appeal, Dupin defended *Le Constitutionnel* and freedom of the press once more. He claimed that "the article was not slanderous, but rather simply one of opposition. Its reproches were generalized," rather than aimed at specific institutions or individuals. "The accusation of slander is therefore wrong," concluded Dupin. *Le Constitutionnel*'s lawyer portrayed censorship as a "monstrous creation," asserting that "The press is oppressed. Because of that, everything constitutes an obstacle. Everyone is worried because everyone is threatened. The most alarming rumors are circulating and gain currency because of the effort made to refute them."

With the full support of Rousselin de Saint-Albin and the rest of the editorial team, Dupin put the practice of censorship itself on trial: "This censorship has been applied in a violent manner." He demanded, "What maneuvers have not been employed, not only to thwart *Le Constitutionnel* as the principal voice of the opposition, but also to destroy its value as private property?" Dupin complained that "all the political articles are crossed out entirely or mutilated in their most important parts. What was strong became weak. Stories were eliminated and news prevented from spreading. Things permitted to others were forbidden to *Le Constitutionnel*," such as reprinting articles from other papers or avoiding the censorship regulations to report breaking news. "Formerly," Dupin exclaimed, "you will remember that censors effaced what did not please them with a red pen. In our pleas over the last year, we have often indicated this manner of suppression. This year, the censors returned to their favorite instrument. They have taken up their redoutable scissors!" They searched for "a pretext to suspend" the paper. The spectators' laughter as Dupin mocked the practice of censorship did not impress the judges.

The paper had no recourse. The editors asked repeatedly to consult the censors: "This was a sacrifice that they were unwilling to make," claimed Dupin. "Nor would the censors allow mention in the paper that the editors had asked for a consultation." To drive the point home, Dupin recounted that "a peer of France, the duc de Choiseul, wrote a letter to *Le Constitutionnel* that the censor crossed out. The duc complained to the vicomte de Bonald, his colleague in the Chamber of Peers [who oversaw censorship]. The censor did not even permit mention of the complaint."[52]

Dupin's spirited defense was mostly in vain. The civil suit was dismissed because Cophignon was "unnamed in the articles." On 17 July, the judges, however, condemned the chief editors of *Le Constitutionnel* and *The Courrier* to fifteen days in prison. The editor of the former was penalized 150 francs and the latter 450 francs. The editors also had to cover all the costs of their unsuccessful appeal—a much heftier sum that was, however, subsidized by the entire editorial team.

With the successful prosecution of these two papers, the Villèle ministry made clear that there was a steep price to be paid for opposing the government's will. Although the papers could afford the penalty and other members of their editorial teams headed by Rousselin de Saint-Albin stepped in to run the papers during the incarceration of one of its members, censorship remained a major problem for the opposition press in the run up to the elections of November 1827.

Le Constitutionnel's ongoing struggles with censorship in 1827 revealed the paranoia regarding even relatively innocent observations exhibited by supporters of the Bourbon state. Anything that might relate to politics or religion was subjected to serious scrutiny. Removal was the default reaction to any word, phrase, or article that was subtle or less than straightforward. This draconian application of censorship seemed intended to remove the mouthpiece of the liberals to leave a clear field for supporters of the Villèle ministry.

Alexandre Rousselin de Saint-Albin was an important part of *Le Constitutionnel*'s defiance of the Bourbon state and its attempt to rein in the ultra-montaine clergy. Throughout the summer and fall of 1827, he wrote many articles and handled most of the correspondance with the censors. He sought to convince them to change their minds and then, all too frequently, he had to bear the bad news about the cuts to the other editors. As was his usual pattern, Rousselin de Saint-Albin allowed others the limelight while he worked diligently and often thanklessly behind the scenes to accomplish his goals.

Getting out the news—not a sanitized caricature of it—was an obsession of liberal journalists. It was their only way to have any political impact, short of joining the legislature. A number of *Le Constitutionnel*'s editors and supporters did just that in the latter years of the Restoration, most notably Charles-Guillaume Étienne and André Dupin, who joined Benjamin Constant and the duc de Broglie at the heart of the liberal opposition. Adolphe

Thiers and Antoine Jay entered after 1830. But Rousselin de Saint-Albin stalwartly remained a journalist; in fact, he never once ran for office. Abstention from formal political activities allowed him to focus on influencing public opinion indirectly and insulated him somewhat from unwanted attention to his past.

The censorship bureau overseeing Paris' newspapers repeatedly removed references to the war in Spain. The censors asserted, "For some time, the opposition papers have suggested that Spain is threatened by an insurrection. Without doubt, this is a means of speaking about the revolutionary hopes spread across Europe." They were "determined to remove all exaggerations or allusions that reflect bad faith." *Le Constitutionnel* was censured so often because it was perceived to be particularly fond of "this type of sedition."[53] The censors also eliminated all references to popularity, whether it was the enthusiastic response of the people of Strasbourg to the arrival of Benjamin Constant on 20 August or the department of the Mayenne's tepid reaction to Charles X's visit, when "only officials and clergy applauded the king."[54]

The censors were obsessed with implications. In an article entitled "words and things," *Le Constitutionnel* "sought to show that men, with only a few exceptions, are almost always influenced by words." The editors wanted to demonstrate "the good intentions and generosity of the liberal party at the expense of the royalist and clerical party." The article was censored for the claim that "it is an abuse of the word to label as 'opposition' the active, laboring majority who love the laws and pay a billion francs in taxes. They are not a party, they are the nation, they are France itself." This statement powerfully echoed Emmanuel-Joseph Sieyès's *What is the Third Estate?* of 1789. For the censors, such references were particularly dangerous because it was combined with praise of "literary princes" widely understood to refer to Louis Bonaparte, Napoleon's younger brother.[55] These "words and things" and the Bonapartist link, with its potent criticism of the king and his ministry, could not be allowed to reach the public, wrote the censors. The bureau took paranoia to extremes by erasing a critical review of a serious book on military tactics under the Empire.

The ministry's successful prosecution of *Le Constitutionnel* did not have the desired effect. Instead of intimidating the liberal press, if anything, it emboldened editors to step up their critiques by challenging the censorship laws several times weekly. The bureau itself "remarked that for the past several weeks, the Parisian papers have been sending more ferocious articles than ever."[56] On 19 September, *Le Constitutionnel* submitted a "very intense article attacking the bureau of censorship." The piece explored France's intervention in Spain, specifically a policy attributed to the heir to the French throne. The coverage combined "praise for the Dauphin with slander of the bureau." Predictably, the censors "removed the slanders aimed at them" but kept the tribute to the duc d'Angoulême. They justified their action by asserting that since the original had not been presented to the bureau, they could not permit any public discussion that might "vilify" the Dauphin.[57] Such measures led *Le Constitutionnel* "to accuse the royal government of imitating the forms of imperial despotism" just a week later, in language reminiscent of Rousselin de Saint-Albin's appraisals of Napoleon Bonaparte. The bureau censored the article: "Today, we cannot allow the press to undermine the formal legality of a royal ordinance."[58] The press was muzzled, though the battle over censorship continued behind the scenes. But liberal lobby groups, and the publication of lengthy pieces not subject to the same form of censorship, ensured that the public heard the opposition's reproaches.

The ministry believed that holding an election in 1827 was more likely to return positive results than waiting until the end of the deputies' terms. The Chamber of Deputies was dissolved in early November, and balloting was scheduled for later that month. At the same time, Charles X named seventy-six new peers to ensure firm support from the legislature's upper chamber. Despite the ministry's many advantages, the election results were disastrous. Although a few deputies shifted back and forth between factions, ministerial supporters won about 180 seats, but so did the liberals, with ultra-royalists taking 70. This result represented a great leap over the 17 liberals elected in 1824. A more moderate chief minister, Jean-Baptiste Gay de Martignac, took office and a liberal, Pierre-Paul Royer-Collard, presided over the Chamber of Deputies.

Formal censorship and prosecution for "tendency" were both abolished in April 1828. Libel remained an issue for the courts to decide. But the new ministry was not defenseless. It revived the practice of "caution money," forcing daily Parisian papers to deposit a whopping 200,000 francs as "the most natural protection . . . which joins interest to wisdom by assuring,.in advance, that any damage to the honor of a citizen . . . can be immediately repaired," claimed the measure's sponsor, Keeper of the Seals Joseph Marie, comte de Portalis.[59] Notwithstanding this weighty limitation on the willingness of newspaper owners, especially those like Rousselin de Saint-Albin who were dependent on the income derived from the paper, to criticize the government, the press emerged from the crisis of 1827 stronger than ever. Over the next two years, the ministry passed a number of measures dear to the liberals such as the institution of local elections and the expulsion of the Jesuits. Charles X and the Villèle ministry won the battle over censorship, but lost the war for public opinion.

Looking at the entirety of Alexandre Rousselin de Saint-Albin's long life, it is difficult to escape the conclusion that the politics of the Restoration were rather bloodless. Debates over press censorship and repeated attempts to shame the ministry or block its dictates through the mobilization of elite public opinion have their own drama, but lacked the stakes—personal, political, and social—of earlier periods. Professor Charles Dupin, the younger brother of *Le Constitutionnel*'s lawyer, provided contemporary insight into why dedicated Revolutionaries like Rousselin de Saint-Albin, Royer-Collard, or Constant were content to see political discussion confined to the propertied who claimed to represent "the people." In 1827, Dupin argued that the most important political divide was not royalists against liberals or ultras versus ministerial supporters. It was actually generational.[60] Dupin divided the exceedingly wealthy French electorate (voters had to pay a certain amount of taxes on property) of perhaps 100,000 men (or so he thought) between those who were at least twenty years old in 1789 and those who were not. Those who experienced the Revolution as adults steadily declined. By 1827, more than 60 percent of the electorate remembered neither the pain nor the promise of 1789. He argued that without having lived through its upheavals, the "young" were more amenable to the ideas and tactics of the Revolutionary and Napoleonic eras. Over time, therefore, the liberal movement became progressively more radical. The obvious conclusion was that a conservative monarchy was doomed to flag and fail due to generational turnover.

In *Le Constitutionnel*'s long review of Dupin's work, which appeared at the height of the censorship crisis of 1827, the editors tried to depoliticize the issue, though they could not resist a jab at the ministry. They commented, "The action of time is extremely seditious. Monsieur de Villèle ought to consider the means of opposing such a coup d'état. What does he think of an ordinance that dismisses the new generation? It is an idea like any other and completely worthy of the wisdom of the ministry." The editors also made clear that the new generation did not intend "the destruction of the Christian faith, the monarchy, the Bourbon dynasty, or even the ministry." Instead the new generation focused on "France's commercial and productive forces, the liberty to work, and the ideas that direct these concerns." Their "great revolution will take place without noise, without effort, unnoticed, irresistable, and quick, like time." *Le Constitutionnel* "regretted that there was nobody in the ministry capable of listening to them." The article concluded that "we should not despair because the capricious actions of the ministry are opposed by the movements of nature . . . . Time will prove stronger than the Jesuits and Monsieur de Villèle."[61] With first-hand experience of the vagaries of Revolution and a deep appreciation of the importance of past models of historical change, the editors of *Le Constitutionnel* settled in for the long-haul, confident that their victory was only a matter of time. Such a perspective was central to how former Revolutionaries like Rousselin de Saint-Albin became liberals.

DESPITE ITS POSITION as the bestselling paper in the world, known for its steadfast opposition to the ministry, the editorial line of *Le Constitutionnel* was in flux after the elections of 1827. The quarrel was over how radical a stance to take. Since a great deal of money was at stake, most of the editors and owners were interested in limiting change to replacing the dynasty. The House of Orléans, headed by Louis-Philippe, provided a moderately liberal alternative to the Bourbons. Along with most of the team, Rousselin de Saint-Albin leaned increasingly in that direction. They were willing to be patient about the pace of change. Another group, headed by Adolphe Thiers and Louis-Augustin-François Cauchois-Lemaire, wanted to criticize Charles X and his government more directly. In March 1830, Thiers made a deal to escape the other editors' constraints. He sold his share and became the chief editor of a new daily, *Le National*, though he remained closely aligned with *Le Constitutionnel* until the late 1830s.

Charles X refused to accept a drift toward a limited, constitutional monarchy. An address to the legislature on 2 March 1830 asserted his prerogatives, alienating many moderates: "The Charter has placed the liberty of the people under the safeguard of my royal rights. These rights are sacred: my duty towards my people is to pass them on intact to my successors. . . . If criminal maneuvers create obstacles to my government that I do not wish to think of, I shall find strength to surmount them in my resolution to maintain law and order." In response, the Chamber of Deputies passed an address written by François Guizot and *Le Constitutionnel* editor Charles-Guillaume Étienne that insisted that "the intervention of the people in the deliberation of public affairs" was a "right," leading Charles to seek a more compliant group of deputies.[62] He dissolved the legislature, but the election results were catastrophic for the royalists. The liberal coalition won an astonishing 274 seats, an increase of 94 from 1827. The ultra-royalists won only 104, a decline of 76 seats.

The king's rejoinder was the so-called July Ordinances issued on 25 July.[63] He and his new ministers, headed by the prince de Polignac, dissolved the Chamber of Deputies once more. Charles X acknowledged the critical role of opposition newspapers in the political process, claiming that "intrigues have been practiced . . . to deceive and mislead electors." He then suspended freedom of the press. The Ordinances instituted separate "government authorization" for both editors and printers of any paper or periodical. This authorization had to be renewed every three months and "can be withdrawn at any time." Papers in violation could be closed permanently and their printing presses sequestered. The suffrage was also limited even further, with greater advantage given to those with landed wealth. This move came at the expense of the commercial, industrial, financial, and professional middle classes that overwhelmingly voted liberal. Romantic writer and diplomat, vicomte François-René de Chateaubriand, a strong supporter of the House of Bourbon, wrote that these measures "displayed a complete ignorance of the actual state of society."[64]

The fourth estate, France's journalists, rejected the government's measures. They searched for means of resisting the state's dictates. On 26 July, the editors of *Le Constitutionnel* did what most businesses do when contemplating a dangerous act: they consulted their lawyer, André Dupin, an acknowledged expert on freedom of the press. In Dupin's account, the delegates from *Le Constitutionnel* were accompanied by editors from two other opposition papers. Dupin asked for time to study the Ordinances and to discuss the matter with other legal authorities. At 11 a.m., a "flood of journalists" gathered to hear him. Dupin and his colleagues were "unanimous that the Ordinances were invalid and that they could rightly be resisted." His legal estimation was even more bellicose: "Only the law is in force. The Ordinances of 25 July cannot abrogate or depart from them. These Ordinances *should not be enacted*. If I were a journalist, *I would resist them* with every means and by right. In my opinion, any newspaper that asks for this sort of authorization [to publish] would not deserve a single French subscriber." That said, he told the journalists to leave his office if they wanted to have a "political meeting."[65]

Fortified by this bracing legal opinion, *Le Constitutionnel*'s editors attended a summit held at the office of Thiers' *Le National*. Forty-four journalists, including Cauchois-Lemaire and Dumoulin, representing eleven daily papers, composed a manifesto that described the ordinances as "a most resounding violation of the laws" and contrary to "people's common sense." Journalists "must be the first to set an example of resistance to the authority which has despoiled the character of the law." The group concluded that "it is for France to decide how far her own resistance should go."[66] A group of opposition deputies led by liberal banker Casimir Périer were inspired to write and publish their own clarion call. Both addresses were printed and placarded all over the city. Impromptu demonstrations in and around the Palais Royal turned into riots whenever the police or high-ranking officials provided convenient targets.

On 27 July, four papers headed by *Le National* appeared, despite the prohibition. Others like *Le Constitutionnel* canceled their editions when they could not obtain permission to publish. The four papers were suspended and their presses seized. Warrants were issued for the arrest of the journalists who signed the previous day's manifesto. While the capital's politicians, journalists, and electors debated, the working classes led by the thoroughly politicized printers took to the streets, provoking a confrontation with troops attempting to maintain order. After the soldiers opened fire, the Revolution was on. Over the next "three glorious days" (27–29 July 1830), barricades arose preventing communication and facilitating the people of Paris's victory over the garrison. The Polignac ministry and the attempt to refurbish the absolutist ramparts of the Bourbon monarchy collapsed with relatively little bloodshed. But what would come next was unclear even to those most involved in resisting Charles X.

Alexandre Rousselin, comte de Saint-Albin welcomed the defeat of the House of Bourbon. By 1830, he, like many of his contemporaries, had already made the transition from Revolutionary to liberal. He feared the consequences of unleashing popular violence on "*les trois glorieuses*." As Chateaubriand remarked, "the praises of the Terror had reminded Frenchmen of 1793 and caused them to recoil."[67] This former terrorist now strongly supported simply changing the dynasty to consolidate a constitutional monarchy, a shift he saw as a necessary step toward an eventual return of the republic. Rousselin de Saint-Albin and other former Revolutionaries had lived through the consequences of going too far too fast. In the crucible of July 1830, he favored making Louis-Philippe d'Orléans the ruler of France.

In 1830, the editors of *Le Constitutionnel* were by no means united in their hopes for the new regime. Although the paper was decidedly "liberal," that term embraced a wide spectrum of belief, from democratic republicans to constitutional monarchists to Bonapartists. With circulation reaching its apogee of 23,300, *Le Constitutionnel* emerged as a major power center during the debates of that heated summer.

Le Constitutionnel played a supporting role in the July Revolution— though certain editors were among the leaders. However, the paper sought to take credit for the turn of events. The editors constantly played up the popularity of the new dynasty with the deputies and in popular opinion more generally. To ensure that the public linked the Revolution of 1830 with *Le Constitutionnel*, the paper championed raising money to care for those wounded during *les trois glorieuses* and to support combatants and their dependents. *Le Constitutionnel* collected more than one million francs, and other papers amassed an additional quarter million.

Rousselin de Saint-Albin strongly supported the new regime. His friends and allies were among its leading lights. He was closely linked to Jacques Lafitte, Casimir Périer, and the marquis de Lafayette, among others including Thiers and the king himself, the godfather of his younger son. On several occasions, he was offered important government posts such as councilor of state and deputy minister of war, but always turned them down. His son Hortensius claimed that "he never sought positions, preferring to preserve complete independence. He believed that journalism truly worthy of the name was both a magistracy and a vocation."[68]

There were personal and practical reasons why Rousselin de Saint-Albin rejected public office. Hortensius increasingly was making a name for himself as a lawyer and as an appeals court judge. He was also extremely active in liberal politics. Rousselin de Saint-Albin was determined to avoid blocking his son's path to prominence.

Though the paper supported the new regime, increasingly referred to as the July Monarchy, it did not endorse all of its actions or plans.[69] *Le Constitutionnel* generally followed Thiers' political lead, which often opposed the ministry. Rousselin de Saint-Albin clashed publicly with Louis-Philippe on a number of issues. Both in private and in print, Rousselin de Saint-Albin urged the King not to appoint his old protector prince Talleyrand as ambassador to London. More fundamentally, he fought against reestablishing the full pomp and circumstance of the Bourbon court. He urged Louis-Philippe not to accept public money from the civil list to support his children. During their friendly argument on the subject conducted in a carriage ride across Paris, Rousselin de Saint-Albin suddenly opened the curtain and gestured, "you, who knows the history of the French Revolution so well, have forgotten that it was at this same place that Laporte, the overseer of the civil list under the former monarchy [before 1792] perished tragically."[70] Although Louis-Philippe respected Rousselin de Saint-Albin's historical knowledge and valued the example of the past, in this instance, the new monarch did not take his advice. In 1835, Rousselin de Saint-Albin pronounced his dissatisfaction with the accomplishments of the new government. The dynasty came to power through "a revolution which made so many promises to liberty and humanity," but it "has encountered cruel disappointments."[71] Nevertheless, Rousselin de Saint-Albin remained part of Louis-Philippe's "kitchen cabinet" of advisors for many years.

Rousselin de Saint-Albin also refused to join the ministry because *Le Constitutionnel* needed him. Several editors and publishers retreated into the background. Dumoulin passed away in 1830, while Jay and Étienne focused on their careers as deputies. Rousselin de Saint-Albin resumed the role of chief publisher, a position he held for most of the next seven years as the paper employed more editors who were not also owners. The other shareholders increasingly meddled in the paper's political positions, leading to conflict with Rousselin de Saint-Albin. The moderate tone and straightforward style of *Le Constitutionnel* fell out of vogue in Paris, though provincial readers proved more loyal. Other papers took the opportunity to rein in the power and influence of what had been France's bestselling paper for more than a decade. They criticized its positions to win over its subscribers. After the July Revolution, the press also played a far different role. Newspapers remained a vital part of the political process, but were no longer the chief bulwark of the opposition. Shifting tastes cut sharply into subscriptions. From its peak of 23,300 in 1830, *Le Constitutionnel* fell to less than 7,000 in 1837. The era of Rousselin de Saint-Albin's greatest influence witnessed the decline—both relative and absolute—of the paper he had helped to found and run.

Despite *Le Constitutionnel*'s close ties to the new regime, government oversight remained a major hurdle. Nominally liberal, the July Monarchy used means other than formal censorship to constrain the press. The libel laws were dusted off and applied thoroughly. In its first three years, the Orléanist government filed 411 cases against journalists and won 143 condemnations (35 percent). In part because of its moderation, and in part because of Rousselin de Saint-Albin's bond with Louis-Philippe, *Le Constitutionnel*'s editors stayed out of jail and did not have to pay huge fines. But the need for restraint surely contributed to the paper's declining political relevance and thus its flagging readership.

ROUSSELIN DE SAINT-ALBIN was rich, powerful, and respected. But he remained vulnerable to criticism regarding his actions as a terrorist during the French Revolution especially once the influence of *Le Constitutionnel* was on the wane. His reputation came under attack from a rather unlikely source, Charles-Antoine Nicolas, comte de Lamotte-Valois, the husband of the woman implicated in the Diamond Necklace Affair, who had been jailed for a year thanks to Rousselin's mission to Troyes.

In 1823, Lamotte-Valois published a memoir that sought to enforce a judgment from 1795 relating to his arrest. Two members of the Revolutionary Army had been convicted of stealing jewelry, fancy weapons, and horses from his mansion. The original judgment sentenced the perpetrators to six years in irons, to 50,000 francs in damages and interest, and to be hung in effigy in Troyes' public square. Rousselin de Saint-Albin was referred to by position, though not by name, in highly unflattering terms. Rousselin was a "young man, deeply attracted to pleasure" who, Lamotte-Valois implied, found female companionship during an earlier visit to his home. Rousselin was also accused of turning a blind eye toward the depredations of the Revolutionary Army.[72]

A second, more detailed and more damaging memoir followed a few months later, after Lamotte-Valois failed to extort money from Rousselin de Saint-Albin to forestall publication. This lengthy piece described him as "the agent, successively of Marat, Robespierre, and Danton." Lamotte-Valois recited Rousselin's actions like his denunciation of the Girondins. Quoting liberally from *Le Moniteur*, France's official newspaper, Lamotte-Valois likened Rousselin's actions in Troyes to those of ultra-terrorist Jean-Baptiste Carrier in Nantes. "It is evident that, for a long time, Rousselin has been tormented by the desire to wrap his conduct during the Revolution in an impenetrable veil to hide in some way from the eyes of his contemporaries. He found it necessary to his interests and to his peace of mind to procure a new name."[73] Lamotte-Valois then described Rousselin's true parentage, including the lies that he had spread about François, such as his emigration to the Caribbean when he had actually died in a Parisian charity hospital. Rousselin's marriage to Clémentine almost two years after the birth of his elder son received much attention. The memoir's vindictive tone illustrated that Lamotte-Valois wanted revenge at least as much as he wanted a payoff.

Rousselin de Saint-Albin immediately mobilized friends and allies to get both of Lamotte-Valois's memoirs suppressed by the courts. Three years later, the memoir was excerpted by another of Rousselin de Saint-Albin's critics, leading him to publish a short pamphlet detailing Lamotte-Valois's untrustworthiness and describing the memoir as a "libel." Again, thanks to the influence of *Le Constitutionnel* and his accuser's reputation as a swindler, the issue could be swept under the rug.

In 1835, an anonymous pamphlet attributed to "a reactionary," Pierre-Jean-Baptiste Nougaret, again associated Rousselin de Saint-Albin with terrorism. Nougaret relied heavily on Lamotte-Valois's suppressed memoir. Several "patriotic" newspapers picked up the story and publicized Rousselin de Saint-Albin's terrorist actions far and wide. He wrote a public letter trying to—from his perspective—set the record straight, but without much success.

Far more dangerous to Rousselin de Saint-Albin's reputation was the publication of volume 33 of the quasi-official *Parliamentary History of the*

French Revolution by Philippe-Joseph-Benjamin Buchez and Pierre-Célestin Roux in 1837. Buchez and Roux repeated Nougaret's accusations of terrorism against Rousselin de Saint-Albin to explain why he had been brought before the Revolutionary Tribunal on 20 July 1794. The Saint-Albins—father and son—immediately sued Buchez and Roux. Such an influential publication was difficult to suppress or censor. The suit was dropped only when volume 35 appeared later that year. It included a lengthy defense by Hortensius and reprinted Alexandre's public letter to the newspapers from 1835 as a kind of preface. The Saint-Albins also forced another influential muckraker, Joseph-Marie Quérard, to print a combination retraction/explanation after he wrote a lengthy diatribe that detailed all of Rousselin de Saint-Albin's terrorist activities and questionable associations. Quérard's popular *Literary Deceptions Unmasked* gave the public all the dirt and nothing but the dirt on their favorite authors. Rousselin de Saint-Albin began looking for someone to buy him out of *Le Constitutionnel*.

Other factors surely influenced Rousselin de Saint-Albin's decision to retire from *Le Constitutionnel*. The paper's loss of influence, declining subscriber base, and ongoing infighting among the ownership group were profoundly discouraging. His son claimed that a serious "argument" divided the editors in this period.[74] At the same time, the business itself was evolving. Two newspapers founded in 1836 changed the rules of the game. Émile de Girardin's *La Presse* had a new business model. He halved the cost of subscription and accepted advertisements. Along with *Le Siècle* started by Armand Dutacq, *La Presse* serialized popular novels. Thus, newspapers swiftly began to look different and had a distinctly different relationship with their readers. *La Presse* soon became a major player in the leftist opposition, the same political terrain occupied by *Le Constitutionnel*. To compete, *Le Constitutionnel* adopted some of the same tactics and abandoned its middle-of-the-road seriousness. After such a long period of success and surrounded by a fractious team, it is not surprising that Rousselin de Saint-Albin preferred to abandon the field rather than learn the new tricks of the trade.

Consideration for his politically engaged son Hortensius likely provides the best explanation for Rousselin de Saint-Albin's decision-making. Member of the Legion of Honor since 1831, Hortensius de Saint-Albin joined the general council of the department of the Sarthe in 1833 where Alexandre had purchased a château in the Loire Valley. Having received one of his father's shares in *Le Constitutionnel* in 1835, Hortensius could support himself with ease and planned to run for deputy in the elections of 1837. He was also angling for an appointment as a judge on the civil court of the department of the Seine that surrounded Paris. The combative son had already shown himself willing to defend his father's legacy; the last thing this ambitious, talented young lawyer needed was constant reminders of his father's check-ered past or his own illegitimate birth. Alexandre's decision to retire from *Le Constitutionnel* can best be understood in this context.

Finding an appropriate buyer was harder. Étienne and Thiers wanted someone who would follow their political line and revive the paper. They heard that Louis-Désiré Véron, a doctor with a fortune earned sel-ling patent medicines who had run the Paris Opera for five years was now looking to buy into a newspaper. Véron's skill at cultivating bourgeois taste as the head of the Opera suggested an astute businessman. Thiers told Véron, "you will rejuvenate this old paper. You can come to see me in the morning, at noon or when I'm getting washed. I'll give you ideas for arti-cles while I'm shaving."[75] Véron did not have the money to buy more than one of the Saint-Albins' shares, so a group of his friends jointly purchased the other but let Véron control it.

With Thiers himself in and out of power, the paper continued to drift into irrelevance. By 1843, *Le Constitutionnel* had only 3,720 subscribers. Véron bought out the other owners for about a quarter of the value per share he paid Rousselin de Saint-Albin. The new owner resuscitated the paper by serializing the novels of popular authors like Eugène Sue, while changing its tone and political content. The name remained the same, but it was a different paper, with different goals, different readers, and different people in charge.

We do not know what Rousselin de Saint-Albin thought about the new *Le Constitutionnel*. His pride in the paper and its accomplishments, however, came through in everything he wrote.

> The services that *Le Constitutionnel* has rendered to the country have been historic. But I will not hide my personal involvement behind a collective screen. I have never diverged from my principles. I defy an-yone to demonstrate that from its beginning until now that I wrote a line in *Le Constitutionnel* or that it published a word that was weak or equivocal or that was contrary to the free expression of my belief in the most extensive and firm form of liberty.[76]

Rousselin de Saint-Albin certainly had other interests to pursue outside of journalism and publishing. When he sold his shares in *Le Constitutionnel* in

March 1838, he was almost sixty-five years old and a grandfather with two teenaged children still at home.

Le Constitutionnel solved many of Alexandre Rousselin de Saint-Albin's problems. As a profession, journalism was an excellent fit for someone educated in Enlightenment who had experienced the troubles and triumphs of the Revolutionary and Napoleonic eras. During the Restoration, the refined, sophisticated elite and middle-class audience of the opposition press provided a superb showcase for Rousselin de Saint-Albin's talents. His beloved classical and literary allusions and profound political engagement were shared by and shaped his readers. In this crucible, middle-class liberalism was forged.

Cooperating with others and operating behind the scenes as part of an ownership-editorial team was second nature to a former secretary general in the Ministries of War and Interior. The paper allowed him to spread his ideas and wield considerable political influence. Both factors assuaged Rousselin de Saint-Albin's burning desire to matter, to become "someone." Although he exercised authority briefly during the Hundred Days, Rousselin de Saint-Albin had spent almost fifteen years in the political wilderness. He had not enjoyed the experience.

Ongoing battles over censorship with the Bourbon government allowed Rousselin de Saint-Albin to fight for something he believed in without fearing to wake the sleeping giant of popular activism. When the behemoth awakened in July 1830, he endorsed a change in dynasty. Louis-Philippe was a liberal alternative to the anarchy that would come from a revival of the republic. Rousselin de Saint-Albin deemed that France was not yet ready to go back to the future. *Le Constitutionnel*'s decline in profitability and as a political force across the 1830s showed that the aging Rousselin de Saint-Albin was increasingly out of step with the times.

Le Constitutionnel made Rousselin de Saint-Albin rich as well as powerful. Even though the benefits declined after the Revolution of 1830, the paper provided a stupendous windfall to its early investors. Rousselin de Saint-Albin's two shares generated a hefty annual income and a considerable fortune when he sold them in 1838. From an impecunious, frequently out of work state employee closely watched by the police, he had become a wealthy press baron. After remarrying, Rousselin de Saint-Albin bought a château and founded a dynasty of nobles. His elder son's successful career as a judge and deputy must have been deeply gratifying. For the illegitimate grandson of a dyer and a washerwoman (and, to be fair, prominent nobles on his mother's side), Hortensius de Saint-Albin's achievements were impressive.

Hortensius's growing prominence brought home the consequences of *Le Constitutionnel*'s waning influence. Rousselin de Saint-Albin could not outrun his past forever. When his revived public notoriety as a terrorist might have threatened his son's career and his involvement with the paper could no longer provide sufficient political cover, Rousselin de Saint-Albin left public life, ostensibly to spend time with his two teenage children and grandchild. Selling his stake in *Le Constitutionnel* also allowed him to escape the squabbles and frustrations of running a flagging daily paper and provided some distance from liberal politics. He determined to use the time to write about the legacy of the Revolution.

6

Remembering and Forgetting the French Revolution

MEMORIES AND MEMOIRS

There is only you and me who know the entire history [of the French Revolution] which so few suspect.

—LOUIS-PHILIPPE D'ORLÉANS, King of the French to Alexandre Rousselin de Saint Albin, c. 1831

THE REVOLUTION WAS never far from Rousselin de Saint-Albin's thoughts or actions. Even when he was most thoroughly involved with *Le Constitutionnel* and the political crises of the day, he remained obsessed by the past. Rousselin de Saint-Albin was actively engaged in both remembering and forgetting the French Revolution. He defended certain aspects and people, while vilifying others. His actions during the Terror, however, were deliberately shunned in hopes that memory of them would end up on the dustbin of history. The successes and failures of these efforts to remember and forget the Revolution reveal the complex legacies of the Revolution in the first half of the nineteenth century.

Controlling the history of the French Revolution mattered. The Revolution was a flash point in public debate. It shaped the possibilities of political action. The centrality of the events and personalities of the Revolution to nineteenth-century politics was also influenced by ongoing censorship and the periodic eruptions of popular anger that threatened the stability of the existing system. The continuity of certain people and families across the period magnified the importance of remembering and forgetting the Revolution. This was true of major players like Lafayette, Talleyrand, and Louis-Philippe, but was perhaps even more common among second-rank figures who did so much of the work of the Revolution, such as Marc-Antoine Jullien and Rousselin de Saint-Albin. Because politics were personal and the Terror was

The Making of a Terrorist. Jeff Horn, Oxford University Press (2021). © Oxford University Press.
DOI: 10.1093/oso/9780197529928.001.0001

identified with certain key figures, in large measure because of the successful scapegoating of Robespierre and his faction, political positioning amidst the chaos of 1793–94 had meaning that was widely shared. For Rousselin de Saint-Albin and a significant part of the political class, memories of the French Revolution influenced their sense of self, their emotional wellbeing, their ongoing careers, and their prospects for the future. Well into the nineteenth century, the French Revolution remained a political touchstone, especially for those who experienced and survived it.

Memory was vital to ending a generation of profound, multi-sided, political and social conflict. One way to understand the French Revolution was as a civil war between adherents of differing visions of what France was and what it ought to be. Revolutionary political culture's dependence on scapegoating, denunciation, and exaggerated rhetoric has obscured this interpretation. The Civil Constitution of the Clergy, the overthrow of the monarchy, the execution of Louis XVI, the rebellion in the Vendée, the Federalist Revolt, the Terror, the White Terror, and dechristianization (among other events) divided the French people and generated demands for vengeance. How each of these actions was remembered, both on their own and in relationship to the others, mattered greatly in nineteenth-century politics.

Ending a civil war is never simply a matter of military victory. Unless one side can maintain that military position across the years, preventing further violence requires some sort of reconciliation between the warring sides. During the French Revolution, there were so many "sides," so many deep-seated conflicts that led to violence, that healing the wounds was exceptionally difficult. The Napoleonic regime built an extremely popular and remarkably powerful government that successfully tamped down those divisions. Some conflicts were papered over, others repressed, and still others merely postponed. The Empire's definitive defeat in 1815 allowed certain grievances to be aired once more.

But the France of 1815 was not the France of 1789, 1793, or 1799, either economically or politically. Hemmed in diplomatically and constrained by the government's lack of support beyond a narrowly circumscribed elite, and with a much smaller and less valuable empire, the French state was no longer a threat to dominate Europe. France was also in a far different position vis-à-vis a rapidly industrializing United Kingdom. The realm of the possible was far smaller than it had been for more than a century. The bitterness of straitened circumstances fanned the embers of the flame of Revolution.

Rousselin de Saint-Albin and like-minded contemporaries focused firmly on the future. Their questions about policy and politics revolved around how to make it come to pass. From 1789 until the first years of the nineteenth century, a certain but varying percentage of the population believed that the future was now. In short, they thought that radical changes could be implemented quickly. What nineteenth-century advocates of change learned from the French Revolution was the dangers inherent in rapid transformation. Down that path lay civil war. After 1800, survival forced Rousselin de Saint-Albin and his cohort to adapt to their surroundings. But they remained remarkably loyal to their principles. They came to recognize that they could only lay the groundwork. Fundamental change took time. Revolutionaries who became liberals disdained the battles of the past in favor of preparing for the future. Liberals were willing to wait because they believed that time was on their side. In nineteenth-century France, popular violence occurred regularly because not everyone was equally patient. To end civil war, liberals sought to build a new consensus. In France's case, that meant awaiting a mature Third Republic.

A vital element of Rousselin de Saint-Albin's activities was protecting the reputations of his friends, allies, and acquaintances. More practically, he sought to help them keep body and soul together in the hostile political environment after 1815. Soon after the Second Restoration, he learned that Jean-Lambert Tallien was living in squalor. This dedicated Revolutionary terrorist of 1793–94 had played a major role in bringing down Robespierre and his coterie before becoming a mainstay of political and social life during the Directory. Rousselin de Saint-Albin convinced a high-ranking Bourbon official, Étienne-Denis Pasquier, to visit his room to see how far Tallien had fallen. Pasquier persuaded Louis XVIII to grant Tallien a pension of 2,000 francs a year. In keeping with the political aims of *Le Constitutionnel*, Rousselin de Saint-Albin also defended Chauvet, a teacher who suffered from official persecution and lost his job for having the same name as the son of a former close collaborator of Bonaparte's. This kind of attention and loyalty reflected Rousselin de Saint-Albin's character and practice. Not all of his activities were quite so selfless or disinterested.

Rousselin de Saint-Albin emerged as an important editorial figure— mostly in a negative way—in the publication of first-hand accounts of the Revolution, particularly for the period after 1794. Almost as soon as Napoleon Bonaparte consolidated power, Paul Barras, the general's former patron and boss, began to worry about keeping his secrets. Barras hoped someday to publish his views on the Revolution and the men and women who made it. In July 1801, Bonaparte sent men to the château of Grosbois, where Barras had been exiled, to seize all correspondence concerning the First Consul and his wife

Josephine, Barras' former mistress. Months before, Barras had anticipated Bonaparte's move by giving his most sensitive letters to Rousselin. The latter's marriage to Barras' cousin Clémentine de Montpezat strengthened their bond. Rousselin also spent a number of years in the region either in hiding or in internal exile plotting with Barras. The consolidation of the Empire seems to have made the mystery of Barras' papers acceptable to the government even after Barras himself was interned in 1810 in Montpellier.

Early in the Restoration, Barras began to revise his memoirs in earnest. He drafted most of the text, then Rousselin de Saint-Albin heavily edited it before Barras approved a final version. Other sections were written by Rousselin de Saint-Albin on the basis of Barras' notes or dictation. During this period, both men actively spread rumors about Joséphine's promiscuity, especially her supposed love for General Lazare Hoche. Many in the know were aware that Barras's memoirs were intended to score points at Bonaparte's expense. Given the Bonapartist stance of *Le Constitutionnel*, its difficulties with official censorship, and the shape of political alliances during the Restoration, neither Rousselin de Saint-Albin nor Barras could afford to set off a potential firestorm by provoking a libel suit from Bonaparte or, after 1821, his heirs.

In June 1825, Barras' lingering illness led the Keeper of the Seals to order that "all Barras's papers that might be of interest to the government should be sealed when the moment comes" as a means of preventing publication. The order remained in place after Barras's recovery. The embittered General died on 29 January 1829 at the age of seventy-three. Once again, Barras made sure that his materials would remain in his protégé's hands rather than under the government's thumb. On the day he died, Barras signed a new testament ordering that "my papers and *Memoirs*, held by one of my friends, be given to him [Rousselin de Saint-Albin], to complete those parts of the *Memoirs* that time has not permitted me to finish." This directive contradicted an earlier instruction that gave an editorial role to Paul Grand, a young lawyer, and assigned some of the financial benefit of publication to his manservant Courtat, "under the orders of my wife."[1] Anticipating a magistrate's arrival the next day, Grand and his brother Pierre brought a huge trunk of materials by carriage to Rousselin de Saint-Albin's home soon after Barras expired.

It took almost seven weeks after the funeral to inventory Barras' sequestered papers. They remained under seal despite the spirited effort of several well-known lawyers to wrest them away. Legal argument focused on the government's arbitrariness and abuses of power. It had been thirty years since Barras held a public position, so why muzzle him now? Even after the Revolution of 1830, King Louis-Philippe refused to order the transfer.[2]

Despite this failure, Marie-Pélagie Templies de Barras, hoped her late husband's *Memoirs* would soon see the light of day.

With the influence of *Le Constitutionnel* at its peak, and Rousselin de Saint-Albin fully occupied in running the paper and liberal politics, Barras' *Memoirs* were relegated to a back burner. Initially, Grand and Templies de Barras tried to use the courts to get Rousselin de Saint-Albin either to finish and publish the *Memoirs* or to allow someone else, such as Grand, to do so. Despite several lucrative offers from prominent publishers to print Barras' "secret history of the Directory," these efforts were in vain.[3] The widow ceded her rights to Rousselin de Saint-Albin in December 1832, leaving him in complete control.

George Duruy, who ultimately published the four-volume *Memoirs* in 1895–96, explained the delay. His explanation was based on unequalled access to the relevant documentation and on family tradition (he married Rousselin's granddaughter). In an 1832 letter, Rousselin de Saint-Albin asserted that the version of the *Memoirs* ready for publication "had been written soon after Barras' death, *under the impression of just resentments that he had expressed during his life, resentments that a strong antipathy against his persecutors led me to continue in a heated composition that concealed both fault and danger.*" His notary, Étienne Damaison, described the text as "the nest of a court case." Damaison consulted a legal advisor of the Bonaparte family who told him "that this socially prominent and rich family will not rest *until it has obtained vengeance and reparation from the courts regarding these* Memoirs."[4] Taking out the sections that might generate legal trouble would distort Barras' thoughts and actions, which his friend and protégé refused do. So, Duruy asserted that Rousselin de Saint-Albin delayed publication to avoid legal action by the Bonaparte family. Duruy also avowed that the version he published was closer to the original written or dictated by Barras than many thought.

Barras's *Memoirs* were not the only account of the period that Rousselin de Saint-Albin kept from the public. In 1814, he learned about the poverty of General Claude-François Malet's widow. Malet had staged an unsuccessful republican coup d'état against Napoleon while the Emperor was on campaign in Russia and was duly executed. Rousselin de Saint-Albin provided some support from his own limited finances and managed to get the Restoration government to restore her husband's military pension and even to pay the arrears. Madame Malet provided Rousselin de Saint-Albin with many of her husband's papers, both in hopes of protecting them and also to entice him to write the story of her husband's conspiracy. Thanks to highly placed sympathizers in the administration, Rousselin de Saint-Albin also consulted certain key government documents. Over the next fifteen years, he wrote several "sketches" describing key moments in General Malet's life and the nature of the resistance to Bonaparte, which were read by a number of his friends and acquaintances. After his mother's death in 1830, Malet's son, Captain Aristide de Malet, sought to get Rousselin de Saint-Albin to either publish his work or to return the documents. After years of frustration, Aristide de Malet filed a court case against Rousselin de Saint-Albin in 1836.

Under oath, Rousselin de Saint-Albin explained to Aristide de Malet that he had not published "for fear of losing your mother's pension by revealing your father's republicanism." The Bourbons believed that anyone who opposed Napoleon supported their cause: Rousselin de Saint-Albin did not want to disabuse them because Madame Malet owed this misconception "her bread, her very existence, and the good fortune of her son."[5] The judge agreed that Rousselin de Saint-Albin had no legal obligation to publish his "sketches." That was the end of the matter until 2017 when I discovered that Rousselin de Saint-Albin's descendants possess a fully realized 739 page manuscript. When it was completed is unclear, but internal evidence suggests that it was not finished until the 1840s. The family even sold the manuscript before repurchasing it in the early 1980s. Perhaps Rousselin de Saint-Albin's account of this fascinating episode will see the light of day, despite the fact that neither he nor his children ever made it available to the public.

Rousselin de Saint-Albin controlled the publication of two other important accounts of the Revolution. During the Consulate, General Jean-Charles Pichegru, an important figure in the Directory, was accused of joining a conspiracy against Bonaparte. His journal and notes were seized by Minister of Police Joseph Fouché who sent them to Barras for safekeeping. The documents were given to Rousselin, who was then writing a defense of Pichegru. He hoped to draw attention to the possibility that Pichegru had been murdered while in prison. Rousselin chose not to complete this work but held onto the materials. Along with Barras' papers, Pichegru's journal passed to his son Hortensius and then to Duruy. The family donated the journal to the French National Archives in 1958. Clearly, for Rousselin de Saint-Albin, some things could be more easily forgotten than others.

He also possessed some of Camille Desmoulins's papers. As Pierre-Joseph-Marcelin Matton prepared to publish what he thought was a previously unknown fragment of Desmoulins's incendiary newspaper, *Le Vieux Cordelier* #8, in 1834, he found out about Rousselin de Saint-Albin's vain attempts to convince Danton and Desmoulins to either take action or flee. Matton confirmed the story with the latter's mother-in-law, Anne-Françoise Duplessis, who described Rousselin de Saint-Albin as "the only friend who remains to me among the ruins that surrounded me. We are, he and I, like the two stalks of wheat that the scythe forgot in a harvested field."[6] Matton then visited Rousselin de Saint-Albin to discuss Danton and Desmoulins. He also expressed support for the proposed amnesty to be extended to former revolutionary figures then being bandied about with the strong support of *Le Constitutionnel.* Somewhat astonishingly, the comte gave Matton Desmoulin's handwritten notes defending himself against the charges levied by Louis-Antoine Saint-Just in April 1794. In a warm account of this interaction that left traces in the works of other authors, Matton paid homage to Rousselin de Saint-Albin as "a generous man, who in one of those spontaneous actions so rare in every time but especially in that period, despite the threat to his own life, dared to save, if he could, the lives of Camille Desmoulins and Danton."[7] Whether Rousselin de Saint-Albin found such a tribute worth waiting forty years for is unknown. For this survivor of the Revolutionary era, certain acts needed to be remembered, but only in the correct way by people sympathetic to his situation.

Rousselin de Saint-Albin was also a prominent collector of Revolutionary memorabilia. According to contemporaries, most notably historian Jules Michelet, Rousselin de Saint-Albin had oil portraits and tableaux that attracted many visitors and much praise. His collection included portraits of military men like Hoche and the famous "boy general" François Séverin Marceau-Desgraviers, along with politicians such as Lazare Carnot, Robespierre, François-Antoine Boissy d'Anglas, Desmoulins, Jean-Antoine-Joseph Fauchet, Bertrand Barère, André and Joseph-Marie Chenier, Michel Lepelletier, Georges Couthon, and Pierre-Gaspard Chaumette. Two pieces took pride of place, a canvas of the composer and singer Panard by Jean-Siméon Chardin and a full portrait of Saint-Just by the famous Jacques-Louis David. Rousselin de Saint-Albin had a complete rogues' gallery of the members of the Committee of Public Safety. He also built an impressive and eclectic library of nearly 60,000 books that contained valuable resources for the history of the period.

The quality of the collection was universally acclaimed. A major public exhibit was later drawn from it. Sara Y. Stevenson, an American heiress, recalled a visit:

> I well remember, as a little girl, being shown some of the choicest pieces
> in the series, among which were interesting original portraits. One
> paper especially made an indelible impression upon my childish mind,
> and I can now recall the feeling of awe with which I gazed upon the

appeal to arms in the name of the Commune, drawn up by Robespierre and his colleagues on the night of the 8ᵗʰ Thermidor, a document which has since been published by M. Duruy in the *Memoires de Barras*. Robespierre had just written the first syllable of his name below those of his colleagues when the Convention was attacked, and the bloodstains which bespattered the sheet, and told of the final tragedy of the leader's life, appealed to my childish imagination, and are still vivid in my memory.[8]

How the dinner party displaying the macabre skull of Charlotte Corday that Rousselin de Saint-Albin supposedly threw for one of Louis-Philippe's ministers fits into the picture is unclear. There can be no doubt, however, of the lingering, haunting power that the Revolution exerted on his thoughts.

ROUSSELIN DE SAINT-ALBIN took an increasingly active role in the historical community. He confirmed details for a significant number of historians, especially concerning Danton and Desmoulins (and his own tragic, quasi-heroic role in their arrest and execution). He wanted to be identified with the victims of Robespierre and the Terror. As part of the same effort, he was in close contact with Thiers, Louis Blanc, Walter Scott, and other important chroniclers who shaped public perception and knowledge of the Revolution. Knowing of his father's esteem, Hortensius de Saint-Albin allowed Michelet, whom he knew socially, to read and even quote from Barras's *Memoirs* many decades before they appeared in print. Michelet also consulted a few of Rousselin de Saint-Albin's unpublished historical works.

Hoping to build on his well-received and successful biographies of Hoche, Chérin, and Marbot from 1797 to 1800, Rousselin devoted a significant proportion of his retirement to composing new material based on the lives and actions of the great men he had known and worked with. He labored assiduously on a massive *Life of Championnet* for a number of years. Biographical fragments about General Jean-Baptiste Kléber, accounts of Malet's plot, and, almost inevitably, some notes on Danton and a sketch of Barras' views on the events of 9 Thermidor flowed from his pen in this period.

The subjects of these works reflected both his experiences and his sense of his actions and legacy. Rousselin de Saint-Albin identified closely with his subjects. He portrayed Hoche as a true "child of the Revolution," while Championnet and Kléber both served with his foster father, Laurent Corbeau, early in the Revolution. Hoche, Championnet, Malet, and Marbot were jailed for political reasons associated with Jacobinism. In 1804,

Rousselin de Saint-Albin's future mother-in-law, the marquise de Montpezat, was arrested for possessing correspondence related to a conspiracy originally involving Pichegru. In the introduction to his *Life of Championnet*, Rousselin de Saint-Albin explained that he chose these particular people from "among those warriors whose actions serve as examples. These men consistently practiced the principles of selflessness and of absolute devotion to their country."[9] Rightly or wrongly, Rousselin de Saint-Albin saw himself in that same light.

Malet, Kléber, and Barras were all victims of Napoleon, while Hoche, Chérin, Marbot, and Championnet had all been pushed aside or at least out of the limelight by Bonaparte's rise to power. Despite his participation in the administration of the Hundred Days and espousal of liberal Bonapartism (when the Emperor was safely exiled to Saint-Helena), Rousselin de Saint-Albin clearly believed that Napoleon had hijacked the Revolution and robbed him of his rightful place as an important public servant. Although he had a prudent fear of the legal reach of the Bonaparte family, his actions as editor and author demonstrated a palpable desire to balance the scales, though he adopted a remarkably long-term perspective in order to do so.

Just as he chose to keep Barras's *Memoirs* and Pichegru's journal under wraps, Rousselin de Saint-Albin never made his mature work as an historian available to the public. There was certainly an audience for such first-hand, patriotic versions of the events of the Revolution and its great men. Relying on the same approach and making heavy use of primary sources as before, Rousselin de Saint-Albin had no shortage of offers to publish. Yet he did not. He did not fear the public eye, nor did he lack confidence in his abilities. Contemporaries validated his self-judgment, as have professional historians of more recent vintage who consider Rousselin de Saint-Albin's histories written in retirement to be solid, albeit Romantic, accounts of events. His work on Danton provides a significant, though hardly unbiased, source of information on this key figure. Perhaps he did not think that the time was right for his work to appear. Perhaps he simply wanted to let sleeping eagles rest. Neither explanation is particularly convincing.

When he died in 1847, Rousselin de Saint-Albin's manuscripts passed to his children, most notably to Hortensius. Like his father, the elder son did nothing with them until 1860 when he released the two volumes of the *Life of Championnet* to considerable success. Thirteen years later, just a few years before his own retirement, Hortensius published several of his father's sketches as part of the deluge of material on the Revolutionary era collected and distributed by historians and amateurs alike during the Third Republic. Yet the most significant pieces of Rousselin de Saint-Albin's literary and historical legacy remained hidden, namely Barras' *Memoirs* and his account of Danton's actions after the overthrow of the monarchy. His grandson-in-law took care of the former, but the latter has never appeared. Was it because this work discussed both Danton's and his own profound engagement with the Terror and revealed that although they ultimately became its victims, master and protégé began as its proponents and executors? That is my suspicion.

During this phase of profound engagement with the history of the Revolution, historian Georges Averal recounted his encounters with "patriot of 1789" Rousselin de Saint-Albin in glowing terms. He was never one of those "political Figaros" who said, "Oh, I am old, pardon the actions of my youth!" Rather he responded to his detractors:

> Who could deny that I was young when the Revolution was young itself? You can exhume some of my ardent or even choleric words when everyone was angry. I cannot retract them any more than I wish to repeat them in a more tranquil period. No, I do not refuse to accept responsibility for having been what the aristocracy names a Revolutionary. I am honored to still be what I was.[10]

These actions and words might be seen as those of a convivial man with time on his hands after retiring from *Le Constitutionnel* in 1838. They can also be understood as an attempt to burnish his legacy. Preventing some accounts from appearing and avoiding public controversy protected his reputation. Rousselin de Saint-Albin certainly had his defenders, especially when he was a powerful journalist, but there were a number of disquieting cracks in the public image that he wished to present to the public and to posterity that needed to be plastered over.

He was accused of hoodwinking his foster father to acquire his title in order to cover up his identity as a terrorist. Horace de Viel Castel described Rousselin de Saint-Albin as

> an old *sans-culotte* whose real name is Bousselin [*sic*], but who found it desirable when the Restoration took place to destroy the identity of the companion of Robespierre, Marat, &c. With this object, and for a certain money consideration, he prevailed upon an old Marquis de Saint-Albin, who was without a *sou* or a rag to his back, to adopt him as his son. He took his adoptive father's name, dropped his own, and then, the better to hide all traces of Bousselin, published an obituary pamphlet containing an account of that worthy's last moments.[11]

The factual inaccuracies of this account notwithstanding, such charges burdened the next generation of the family with consolidating its transition into the highest reaches of the political and social elite.

For polemical purposes, Armand de Pontmartin kept alive the memory of Rousselin de Saint-Albin's "terrorist newspaper, *The Journal of Public Safety*" and how "the citizen Rousselin-Corbeau became, with the passage of years, comte Alexandre de Saint-Albin." Pontmartin recalled Rousselin's role in "denouncing the regulars and actors of the theater of the nation" in 1793. During the Restoration, Pontmartin asserted that by seeking "to forge a sole party from Bonapartism and liberalism," Rousselin de Saint-Albin demonstrated that "he had adored servitude under two different forms: Terrorism and Empire."[12] Pontmartin emphasized that, although Rousselin did not live to see the Second Republic, his younger son devotedly served the Second Empire which destroyed that short-lived dream, just as the original Empire annihilated the Revolutionary republic.

In a muckraking series purporting to "unmask literary deceptions," noted bibliographer Joseph-Marie Quérard devoted a long article to Rousselin de Saint-Albin's life and work. Quérard depicted "Alexandre-Charles Rousselin, former civil commissioner of the Revolutionary government in Troyes during the Year II and former editor of the *Journal of Public Safety* who today impersonates the comte de Saint-Albin," as "an accomplice" of convicted terrorists. Quérard was furious that an earlier work mentioning Rousselin's activities during the Revolution had been censored for referring to a pamphlet that he had "the [political] credit to have prosecuted and condemned as defamatory." "But the true motif," Quérard asserted, "was that the article in question recalled certain writings displaying a very dark republicanism. He [Rousselin de Saint-Albin] took advantage of the situation to make it disappear. In his new social position and, as a rich landowner, Rousselin could negate his past and then seek to destroy the traces." It clearly irked Quérard that his previous book had been taken to Rousselin de Saint-Albin's home where "my disapproving article was replaced by an apology for Rousselin's conduct." He fumed that this "knowing distortion of the truth," "had been imposed" by Rousselin de Saint-Albin. Now Quérard could cleanse his conscience by publicizing those actions once more.

This "hero of the Terror under the name of Rousselin" was the son of the dyer François, wrote Quérard. Making heavy use of primary sources, Quérard got some minor details wrong, but his account of Rousselin's actions in Provins and Troyes is generally accurate. The charges that he had "brought a young girl with him for his baser pleasures" as well as his oppression of adherents of the old régime, were, however, given pride of place. Quérard reported that "the horror that the name of Rousselin still inspires in Troyes with the elderly who were contemporaries of the proconsul's mission or among the descendants of his victims proves that the truth cannot be destroyed by autobiography." With repeated quotes from Rousselin's own writings, such as the denunciation of the Girondins in May 1793, Quérard made the damning case that Rousselin de Saint-Albin had been an ardent Revolutionary and terrorist, though he did note his service to Bernadotte, his biographies, and his literary activities after 18 Brumaire. The quantity of evidence made it hard to dispute and harder to dismiss his description of Rousselin as a committed terrorist.[13]

Prominent Catholic intellectual and historian Geoffroy de Grandmaison kept memories of Rousselin de Saint-Albin as a prominent terrorist alive. In evaluating the *Memoirs*, he noted that Rousselin de Saint-Albin "shared Barras' thoughts against Napoleon" before getting to the heart of his critique. Grandmaison described Rousselin de Saint-Albin as having "a rather shady personality and a mediocre soul" which had allowed him to "pretend to be a moderate during the Revolution." However, Grandmaison concluded, "all his life, he carefully hid his role during the Revolution and even more carefully eluded questions of his birth and his 'nobility.'" "To pierce the mystery," a discussion of his father François and his mother's liaison with Corbeau de Saint-Albin followed. Their affair "enlightened his personality no less than his opinions." Grandmaison detailed Rousselin's actions during the Terror in Provins and Troyes, citing "a likeable woman, very indulgent for such debris of the Revolution, who avowed that he [Rousselin] had been misled at the age of 18." Then Grandmaison got nasty. He baldly stated that Hortensius had been born out of wedlock in 1805 from a relationship formalized two years later. And Rousselin was poor. "Everyone knew that this shady character lived at Barras' expense." After his adoption by Saint-Albin, "who was absolutely nothing to Alexandre Rousselin," "the former Jacobin became Monsieur, le comte." Grandmaison emphasized that Rousselin de Saint-Albin's children by his second marriage "have no stain and at least have the honor not to be related to Barras." Returning to the *Memoirs*, Grandmaison concluded, "in chapter after chapter, one encounters a laudatory appreciation, an enthusiastic note, or a trait of virtue or honor of Rousselin de Saint-Albin. Who would know his virtues better? It was his hand that held the pen."[14] By this time, Rousselin de Saint-Albin had been dead for more than fifty years. He may have been gone, but he, like the Revolution itself, was not forgotten.

Memory can be tricky. Especially in retirement, Rousselin de Saint-Albin could not escape recollections of his actions during the French Revolution. Nor did he wish to, as his thorough engagement in writing and editing history demonstrates conclusively. His goals were, however, not simply either remembering or forgetting. He had more difficult tasks in mind: to generate and disseminate a particular image of the French Revolution and of his own activities. Here Rousselin de Saint-Albin was less interested in "the truth" of what actually happened. He was more engaged in how things ought to have been. For Rousselin de Saint-Albin, this intent was less a deliberate factual distortion of the course of events—though it was that too—than a response to the disappointed hopes of his youth. He also hoped to pass along a legacy of devoted public service and noble intentions to his descendants. Although he had considerable success in propagating a reputation as a victim of the Terror rather than a terrorist, especially when he was involved with *Le Constitutionnel*, Rousselin de Saint-Albin and his family had to cope with the persistence of others' memories of the French Revolution.

Remembering and forgetting were the intertwined double helix of how the French dealt with the legacy of Revolution. The possibility of enabling society to achieve its potential, of facilitating the emergence of France as it should be—that was the very project of the Revolution itself. For former Revolutionaries turned liberals, such as Rousselin de Saint-Albin and the cohort who survived the Revolution, exercising a selective memory toward their earlier ideas and actions was not an abandonment of the commitments of their youth. Such selectivity might be understood as a more realistic view of how to make the ideal France of their dreams into a reality while working within the narrowed political constraints that marked the first half of the nineteenth century. In many ways, during the Restoration and the July Monarchy, a liberal was a Revolutionary who both wanted France to achieve its potential and feared the consequences of the means necessary to achieve that goal.

Conclusion

SATISFACTIONS AND REGRETS OF A LIFE
IN REVOLUTION

COMTE ALEXANDRE-CHARLES ROUSSELIN de Saint-Albin lived an
extraordinary life. His public career and private pleasures brought him fame,
fortune, and personal gratification. He had a supportive wife and three children, two of whom he was particularly close to. He also had plenty of interesting things to do, as well as the time and resources to enjoy those pursuits.
Unwilling and unable to abandon a lifetime of political engagement, he nonetheless allowed himself to fade from public view after retirement. Rousselin
de Saint-Albin's decisions about publishing, from Barras' *Memoirs* to his own
works, reflect a deliberate choice to keep a low profile. He most likely did
so to protect his children, especially his son Hortensius, from some of the
consequences of his earlier actions.

Surrounded by his books and manuscripts, with evocative images of people
who had shaped the Revolution looking down from the walls and the skull
of Marat's murderer for company, Rousselin de Saint-Albin rejected Hamlet's
angst about the past. This budding patriarch had good reason to be pleased
with his family and its prospects. Hortensius was a well-regarded politician
who had already emerged as a close collaborator in protecting the family
name. Sharing his father's devotion to public service, he served on the Sarthe's
departmental council, and for twelve years (1837–1849) as a deputy. He was
also a judge, primarily with Paris' influential appeals court, from 1837 to 1876.
In 1831, he had married a talented still-life painter whose works were publicly
displayed in Paris' salons under the name of Cécile de Saint-Albin. The couple
had a daughter, Marie, who seems never to have married. Hortensius served as
his father's literary executor.

The Making of a Terrorist. Jeff Horn, Oxford University Press (2021). © Oxford University Press.
DOI: 10.1093/oso/9780197529928.001.0001

Sophie, Rousselin de Saint-Albin's much younger wife, gave him two children. Louis-Philippe, born in 1822, had as godparents the future king and queen. He was a scholarly youth who either accommodated or had no alternative to working for the Bonaparte family. Known as the vicomte de Saint-Albin, Louis-Philippe de Saint-Albin served for many years as personal librarian to the active and engaged Empress Eugènie, the consort of Napoleon III. This quiet, unassuming man was content with his books and uninterested in publishing his father's works. He never married.

Rousselin de Saint-Albin doted on his daughter Hortense, born in 1824. Devoted to her father, she lived at home until after his death, but had excellent expectations of a good marriage. She wed Achille Jubinal, a prominent professor of medieval history, writer on contemporary topics, and republican politician, in 1855. They had two children: Marc, born out of wedlock in 1851, and in 1860 Amélie, who later married Georges Duruy. Rousselin de Saint-Albin's numerous contemporary descendants descend from this branch of the family tree. When he died, intellectually active though somewhat enfeebled, in June 1847, he had much to be proud of.

Some of this dynastic success—the superb educations and the funds to support the early stages of Hortensius' career and Hortense's dowry—stemmed from the fortune Rousselin de Saint-Albin made from Le Constitutionnel. The paper's immense profits allowed him to purchase, restore, and furnish a beautiful historic home in fashionable central Paris as well as to buy books, paintings, and memorabilia, all while enjoying a noble lifestyle. The influx of capital from the sale of his two shares in the paper buttressed the family's long-term financial position. His journey from an impoverished young man to seeing his children firmly ensconced in the French elite must have given him considerable satisfaction.

Yet recognizing the existence of certain concerns on the horizon might help to reveal how haunted Rousselin de Saint-Albin was by his past as well as his fears for the future. He did everything he could to cover up or distract attention from three aspects of his early life. First, he disassociated himself from extreme republicanism and the Terror, except as a victim. Using the courts with skill and precision, he successfully muzzled many of his critics. For example, in 1843, Quérard published a full retraction of certain parts of his article. "To avoid the continuance of an unfortunate lawsuit," Quérard added materials written by Hortensius to the article in any unsold copies of the book and gave permission for Saint-Albin to fix those "that have been sold or are in libraries where you see fit." He also admitted that his article contained errors because he had focused too much on two contemporary pamphlets critical of Rousselin's actions in Troyes. Ten years later, after Rousselin de Saint-Albin's death, Quérard apologized for the "sorrows" he had caused and expressed his personal esteem for Hortensius.[1] The apology for not confirming sources seemed genuine, but the damage was done.

Second, in almost every contemporary printed reference, Alexandre-Charles Rousselin de Saint-Albin was described as the son of artillery officer Antoine-Pierre-Laurent de Corbeau and grandson of marquis Antoine-Laurent de Corbeau de Saint-Albin, scion of an old Dauphinois noble family. Rousselin de Saint-Albin referred to Corbeau as a "remarkable man." This idea should not "be suspect of partiality because he was linked to this virtuous citizen by the bonds of a close kinship." In writing history, Rousselin de Saint-Albin refused "to omit important facts because they honored the memory of his father."[2] These warm words, however, only saw print fourteen years after Rousselin de Saint-Albin's death.

Finally, Rousselin de Saint-Albin, again with impressive success, sought to suppress the fact that his son Hortensius had been born out of wedlock. Although far from unusual at the time or later, Rousselin de Saint-Albin was determined to help his son evade any challenges to the public positions of trust and responsibility he seemed destined to fulfill. Fudging the date of marriage was possible, but avoiding the topic altogether was the family's favored approach. A police document of 1815 observed that Rousselin de Saint-Albin always "made his [first] marriage in Normandy a mystery."[3]

Rousselin de Saint-Albin's sensitivity on this issue is revealing. Although he loved and respected his foster father, he may have carried powerful and deep-seated scars from his mother's actions during his youth. It is easy to imagine Rousselin's life as a schoolboy taunted by aristocrats for having the accent and manners of a working-class Parisian. That his tuition was paid by a noble artillery officer so frequently absent from the scene probably did not help matters. Perhaps Rousselin de Saint-Albin never moved past these formative worries about propriety and position. Given his lifelong resistance to the dictates of the Roman Catholic Church, he may not have wanted his children or grandchildren to face the hypocrisy and social shunning that might stem from an illegitimate birth.

Most likely, Rousselin de Saint-Albin deliberately attempted to obscure those aspects of the past that did not fit with the identity he sought to create for himself and his family. His unceasing, remarkably effective efforts to remake himself and the world around him were challenged by his past behavior. So he did his best to bury them.

Many of Rousselin de Saint-Albin's choices make more sense if we pay close attention to his construction of a noble heritage and a past as a moderate liberal activist whose public service was linked to his experience as a victim of the Terror. The decisions neither to run for office during the Restoration nor to accept any official position under the July Monarchy allowed Rousselin de Saint-Albin to avoid a great deal of public scrutiny and paved the way for Hortensius to enter the electoral lists in a department away from Paris, where the facts of his background would be harder to find and disseminate. Court cases lodged in the 1820s, 1830s, and 1840s sought to establish his version of events as the official record, providing a certain kind of confirmation of this objective. Rousselin de Saint-Albin's decision to retire just as his son acquired a new more prominent place in French society offers another kind of support. His unwillingness to publish Barras' *Memoirs* or his own histories also fits this decision to worry less about the past and more about the future, particularly that of his family.

By deferring to his elder son and protecting his reputation and heritage, Rousselin de Saint-Albin made a critical set of choices that reflected a diminished confidence in the course of current events. With the government of Louis-Philippe increasingly turning its back on the ideals of the French Revolution in favor of the emerging *"juste milieu"* in which the pace of change slowed to a hesitant crawl, Rousselin de Saint-Albin understood that many of his youthful hopes and dreams were doomed to disappointment. In Hortensius, Rousselin de Saint-Albin saw a prominent jurist and legislator already well able to maintain the public prominence of the family name. At retirement he had one grandchild, and his two younger children had superb prospects. It seemed like only one thing could get in their way: his past.

Although he never fully lost his hope for the future or in the achievements of the French Revolution—his final public act was to sign a petition to liberate France's slaves once more, as had been done in 1794—Rousselin de Saint-Albin subordinated those prospects to protecting and perpetuating the position of his children and grandchildren. It would be a gross exaggeration to say that Rousselin de Saint-Albin came to embody the domestic, bourgeois values that emerged so strongly in this period, in part because of the lack of possibilities for more drastic social or political change. Yet such a perspective does seem to apply to certain choices made by this budding patriarch. In some ways, being a good parent came to outweigh being a good politician or public advocate. He requested that the phrase "He loved us" be inscribed on his tombstone.[4]

Rousselin de Saint-Albin's pessimism about the prospects for improving society in the 1840s intersected with his growing and well-founded optimism about the potential longevity of the success that he and his family had achieved. Perhaps this shift in view happens naturally to a Revolutionary terrorist whose star-crossed career illuminates the turbulent period from the Enlightenment to the eve of the Revolution of 1848. It certainly happened to comte Alexandre-Charles Rousselin de Saint-Albin and those of his contemporaries who came of age during the French Revolution, and lived to tell the tale of how a relatively small group of French people changed the world.

APPENDIX

Alexandre Rousselin and the Historians

What was Revolutionary about Alexandre Rousselin's life? Almost everything. Restating an approach popularized by Robert Darnton suggests how historians might evaluate this young, intellectually minded Parisian's efforts to made sense of the social and cultural trauma that accompanied the collapse of the old régime.[1] His biography illuminates key elements of the energy unleashed in 1789. Rousselin absorbed a larger dose of the drive to build something new and better than most of his contemporaries, and never really lost it. From the Year II, through the Directory and Napoleonic era, into the Restoration and the July Monarchy, Rousselin engaged in a constant struggle to matter, to be part of something bigger than himself. His political acuity, emotional responses, and remarkable durability furnish insights into the interpretation of Revolutionary regimes.

Alexandre Rousselin was no ordinary citizen.[2] Yet he has been almost completely forgotten by historians despite his frequent position as an eyewitness to events. Even during his lifetime, he was relatively unknown outside of certain circles of liberal intellectuals, Parisian politicians, and journalists. Rousselin was also notorious in the department of the Aube and with a small group of other victims of the Terror like the comte de Lamotte-Valois. Unlike many Revolutionaries, beyond his literary endeavors, after 1793 he shied away from public exposure and never ran for office, a rare combination for someone of his influence and stature. Among his contemporaries, those choices were distinctive; they underscore how militants who were proximate to power or who only briefly held the reins themselves made the transition from Revolutionary to liberal. These important features of political culture affected thousands of people active in the Year II, but have received little scholarly attention.

Rousselin was inspired by 1789, but even more by the dynamics of Paris' popular movement. He came of age politically in the sections and clubs and was alive to their nuances. After the fall of 1793, he also recognized their strengths and weaknesses.

The Committee of Public Safety's decision to let him edit its newspaper and then send him on two missions to Champagne rewarded his activities in the popular movement and recognized his extraordinary ability to find influential mentors and patrons. In 1792–1794 Rousselin was part of a group of mostly young, mostly educated militants who functioned as a transmission belt between groups, factions, and institutions. He shows how much these activists mattered to the work of the Revolution, both in Paris and in the provinces, where they energized the popular societies and directed the Revolutionary Army. Could France have survived the crisis without them?

Morris Slavin's 1994 book on the Cordeliers was the last gasp of a rich historiographical tradition focused on the popular movement exemplified by Albert Soboul and Richard Cobb.[3] Since the bicentennial, historians have focused more on the deputies' motivations and rhetoric and delineated Revolutionary political culture and ideology including the role of emotions.[4] But the popular movement never completely faded from view. Michael L. Kennedy's four volumes on the Jacobins reveal the diverse intersections between the clubs and the popular movement while Samuel Guicheteau's study of workers in Nantes along with Dominique Godineau's and Katie Jarvis' examinations of women workers and market women of Paris respectively, kept issues of work and market relations on the agenda.[5] Colin Jones' long-awaited book on the day of 9 Thermidor will examine the politics of the sections and their relationship to the factions in the National Convention to show how the popular movement had largely been muzzled by late July 1794. People like Rousselin bridged the gaps between and among the various groups both within Paris and between the provinces and the capital. They relied heavily on festivals and other forms of symbolic politics to spread ideas or concepts and to gather ground-level feedback.[6] Journalist, personal secretary, police spy, commissioner of the Committee of Public Safety, militant in the sections and clubs: Rousselin's overlapping roles and identities illustrate how idealism, personalities, and institutional rivalries shaped the course of the Revolution's relationship with the popular movement. In this sense, his biography goes beyond a single life to consider how Revolutionary politics worked.

Historians of the Directory and Napoleonic era headed by Isser Woloch have explored the subsequent political behavior and survival of networks of activists from the early stages of Revolution, as well as from the Terror.[7] Studies of local elites or particular social groups and professions have traced continuity and change in political engagement and the survival of Revolutionary activists.[8] Most such studies cover 1794 to 1799 or stop in 1804 or 1815, or they begin in 1799 or 1800. Rousselin's trajectory suggests a different time frame. How many nineteenth-century liberals were disappointed young Revolutionaries, especially in the 1815–1830 era? Rousselin was only sixteen in 1789 and he was exceptionally young for the posts he held, but his cohort or generation deserves investigation. Did this group have a "particular historical identity," as Alan Spitzer argued for Frenchmen born between 1792 and 1802, because of "the trauma of growing up in an age of transition"? Rousselin's cohort merits the kind of extended prosopographical analysis and cultural assessment modeled by Spitzer and Jean-François Sirinelli.[9]

THE EXTRAORDINARY EVENTS from 1792 to 1794 are at the heart of this book, in part because it was the pivot of Rousselin's life and career. This era also played a vital role in the work of revisionist historians who followed in the wake of François Furet to stress the centrality of political language and ideology. Rousselin's experiences suggest that revisionists take their interpretation a step too far when they argue that the language deployed in 1789 "structured" or "patterned" the Terror or the Revolution itself.[10] At age sixteen Alexandre Rousselin could not have imagined the rhetoric he deployed, much less the actions he took a mere four years later. To see a deterministic inevitability to the onset of political violence is to ignore the shifting context of language and behavior. For Rousselin and most others, Revolutionary events like the *Declaration of the Rights of Man and Citizen*, the flight of the king, foreign invasion, the execution of Louis XVI, and the onset of civil war, among other events, changed the meanings of words. The militants' deep commitment to the survival of the Republic and of the Revolution, not to mention the persistence of their own lives and political careers, naturally evolved. For activists like Rousselin, the meaning of words like "treason" or "terror" cannot be divorced from the contingency of political choice nor from the ebb and flow of the Revolutionary crisis on the battlefield, in the streets, and in political discourse. These meanings changed, not once but several times. The rapid pace of change in political terminology and practice was one of the most Revolutionary aspects of the French Revolution. This biography asserts that the emergence of Revolutionary violence was based on the circumstances of that tumultuous time. Rousselin and his cohort would have been appalled by the notion that such violence, such actions, or such a crisis were in any way structured or patterned in the ideas of 1789.

Responding to revisionism, Michel Biard, Jean-Clément Martin, and Marisa Linton argue that the Terror never became "the order of the day." Martin's discussion of this "national myth" focuses on how violence stemmed from the weakness of the Revolutionary government, rather than expressed its strength. His combative formulation places the events of 1793–94 in a longer-term perspective and decenters 1793–94 as the sole era marked by widespread state violence. Biard and Linton's new book convincingly demonstrates the nineteenth-century origins of the term, effectively following up on Ronald Schechter's linkage of the origins of the discourse of the Terror to the judicial terminology of the old régime. Biard and Linton also stress that use of the term "the Terror" is often intended to discredit the Revolution itself. Martin even characterizes the Terror as "fake news, a creation that has succeeded in anchoring itself in collective memory."[11] Preference for "the terror" has become a new orthodoxy among those working on the Year II.[12]

Of course, myths can have great power, and for Alexandre Rousselin, the Terror was anything but fake news. He recognized the makeshift quality of many Revolutionary institutions. Legal precedent could not keep pace with deeds on the ground. His missions also show how the actions of the Revolutionary Army and of various agents of the central state were experienced as a system by both those people like Rousselin who implemented government policies and, more importantly, by the far greater number of French who experienced this "terrorism."[13] Inhabitants of the departments of the Seine-et-Marne and Aube neither fully realized nor truly cared about the provisional nature of the tactics used repeatedly by representatives on mission, commissioners of the Committee of Public Safety, detachments of the Revolutionary Army, or popular societies. The Champenois experienced the Terror as deliberate state policy and Rousselin's actions as its expression, no matter the official phrasing or legal foundation. After all, on 22 November 1793, Rousselin asserted, "I have made terror the order of the day." Both the form and content of the Troyens' recurring denunciations of their tormentors for "terrorism" conclusively demonstrate this lived reality.

In approaching "the Terror" as part of "a political culture of violence among the leadership," Timothy Tackett provides a superb model. For Tackett, this "attitude or *mentalité . . .* preceded the Terror and made the option of 'state-sponsored violence on an unprecedented scale' seem almost inevitable and necessary." He shows how Revolutionaries "became terrorists"[14] building on microhistories of the provincial Terror like that of Colin Lucas and broader studies like Biard's work on representatives on mission. For generations, the myth of the Terror as "the order of the day" was universally accepted. Perhaps this particular myth became so pervasive and proved so enduring because it epitomized the perceptions and experiences of both terrorists and the terrorized. From Rousselin's perspective, the Terror deserved capitalization because it grew out of militants' efforts to preserve the Revolution. He never conflated the Terror with the Revolution, but he also knew that the Revolution could not be isolated from the Terror. By extending the consequences of that *mentalité* over a career stretching forty-plus years after 1794, Rousselin illustrated how an idealistic youth became first a Revolutionary, then a terrorist, and finally, a liberal.

It was a bumpy ride. Rousselin provides a test case for some of the arguments about emotions during the Revolution and specifically during the Terror.[15] Linton highlights the roles of friendship and fear in determining political choices. In Rousselin's case, emotions especially fear of denunciation, dictatorship, failure, and later, for his children marked his behavior both during and after the Terror. The intensity of his emotional reactions may have been greater when he was younger, but these feelings had an enduring influence on his actions.

Evaluating emotions requires historians to rethink individual and collective relationships in ways that usually depend heavily on certain types of sources. For Rousselin, it is often difficult to glean emotional content from official reports or his published work.[16] Reliance on personal correspondence, however, raises questions of separating rhetoric from reality. How should we evaluate the overblown claims of eternal friendship and abiding love in the letters between Rousselin and Benjamin Constant? Was it a shooting star of a friendship, or did it reflect the emotional tenor of the times as people cast about for anchors to resist the attractions of Bonaparte and his regime?[17] In this biography, the methodological response to lack of direct evidence and soaring rhetorical flourishes was to consider the consistency of behavior over time to assess what might be missing that might plausibly be attributed to emotions. Despite the blandness of the bulk of the surviving documentation, Rousselin's fears about the fate of Revolution, the costs of inaction, and later of denunciation and irrelevancy emerge from his deeds. After 1815, love of family strongly influenced his behavior. The history of emotions can be evaluated in different ways and deserves to be widened beyond its period of greatest intensity.[18]

Tackett sketches a baseline emotional politics for decision-makers between 1789 and 1794 that depends heavily on the survival of certain types of sources.[19] Rousselin almost definitely oscillated between fear, hope, anger, and joy during the upheavals of 1789–96, though the available evidence makes it difficult to demonstrate. Did the choice first to create and then to ensure the survival of such sources denote a particular psychology that may or may not have typified the Revolutionaries? Has that personality type been vastly over-represented in our understandings of Revolutionary *mentalité*? Rousselin's choices of what to write and his decision to purge the historical record raise important questions about the history of emotions.

When read against the grain, Rousselin's missions in Champagne highlight other aspects of the history of emotions during the Terror. Parisian friendship networks, club conflicts, and rivalries among the deputies played out publicly in the provinces. Emissaries of the central state and the inhabitants of Provins and Troyes certainly felt fear, and it showed. But when reconstructing the Troyens' actions in 1793–94, the difference in their emotional tenor from the Parisians is remarkable.[20] Even though the Aube endured visits by multiple representatives on mission and commissioners of the Committee of Public Safety as well as detachments of the Revolutionary Army, Alexandre Guélon displayed surprising little fear when he went to Paris in June 1794 to denounce Rousselin and his supporters for "terrorism." He was undeterred by having been jailed for months as a "moderate." It never occurred to him that he could be sent before the Revolutionary Tribunal and survived only because of 9 Thermidor. Fear was a driving force of Revolutionary politics, but it had different emotive power in the provinces—and in different departments—than it did in the hot-house atmosphere of Paris. Rousselin's experiences underscore the longitudinal and latitudinal emotional responses revealed by a longer-time frame and a comparative approach.

BIOGRAPHIES DEPICTING THE outsize characters and extraordinary actions of the Revolutionaries have always been part of the story of how to construct a new regime and uncover its meaning both for participants and for those who followed in their footsteps. As a subject, Alexandre Rousselin is unusual because he served—and survived—so many governments. Unlike most higher-level former Revolutionaries, he was not a pariah when the Bourbons returned to the throne. He chose not to return to public service despite several invitations to do so. The Revolutionary decade may have been the high point of his political engagement, but it was not the apex of his political career or of his influence. His ability to survive and thrive through connections, hard work, aptitude, and sheer luck was unparalleled.

Rousselin's career evokes the fate of a "missionary of the republic" after their missions were over and later once there was no longer a republic. In his case, facing his victims' vengeance and rehabilitation were two sides of the same political coin.[21] He could not escape the consequences of Revolutionary action. Political transitions posed a threat that his past would once again become a liability.

With one exception, the recent spate of biographies of less iconic revolutionaries remains focused on high politics. Camille (though not Lucile) Desmoulins, Nicolas-Louis François de Neufchâteau, Pierre-Antoine Antonelle, Philippe-Antoine Merlin de Douai, and Léonard Bourdon were all deputies.[22] Through vignettes, case studies, or collective biography, more venerable scholarship depicted the Revolution from the bottom up highlighting the Terror or 1789–95.[23] Biographies of pivotal figures, especially Robespierre and Bonaparte, have appeared at regular intervals, deepening and refining our sense of their motivations, actions, and contributions, but again the time frame under consideration is limited.[24] Alexandre Rousselin experienced not only the emergence of Revolutionary politics, but also how the republic became a constitutional monarchy, along with each stop along the way. He lived the Revolution from the middle out and represents an important layer of bureaucrats and activists who made the various regimes work.[25]

Only one other "middling" figure of the era has been the subject of a full biography: Marc-Antoine Jullien (1775–1848), the individual whose life most closely mirrored Rousselin's.[26] Both young, both provincial "missionaries of the republic," both victims of reaction, both interested in education as a means of remaking society, both writers, both forever tarred with the reputation as terrorists, both became liberals after 1815. Among historians, Jullien is far better known, in large measure, because of R. R. Palmer's interest, and because historians of education have rediscovered his ideas. His trajectory highlights how unusual Rousselin's accomplishments were.

Jullien enjoyed a leg up because his father was a deputy to the National Convention. His missions in Bordeaux were bloodier, and his fear of counter-revolutionary/foreign plots even more impassioned than Rousselin's. Closely attached to Robespierre, 9 Thermidor began "a career of personal exculpation that lasted the rest of his life," wrote Palmer. Denounced two days later, Jullien spent fourteen months in jail. Soon after his release, he was censured anew as a suspected accomplice of Gracchus Babeuf's abortive Conspiracy of Equals and by Louis-Marie Prudhomme's history of the Revolution for his role in the Terror at Bordeaux. He went to Egypt with Bonaparte and worked in military supply, mostly in Italy, for much of the Consulate and Empire, while starting a family and writing about education. Jullien became a liberal supporter of constitutional monarchy and ran unsuccessfully for office (in 1815, 1817, 1824, and 1831). He made ends meet as an editor of the *Revue Encyclopédique*. Portraying himself as a victim of "misunderstandings," he sought to influence public opinion by publishing advice to various electoral colleges and foreign polities. His publications, whether on politics or education had little contemporary impact. Palmer concluded that, after the Terror,

> He was marginal to every successive regime. Feeling excluded, he fell into a mood of chronic self-pity and self-justification; probably he had an exaggerated idea of his own abilities and his own importance. He was marginal also to the educational theorists and practitioners of his day, and to the sciences that he greatly admired. But he was more than a marginal man, and certainly not a nonentity. He was an intelligent expositor and publicist for the work of others. To be such is a useful social role.[27]

Palmer bent over backward to stress that after 1794, Jullien was "not a nonentity." The similarities and differences of their parallel lives highlights Rousselin's extraordinary journey. Although marginalized under Napoleon—for his close ties to Joséphine Beauharnais, Benjamin Constant, Germaine de Staël, Joseph Fouché, and Paul Barras—he did not remain so. Through hard work, great connections, and luck, Rousselin helped to build the world's bestselling newspaper, engineer a revolution, and protect parts of the Revolutionary legacy through an embrace of liberalism. Jullien supported liberal constitutionalism as a last resort in a final effort to matter. Rousselin reached the same political place, but his pathway was, at the same time, more pragmatic and more idealistic. After 1800, they each recognized that the fulfillment of their youthful dreams for a more equitable society was rather far in the future. For historians, the divergence of these trajectories suggest the utility of reexamining the political role of patronage and the position of the press in the emergence of liberalism, but from a longer-term perspective that includes Revolutionary involvement.

Rousselin and Jullien wondered endlessly about how to seal the fissures that separated republicans and how to reunite the French elite divided by the Revolution. While historians have explored these topics in depth to delineate the difficulties of ending the cycle of violence, Rousselin's career encourages their consideration both from a longer-term perspective and with a focus on the differences between and among "Revolutionaries" and "terrorists."[28] The persistence of denunciation for "terrorism" well into the 1830s makes clear that the enduring fear fostered by the Revolution shaped individual decision-making for decades. How many people found ways to matter outside of high office or the summit of the bureaucracy, far from the public eye? How many others like Rousselin were there? The tendency to separate historical inquiry into old régime, Revolution, and nineteenth century means that scholars do not always recognize when individual careers or political cohorts cross those divides.

Idealism shaped Rousselin's life and career, but he was also a pragmatist dedicated to keeping the wheels of government turning. To borrow Pierre Serna's term, he was a *"girouette"* (weathervane) or "chameleon" of the "extreme center" whose competence and drive made him a model public servant. Serna highlighted 1814–16 as a liminal period for such people, and so it was for Rousselin.[29] When he accepted Lazare Carnot's job offer to become general secretary of the Ministry of the Interior as comte de Saint-Albin and participated in the founding of the liberal *Le Constitutionnel*, Rousselin reinvented himself at least twice in 1815. By providing some insight into the long-term motivations of such chameleons, Rousselin shows that they were more than just power-seekers. Rousselin's life was chockablock with such liminal moments; only by exploring how they affected different people from different political groups, sets of experience, and age cohorts can historians plumb the depths of the complexities surrounding the Revolutionary legacy.

Biographies allow other historians to use the experiences, actions, and ideas of an individual as evidence for or against their propositions. Only in the context of other scholarship can Rousselin's true significance, either as unique example or as an exemplar of a cohort, emerge. Unlike so many of the people who developed and implemented the institutions of Revolutionary violence, Rousselin lived to tell the tale as he perceived and witnessed it. The Revolutionary era was marked by ideas and initiatives cut short of fulfilling their potential, but Rousselin survived to reinvent himself as a liberal noble and recover an important position in French society. Alexandre Rousselin may or may not have been an extraordinary man, but he lived an extraordinary life in an extraordinary time. His paranoia, his emotions, and his pragmatism would have been familiar to those who experienced the ebbs and flows of politics in Revolutionary Russia or China. His life has much to tell us about such periods of drastic change.

Timelines

Year	Alexandre Rousselin and family	French politics
1731	Birth of François-Charles Rousselin	
1747	Birth of Nicole-Antoinette Marchand	
1750	Birth of Antoine-Pierre-Laurent de Corbeau	
1754–1763		French and Indian War
1762		Rousseau publishes *The Social Contract*
1767 25 November	Marriage of François and Nicole	
1773 March 5	Alexandre-Charles-Omer Rousselin born	
1777		French entry into War of American Independence
1783	Probable entry of Rousselin at the Collège d'Harcourt	End War of American Independence
1786		Anglo-French Commercial Treaty
1789 5 May 17 June 14 July 26 August December		Estates-General openned National Assembly proclaimed Fall of the Bastille *Declaration of the Rights of Man and Citizen* approved Formation of the Jacobin Club

Year	Alexandre Rousselin and family	French politics
1790 April	Rousselin becomes Desmoulins' secretary	Cordeliers Club founded
1791 20–25 June 17 July September	Rousselin becomes Danton's secretary	King's flight to Varennes Champ de Mars massacre
1792 20 April 25 July 10 August August–September 2–5 September 21 September November-December	Roussselin is secretary of Unity section Rousselin employed at the Ministry of the Interior	War with Austria and Prussia Brunswick Manifesto Overthrow of the Bourbon monarchy Danton heads provisional government Prison massacres France proclaimed a republic Trial of King Louis XVI
1793 21 January March April–December 6 April 15 April 24 April 31 May–2 June 13 July 2 August August September 2–11 October 15 November	Rousselin presents petition of 35 sections Rousselin on Central Revolutionary Committee; publicly denounces Girondins Founding of the *Journal of Public Safety* with Rousselin as coeditor Rousselin takes over coordinating reports from Paris' police spies Review of *Pamela* Mission to Provins Mission to Troyes begins	Louis XVI executed Rebellion in the Vendée region Federalist Revolt Establishment of Committee of Public Safety Jean-Paul Marat acquitted Coup against the Girondins Murder of Marat by Charlotte Corday Universal draft instituted Law on Suspects passed
1794 2 January 4 February 4 April 25 May 8 June 10 June 26 June 20 July 22 July 27 July 11 December 13 December	End of Rousselin's mission to Troyes Rousselin expelled from Jacobin Club Order for Rousselin's arrest; imprisoned Acquitted by the Revolutionary Tribunal Rousselin jailed for second time Rousselin freed from prison Rousselin jailed for third time Divorce of Nicole and François Rousselin	Abolition of slavery in French colonies Danton and Desmoulins executed Festival of the Supreme Being Law of 22 Prairial; Great Terror begins French victory at Fleurus Coup against Robespierre

Year	Alexandre Rousselin and family	French politics

1795
2 January
27 January
3 May
13 June
27 July
25 October
	Marriage of Nicole and Laurent
	   Corbeau
	Rousselin freed from prison
	Rousselin jailed for fourth time
	Rousselin freed from prison
	Rousselin jailed for fifth time
	Rousselin freed for the last time
		General amnesty of
		   prisoners

1796
January–May
June
July
September
	Rousselin is secretary-general of
	   the department of the Seine
	Rousselin is military supply
	   officer/secretary to General
	   Lazare Hoche
	Death of Nicole Corbeau
	Death of François Rousselin	

1797
4 September
19 September
October
December
	Rousselin is military supply
	   officer/secretary to
	   General Louis-Nicolas-
	   Hyacinthe Chérin
	Rousselin's biography of Hoche
	   appears
		"Anti-Royalist" Coup of 18
		   Fructidor
		Hoche's death

1798
September
November
December
	Second edition of *Hoche* appears
	Rousselin is military supply
	   officer/secretary to General
	   Jean-Baptiste Bernadotte
	Rousselin meets Julie Talma,
	   Benjamin Constant, and
	   Germaine de Staël	

1799
February–June
11 May
June
July–September
9 October
9 November
	Rousselin returns to Chérin's staff
	Third edition of *Hoche* appears
	Rousselin is secretary-general,
	   Ministry of War
		Purge of Jacobin deputies
		   from legislature
		Bonaparte returns
		   from Egypt
		Bonaparte's coup;
		   Consulate founded

1800
August
October
	Rousselin serves on Émigré
	   Commission
	Fourth edition of *Hoche* and *Notice
	   on Chérin* appear
	Notice on Marbot appears	

Year	Alexandre Rousselin and family	French politics
1804 December	Rousselin appointed consul for Damietta, Egypt	Napoleon crowned Emperor
1805 25 December	Rousselin begins relationship with Clémentine de Montpezat Hortensius Rousselin born (d. 1878)	
1806	Rousselin begins to spy for the Minister of Police	
1807 27 July	Rousselin and Clémentine marry	
1809 December		Napoleon divorces Josephine
1811 March	Internal exile begins, lasts until April 1814	
1812 October 28 December	Rousselin adopted by Laurent de Corbeau	Malet conspiracy
1813 7 October	Corbeau dies, leaving his title to Rousselin	
1814 April June	Libretto for *Charles Martel or the Parisienne* performed Rousselin writes the popular song *France Delivered or the Lyonnais: A National Song*	Napoleon deposed; Louis XVIII restored to the throne
1815 March 1 May July	Rousselin is secretary-general of the Ministry of the Interior for Napoleon Rousselin helps found *L'Indépendent*, which becomes *Le Constitutionnel*	Napoleon's return from exile; Empire restored for 100 Days Second Restoration of the Bourbons
1816	Clémentine dies.	
1820 June	*Le Constitutionnel* convicted of libel	
1821 4 January	Rousselin marries Sophie Marc (1799–1864)	
1822 9 June	Birth of Louis-Philippe Rousselin de Corbeau (d. 1879)	
1824	Birth of Hortense Rousselin de Corbeau (d. 1885)	Death of Louis XVIII, Charles X becomes king

Year	Alexandre Rousselin and family	French politics
1825 December	*Le Constitutionnel* is world's bestselling daily newspaper *Le Constitutionnel* is acquitted for anti-clericalism	
1827 July	*Le Constitutionnel* is again convicted of libel	
1829	Death of Barras; Rousselin gets his papers	
1830 July		Charles X ousted-Louis-Philippe d'Orléans becomes king
1833	Hortensius de Saint-Albin first elected to public office	
1838	Rousselin sells shares in *Le Constitutionnel* to Louis Véron	
1847 15 June	Death of Alexandre Rousselin de Corbeau, comte de Saint-Albin	
1848		Louis-Philippe overthrown; creation of Second Republic
1851		Coup of Louis-Napoleon Bonaparte; creation of Second Empire
1855	Marriage of Hortense Rousselin de Corbeau to Achille Jubinal	
1860	Posthumous publication of Rousselin's *Life of Championnet*	
1870		Collapse of Second Empire; Third Republic established
1873	Publication of several of Rousselin's historical sketches by Hortensius de Saint-Albin	
1895	Publication of Barras' memoirs by Rousselin's grandson-in-law, Georges Duruy	

Notes

ABBREVIATIONS

AN   Archives Nationales de France
BN   Bibliothèque Nationale de France

INTRODUCTION

1. Cited by Henri d'Almeras, *Charlotte Corday d'après les documents contemporains* (Paris: Librarie des annales, 1910), 237. Unless otherwise noted, all translations are my own.
2. There is a debate among historians about whether to use the term "the terror" or "The Terror" that is discussed in the appendix.
3. The quotes are cited by Brian Massumi, *The Politics of Everyday Fear* (Minneapolis: University of Minnesota Press, 1993), 205.
4. The quotes in this and the previous paragraph are cited in Jules Claretie, ed., *Oeuvres de Camille Desmoulins*, 2 vols. (Paris: Charpentier, 1874), II: 392–94.

CHAPTER 1

1. Cited by Henri-Louis Bouquet, *L'Ancien collège d'Harcourt et le lycée Saint-Louis* (Paris: Delalain frères, 1891), 419.
2. *Discours d'Alexandre Rousselin prononce le jour de l'inauguration des bustes de Marat et Lepelletiers, martyrs de la liberté, faite par la Section de l'Unité, Décadi Brumaire, l'an deuxième de la République Française, une, indivisible, et imprimé par ordre de la Section*, BNF Réserve Lb40 2189, 6.
3. From Book III, Chapter 15 of *Du Contrat social* (1762).
4. Quoted by Bernard Manin, "Rousseau," in *Dictionnaire critique de la Révolution française: Idées*, ed. François Furet, Mona Ozouf, and collaborators (Paris: Flammarion, 1992 [1988]), 476.

5. For more on this world and people who inhabited it, see Robert Darnton, *The Literary Underground of the Old Regime* (Cambridge, MA: Harvard University Press, 1982).

6. Hortensius de Saint-Albin, ed., *Documents relatifs à la Révolution française extraits des oeuvres inédites de A. R. C. de Saint-Albin* (Paris: E. Dentu, 1873), 110.

7. This explanation of the growth of unrest as a "revolution of rising expectations" is associated with Alexis de Tocqueville in *The Old Régime and the French Revolution*, trans. Stuart Gilbert (New York: Penguin Books, 1955 [1856]).

8. On the role of privilege in French society, see Jeff Horn, *Economic Development in the Age of Revolution: The Privilege of Liberty, 1650–1820* (Cambridge: Cambridge University Press, 2015).

9. The most accessible recent biography of Desmoulins is Hervé Leuwers, *Camille et Lucile Desmoulins: Un rêve de république* (Paris: Fayard, 2018); there is no comparable work in English. Based on matters of fact and interpretation, I am dissatisfied with all the biographies of Danton. Frédéric Bluche, *Danton* (Paris: Librarie Perrin, 1984) is the most readable. See also Michel Biard and Hervé Leuwers, eds., *Danton: Le mythe et l'histoire* (Paris: Armand Colin, 2016) for recent historiography on this important figure of the French Revolution.

10. How historians have treated the importance of fear in motivating action is discussed in the appendix.

11. Although this account has clear biases, Duval's close affiliation with Rousselin and the Collège d'Harcourt explain why this account is given pride of place here over other contemporary versions of events.

12. The first three quotes in this paragraph are from Georges Duval, *Souvenirs de la Terreur de 1788 à 1793*, 4 vols. (Paris: Werdet, 1841), I: 35–36, 37–38, and 41. The final quotation is undated; see Pierre-Joseph Matton, ed., *Correspondance inédite de Camille Desmoulins, député à la Convention nationale* (Paris: Ébrard, 1836), 18.

13. Matton, ed., *Correspondance inédite de Camille Desmoulins*, 21–22.

14. Duval, *Souvenirs*, I: 42.

15. These two quotes are cited by Matton, *Correspondance inédite de Camille Desmoulins*, 27–28.

16. Quoted by Duval, *Souvenirs*, I: 51.

17. The quotes are from Félix Godart, *Camille Desmoulins d'après ses oeuvres* (Paris: E. Dentu, 1889), 34–35 and Matton, *Correspondance inédite de Camille Desmoulins*, 50.

18. Cited by Édouard Fleury, *Camille Desmoulins et Roch Marcandier: La presse Révolutionnaire*, 2nd ed., 2 vols. (Paris: Didier, 1852), I: 77.

19. Quoted by Claretie, *Camille Desmoulins, Lucile Desmoulins*, 94.

20. From 7 January 1794, quoted by Philippe-Joseph-Benjamin Buchez and Pierre-Célestin Roux, *Histoire parlementaire de la révolution française; ou, Journal des*

assemblées nationales, depuis 1789 jusqu'en 1815, 40 vols. (Paris: Paulin, 1834–38 [1837]), XXXII–XXXIII: 171–72.

21. Hippolyte Carnot and David d'Angers, eds., *Mémoires de Barère* (Paris: Jules Labitte, 1843), III: 189.

22. The best account of this event and its impact is by Timothy Tackett, *When the King Took Flight* (Cambridge, MA: Harvard University Press, 2003).

23. Quoted in Stewart, *A Documentary Survey of the French Revolution*, 218.

24. Antoine-Claire Thibaudeau, *Mémoires [avant ma nomination à la Convention] 1765–1792* (Paris: Niort, 1875), 110.

25. The emphasis was in the original. Quoted by Robert Christophe, *Danton: A Biography*, trans. Peter Green (New York: Doubleday, 1967), 11.

26. This is in the words of a fellow lawyer, Christophe Lavaux, *Les Campagnes d'un avocat, ou Anecdotes pour servir à l'histoire de la Révolution*, 2nd ed. (Paris: Panckrouke, 1816), 4.

27. Thibaudeau, *Mémoires [avant ma nomination à la Convention] 1765–1792*, 110.

28. The quotes in this and the previous paragraph are cited in the documents reproduced in Jean-François-Eugène Robinet, *Danton, homme de l'État* (Paris: Charavay frères, 1889), 258–59, 261–62.

29. Quoted by Christophe, *Danton*, 143.

30. Dominique-Joseph Garat, *Mémoire sur la Révolution, ou Exposé de ma conduite dans les affaires et dans les fonctions publiques* (Paris: Smits, 1796), 190.

31. André Fribourg, ed., *Discours de Danton* (Paris: Société de l'histoire de la Révolution française, 1910), 132.

32. The manifesto is reproduced in Stewart, *A Documentary Survey of the French Revolution*, 307–11: 308, 310.

33. Quoted by Claretie, *Camille Desmoulins, Lucile Desmoulins*, 199.

34. Quoted by Louis Madelin, *Danton*, trans. Mary Loyd (New York: Alfred A. Knopf, 1921), 108.

35. Quoted by David Lawday, *The Giant of the French Revolution: Danton, A Life* (New York: Grove Press, 2010), 129.

36. Quoted by Claretie, *Camille Desmoulins, Lucile Desmoulins*, 200.

37. Quoted by Matton, *Correspondance inédite de Camille Desmoulins*, 139.

38. Quoted by Hampson, *Danton*, 77 from her *Mémoires*, ed. Armand-Prosper Faugère, 2 vols. (Paris: Hachette, 1864), I: 97 though actually from 96–97.

39. Cited by Corbeau de Saint-Albin, *Pétition à l'Assemblée nationale*.

40. *Rapport fait à la société des amis de la constitution de Valence, par MM. Corbeau et Trie, de leur mission dans le ci-devant Comtat-Venaissin*, 4 March 1791, BNF 8-Lb40-1124, 31 and 38.

41. Saint-Albin, *Documents relatifs à la Révolution française*, 116.

CHAPTER 2

1. The most recent treatment of the political actions of the Cordeliers is Morris Slavin, *The Hébertistes to the Guillotine: Anatomy of a "Conspiracy" in Revolutionary France* (Baton Rouge: Louisiana State University Press, 1994).

2. For consideration of the evolving role of conspiracy in this period, see Peter Campbell, Thomas Kaiser, and Marisa Linton, eds., *Conspiracy in the French Revolution* (Manchester: Manchester University Press, 2007).

3. The best account of this process is Timothy Tackett, *The Coming of the Terror in the French Revolution* (Cambridge, MA: Belknap Press of Harvard University Press, 2015).

4. The first quote is cited by Louis-Marie Prudhomme, *Histoire générale et impartiale des erreurs, des fautes et des crimes commis pendant la Révolution française,* 6 vols. (Paris: no press, 1797), IV: 94 and the second is cited by Tackett, *The Coming of the Terror,* 212.

5. Although his name is not on this pamphlet, France's Bibliothèque Nationale has identified this piece as the work of Alexandre Rousselin. Internal evidence confirms this assertion. I am treating it as his interpretation of events. The quotes in this and the five previous paragraphs are from Jean-Claude-Hippolyte Méhée de La Touche, *La Vérité toute entier sur les vrais acteurs de la journée du 2 Septembre et sur plusieurs Journées et Nuits secrets des anciens Comités de Gouvernement* (Paris: Bureau de l'Ami des Citoyens, 1794), 12, 19–24, 26–28, 36, 40, 44–46. All italics were in the original.

6. Historians' interpretation of the importance of Revolutionary rhetoric and ideology is discussed in the appendix. For a novel interpretation of its development, see Robert Blackman, *1789: The French Revolution Begins* (Cambridge: Cambridge University Press, 2019) and the pugnacious Jonathan I. Israel, *Revolutionary Ideas: An Intellectual History of the French Revolution from The Rights of Man to Robespierre* (Princeton, NJ: Princeton University Press, 2014).

7. Maximilien Robespierre, "Speech on Political Morality" (5 February 1794), Center for the History of New Media, https://revolution.chnm.org/exhibits/show/liberty--equality--fraternity/item/437.

8. *Réimpression de l'ancien Moniteur seule histoire authentique et inaltérée de la Révolution française depuis la reunion des états-généraux jusqu'au consulat (Mai 1789–Novembre 1799) avec des notes explicatives,* vol. 16 (Paris: Henri Plon, 1860), 156–57.

9. Quoted in Louis Mortimer-Ternaux, *Histoire de la Terreur 1792–1794: d'après des documents authentiques et inédits,* 8 vols. (Paris: Michel Lévy frères, 1869), VII: 313.

10. "Extrait du registre des procès-verbaux du Comité révolutionnairede la section de la Réunion," 5 June 1793, reprinted in Alexandre Tuetey, ed., *Répertoire général des sources manuscrites de l'histoire de Paris pendant la Révolution française,* 11 vols. (Paris: Imprimerie nouvelle, 1908), VIII: 470.

11. *Feuille du salut public* 37 (6 August 1793), 3.

12. Quoted in François-Alphonse Aulard, ed., *Recueil des Actes du Comité de Salut public avec la corresponance officielle des Représantants en mission et le registre du Conseil executive provisoire*, vol. 5, *19 Juin 1793–15 Août 1793* (Paris: Imprimerie nationale, 1892), 506.

13. *Feuille du salut public puis de la République*, 1 July 1793–30 Ventôse, an II (1–260), 7.

14. The quotes are reprinted in Pierre Caron, "Les publications officieuses du Ministère de l'Intérieur en 1793 et 1794," *Revue d'histoire moderne et contemporaine* XIV (1910): 5–43, 9, 12.

15. The issue of whether a separate measure establishing "Reign of Terror" was actually passed by the National Convention is discussed in the appendix.

16. No copy of this issue of the *Journal of Public Safety* survives. The fragments quoted here are cited by Ernest Hamel, *Histoire de Robespierre d'après des papiers de famille, les sources originales et des documents entièrement inédits*, vol. 3, *La Montagne* (Paris: Chez l'auteur, 1867), 111; Armand de Pontmartin, *Derniers Samedis*, 2nd series (Paris: M. Levy, 1892), 82–83; and Emmet Kennedy, *A Cultural History of the French Revolution* (New Haven, CT: Yale University Press, 1989), 179, who translates an excerpt found in Arthur Pougin, *La Comédie française et la Révolution: scenes, récits et notices* (Paris: Gaultier, Magnier et Cie, 1902), 103.

17. Anonymous [Alexandre Rousselin], *Correspondance originale des Émigrés, ou les émigrés peints par eux-mêmes. (Cette Correspondance, deposée aux archives de la Convention Nationale, est celle prise par l'avant garde du Général Kellermann à Longwy et à Verdu, dans le Porte-feuille de Monsieur, et dans celui de M. Ostomme, Secrétaire de M. de Calonne.). On y a joint des Lettres curieuses, et des Papiers saisis en Savoie sur les Emigrés, et également déposés aux Archives de la Convention* (Paris: Buisson, 1793), vi.

18. Lynn Hunt's *Politics, Culture, and Class in the French Revolution* (Berkeley: University of California Press, 1984) provides a superb introduction to the importance of political symbols.

19. *Discours prononcé à la Société populaire de la section de l'Unité par un élève du citoyen Maignien* [Alexandre Rousselin], (Paris: Mioneret, n.d. [1793]) and *Discours d'Alexandre Rousselin prononcé le jour de l'inauguration des bustes de Marat et Lepelletier, martyrs de la liberté*, October 31, 1793, a copy of which is found in *Brochures sur les fêtes en l'honneur de Lepeletier et Marat* (s.l., s.d.[1793]).

20. *Discours d'Alexandre Rousselin, Auteur de la Pétition des Sections de Paris contre les 22 députés fédéralistes et rédacteur de la* Feuille du Salut Public *sur les mesures de salut public qui doivent accompagner et suivre l'acceptation de l'acte constitutionnel, et sur les précautions de prendre contra sénsibilité nationale et l'indulgence plénière, à l'époque du 10 août* (Paris: Guillot, 1793), 3–4, 10.

21. On this key institution, see Richard Cobb's magisterial *The People's Armies: The armées révolutionnaires: instrument of the Terror in the departments April 1793 to*

Floréal Year II, trans. Marianne Elliott (New Haven, CT: Yale University Press, 1987 [1961, 1963]).

22. The quotes are cited by François-Alphonse Aulard, ed., *Recueil des Actes du Comité de Salut public avec la corresponance officielle des Représantants en mission et le registre du Conseil executive provisoire*, vol. 7, *22 septembre 1793–24 octobre 1793* (Paris: Imprimerie nationale, 1894), 165–66.

23. The quotes in this and the previous paragraph are cited by Edmond Campagnac, "Un cure rouge: Métier délégué du représentant du peuple Du Bouchet," *Annales révolutionnaires* 6, no. 4 (1913): 476–505, 477.

24. The quotes are cited by Henri Wallon, *Les représentants du peuple en mission et la justice révolutionnaire dans les départements en l'an II (1793–1794)*, 5 vols. (Paris: Hachette, 1889–90), I: 60.

25. *Feuille du salut public* 105, 22, 1er mois, l'an 2 (13 October 1793), 2.

26. The quotes are from *Réimpression de l'ancien Moniteur seule histoire authentique et inaltérée de la Révolution française depuis la reunion des états-généraux jusqu'au consulat (Mai 1789–Novembre 1799) avec des notes explicatives*, vol. 18 (Paris: Henri Plon, 1860), 115, #24, 24 1er mois, an II (Octobre 15, 1793); François-Alphonse Aulard, ed., *La Société des Jacobins: Recueil de documents pour l'histoire du club des Jacobins de Paris*, vol. 5, *Janvier 1793 à Mars 1794* (Paris: Cerf-Noblet, 1895), 454, and *Feuille du salut public* 105, 22, 1er mois, l'an 2 and 129, 17 Brumaire, an II.

27. The best introduction to this phenomenon is Michel Vovelle, *The Revolution Against the Church: From Reason to the Supreme Being*, trans. Alan José (Columbus: Ohio State University Press, 1991 [1988]).

28. The festive politics of such events have been explored by Mona Ozouf, *Festivals and the French Revolution*, trans. Alan Sheridan (Cambridge, MA: Harvard University Press, 1988 [1976]).

29. The quotes are cited by Adolphe Granier de Gassagnac, *Histoire des Girondins et des massacres de septembre d'après les documents officiels et inédits, accompagnée de plusieurs fac-similé*, 2 vols. (Paris: E. Dentu, 1860), II: 128–29 and the second is from *Réimpression de l'ancien Moniteur seule histoire authentique et inaltérée de la Révolution française depuis la reunion des états-généraux jusqu'au consulat (Mai 1789–Novembre 1799) avec des notes explicatives*, vol. 18 (Paris: Henri Plon, 1860), 115, #24, 24 1er mois, an II (15 Octobre 1793) and *Feuille du salut public* 129, 17 Brumaire, an II (7 November 1793).

30. The first quote is cited by Félix Bouquelot, *Histoire de Provins*, 2 vols. (Provins: Lebeau, 1840), II: 343 and the second is from *Feuille du salut public* 22, 1er mois, l'an 2.

31. This is the term used by Michel Biard in his study of the collective activities of the representatives on mission. See his *Missionnaires de la République. Les représentants du peuple en mission (1793–1795)* (Paris: CTHS, 2002).

32. The first quote is from *Réimpression de l'ancien Moniteur seule histoire authentique et inaltérée de la Révolution française depuis la reunion des états-généraux jusqu'au consulat*

(Mai 1789–Novembre 1799) avec des notes explicatives, vol. 18 (Paris: Henri Plon, 1860), 411, #54, 14 November 1793. The second is from François-Alphonse Aulard, ed., *Recueil des Actes du Comité de Salut public avec la corresponance officielle des Représantants en mission et le registre du Conseil executive provisoire*, vol. 8, *25 octobre 1793–26 novembre 1793 (4 Brumaire an II-6 Frimaire an II* (Paris: Imprimerie nationale, 1895), 250.

33. *Rapport de la Mission d'Alexandre Rousselin, Commissaire Civil National du Comité de Salut public de la Convention Naitonale, à Troyes, Département de l'Aube, sur ses operations dans cette Commune et sur les troubles qui y ont existés* (Troyes: Sainton, n.d. [1794]).

34. The quotes in this and the previous paragraph are from *Registre des procès-verbaux deu Comité révolutionnaire établi dans le district de Troyes par Garnier, représentant du Peuple et declare central pour tout le département de l'Aube par Rousselin, commissaire civil national*, 12 Brumaire, an II—9 Nivôse, an II, AN F7 4421, 396. For the issues dividing the Aube's political class, see Jeff Horn, « *Qui parle pour la nation?* » *Les élections et les élus de la Champagne méridionale, 1765–1830* (Paris: Société des études robespierristes, 2004).

35. See Sarah Maza, *Private Lives and Public Affairs: The Causes Célèbres of Prerevolutionary France* (Berkeley: University of California Press, 1993).

36. Marc-Antoine Lamotte, *Réclamation*, 28 Prairial, an II, AN F7 4553 reproduced in the Robert Mennevé Collection, Isabelle C.P. Lacorne Family Archives, 212–14.

37. Cited by Albert Babeau, *Histoire de Troyes pendant la Révolution*, 2 vols. (Paris: Dumoulin, 1873–74), II: 127.

38. The first two quotes are from Alexandre Rousselin, *Lettre au Représentans révolutionnaires*, 27 Brumaire, an II, AN AFII 412 (3316) and the rest are from Alexandre Rousselin, *Discours d'Alexandre Rousselin, commissaire civil national dans le Département de l'Aube, en renouvellant le Département, séant à Troyes* (Troyes: Sainton, 1793).

39. The quotations are from *Registre des procès-verbaux du Comité révolutionnaire établi dans le district de Troyes par Garnier, représentant du Peuple et declare central pour tout le département de l'Aube par Rousselin, commissaire civil national*, 12 Brumaire, an II—9 Nivôse, an II, AN F7 4421, 146–50.

40. The quotes in this and the previous paragraph are from *Registre des procès-verbaux du Comité révolutionnaire*, 154, 166–67.

41. The quotations in this paragraph are from the "Arrêté de Rousselin du 15 frimaire an II," reprinted in Babeau, *Histoire de Troyes*, II: 519–20.

42. The quotes are from the *Registre des procès-verbaux du Comité révolutionnaire*, 316, 325, *Lettre d'Alexandre Rousselin aux citoyens membres composants le Comité révolutionnaire central à Troyes*, 26 Brumaire, an II, AN F7 4421, *Proclamation de Rousselin, commissaire civil dans le Département de l'Aube*, 28 Brumaire, an II, *Déclaration des ministers du Culte Catholique de la ville de Troyes*, n.d. [Brumaire, an II], AN F1bII Aube14, *Procès-Verbal de la séance du 25 Brumaire*, AN AFII412 (3316), and *Rapport de la Mission d'Alexandre Rousselin*.

43. *Lettre d'Alexandre Rousselin aux citoyens membres composants le Comité révolutionnaire central à Troyes*, 26 Brumaire, An II, AN F7 4421.

44. *Deposition de Jean-Baptiste Flamant*, 7 Frimaire, an II, AN F7 4421.

45. *Deposition de Jean Guenin et Nicolas-Simon Bergerat sur Nicolas Pilon*, 24 Brumaire, an II, AN F7 4421.

46. Alexandre Rousselin, *Lettre aux citoyens membres composant le Conseil executive provisoire*, n.d. [25 Brumaire, an II], AN AFII 412 (3316) and *Lettre d'Alexandre Rousselin aux citoyens membres composants le Comité révolutionnaire central à Troyes*, 2 Frimaire, an II, AN F7 4421.

47. *Feuille du salut public* 143, 1 Frimaire, an II.

48. *Arrêté du directoire du département de l'Aube*, 17 Frimaire, An II, AN F7 4421.

49. Guyot, *Lettre aux citoyens administrateurs du département de l'Aube*, 31 December 1793, AN DIII23.

50. *Rapport de la Mission d'Alexandre Rousselin*.

51. The quotes are cited by Babeau, *Histoire de Troyes*, II: 187–88.

52. François-Alphonse Aulard, ed., *Recueil des Actes du Comité de Salut public avec la corresponance officielle des Représantants en mission et le registre du Conseil executive provisoire*, vol. 9, *27 novembre 1793–31 décembre 1793 [7 frimaire an II–11 nivôse an II* (Paris: Imprimerie nationale, 1895), 654–55.

53. Henri Wallon, *Les représentants du peuple en mission et la justice révolutionnaire dans les départements en l'an II (1793–1794)*, 5 vols. (Paris: Hachette, 1890), III: 358; François-Alphonse Aulard, ed., *Recueil des Actes du Comité de Salut public avec la corresponance officielle des Représantants en mission et le registre du Conseil executive provisoire* (Paris: Imprimerie nationale, 1895, 1897), X: 41 and IX: 767–68.

54. The quotes in this paragraph are from Aulard, ed., *Recueil des Actes du Comité de Salut public*, IX: 767–68.

55. All quotes relating to this festival are from the *Journal du département de l'Aube* 2 and 3, 14 Nivôse, Year II (13 January 1794).

56. *Rapport de la Mission d'Alexandre Rousselin*.

57. Jean-Clément Martin emphasizes the depth of state violence in this region. See his *La Vendée et la France* (Paris: Seuil, 1987).

58. Jullien's career and its similarities to Rousselin's are discussed in depth in the appendix.

59. *Archives parlementaires* 84, *du 9 au 25 pluviôse An II (28 janvier au 13 février 1794)* (Paris: CNRS, 1962), 443.

60. *Rapport de la Mission d'Alexandre Rousselin*.

CHAPTER 3

1. David Andress, *The Terror: The Merciless War for Freedom in Revolutionary France* (New York: Farrar, Straus, and Giroux, 2005) provides a lively account of these issues.

2. Quoted in James H. Robinson, ed., *Readings in European History*, 2 vols. (Boston: Ginn, 1906), II: 443–45.

3. Colin Jones has been working for years on an eagerly awaited study of 9 Thermidor that will clarify the stakes in interpretations of the fall of Robespierre. The issue is also discussed in the appendix.

4. *Archives parlementaires* 84, *du 9 au 25 pluviôse An II (28 janvier au 13 février 1794)* (Paris: CNRS, 1962), 443.

5. This tense period is the subject of Morris Slavin, *The Hébertistes to the Guillotine: Anatomy of a "Conspiracy" in Revolutionary France* (Baton Rouge: Lousiana State University Press, 1994).

6. Philippe-Joseph-Benjamin Buchez and Pierre-Célestin Roux, *Histoire parlementaire de la révolution française; ou, Journal des assemblées nationales, depuis 1789 jusqu'en 1815*, 40 vols. (Paris: Paulin, 1834–38 [1837]), XXX: 461.

7. Philippe-Joseph-Benjamin Buchez and Pierre-Célestin Roux, *Histoire parlementaire de la révolution française; ou, Journal des assemblées nationales, depuis 1789 jusqu'en 1815*, 40 vols. (Paris: Paulin, 1834–38 [1837]), XXXI: 325.

8. Cited by Alexandre Tuetey, ed., *Répertoire général des sources manuscrites de l'histoire de Paris pendant la Révolution française*, 11 vols. (Paris: Imprimerie nouvelle, 1910), X: 536 and XI: 39.

9. Cited by Slavin, *The Hébertistes to the Guillotine*, 96 and Buchez and Roux, *Histoire parlementaire de la révolution française*, XXXI:356–57.

10. Ernest Hamel, *Histoire de Robespierre d'après des papiers de famille, les sources originales et des documents entièrement inédits*, 5 vols. (Paris: Chez l'auteur, 1867), III: 431.

11. Cited by Tuetey, *Répertoire général*, XI: xcviii.

12. Except where noted, these quotes are from Adolphe Schmidt, ed., *Tableaux de la Révolution française publiés sur les papiers inédits du département et de la police secrète de Paris*, 3 vols. (Leipzig: Veit, et Co., 1869), II: 169–70.

13. The quotes in this and the previous paragraph are from Marc Bouloiseau and Albert Soboul, eds., *Oeuvres de Maximilien Robespierre*, vol. 10, *Discours (27 juillet 1793–27 juillet 1794)* (Paris: Société des etudes robespierristes, 1967), 386–87 and *Feuille du Salut public* 261, 1 Germinal, an II.

14. Cited by Andress, *The Terror*, 268.

15. Cited by Slavin, *The Hébertistes*, 130.

16. Marisa Linton puts friendship at the center of her account of Revolutionary politics in *Choosing Terror: Virtue, Friendship and Authenticity in the French Revolution* (New York: Oxford University Press, 2013).

17. Maximilien Robespierre, "On the Principles of Morality that Ought to Guide the National Convention in the Internal Administration of the Republic," delivered on February 5, 1794, cited by Richard T. Bienvenu, ed., *The Ninth of Thermidor: The Fall of Robespierre* (New York: Oxford University Press, 1968), 33.

18. François-Alphonse Aulard, ed., *La Société des Jacobins: Recueil de documents pour l'histoire du club des Jacobins de Paris*, vol. 6, *Mars à Novembre 1794*, 6 vols. (Paris: Cerf-Noblet, 1897), 2–3.

19. The quotes are cited by Nicolas Villiaumé, *Histoire de la Révolution française 1789–1796*, 5th ed. 4 vols. (Paris: S. Raçon et comp., 1852), III: 278; Jules Claretie, ed., *Oeuvres de Camille Desmoulins*, 2 vols. (Paris: Charpentier, 1874), II: 393; and Norman Hampson, *Danton* (London: Gerald Duckworth, 1978), 161.

20. Charles Vellay, ed., *Oeuvres completes de Saint-Just*, 2 vols. (Paris: Charpentier et Fasquelle, 1908), II: 326, 330–31.

21. Cited by Tuetey, *Répertoire général*, X: 475.

22. Cited by Hampson, *Danton*, 169, 174. Desmoulins' quotation is cited by Villiaumé, *Histoire*, III: 74.

23. Méhée de La Touche [Rousselin], *La Vérité*, 58–59.

24. Nicolas Ruault quoted by Timothy Tackett, *The Coming of the Terror in the French Revolution* (Cambridge, MA: Belknap Press of Harvard University Press, 2015), 334.

25. François-Alphonse Aulard, ed., *Recueil des Actes du Comité de Salut public avec la correspondance officielle des Représentants en mission et le registre du Conseil executive provisoire*, vol. 12, *16 Mars 1794—22 Avril 1794 [26 Ventôse an II–3 Floréal an II* (Paris: Imprimerie nationale, 1899), 261.

26. *Supplément à la Feuille de la République*, 21 May 1794 [2 Prairial, an II].

27. Cited by Peter McPhee, *Robespierre: A Revolutionary Life* (New Haven, CT: Yale University Press, 2012), 200.

28. Aulard, *La Société des Jacobins*, VI: 155.

29. Cited by André Prévost, *Histoire du diocèse de Troyes pendant la Révolution*, 2 vols. (Troyes: Gustave Frémont, 1908), II: 533.

30. "Motifs d'arrestation des citoyens ci-après désignés : sixième section," cited in the Robert Mennevé Collection, Isabelle C.P. Lacorne Family Archives, 285.

31. Except where noted quotes in this and the previous paragraph are from the *Adresse d'Augustin Guélon, le jeune, aux membres composant le Comité de Salut public de la Convention Nationale*, 13 Prairial, An II (1 June 1794) (Paris: Brousse lard, 1794).

32. Henri Wallon, *Les représentants du peuple en mission et la justice révolutionnaire dans les départements en l'an II (1793–1794)*, 5 vols. (Paris: Hachette, 1890), III: 442.

33. *Rapport du 17 Messidor, l'an deux de la République de la Bureau de la Surveillance administrative de la police générale*, AN F7 3821.

34. Aulard, *La Société des Jacobins*, VI: 176–80.

35. Cited by Daniel Guérin, *La lutte de classes sous la Première République 1793–1797*, 2 vols. new, expanded edition (Paris: Gallimard, 1968), II: 239.

36. Alexis Dumesnil, ed., *Révélations puisées dans les cartons des comités de salut public et de sureté générale; ou Mémoires (inédits) de Sénart*, 2nd ed. (Paris: chex les principaux libraires de France et de l'étranger, 1824), 143.

37. *Adresse d'Augustin Guélon le jeune aux membres composant le Comité de Salut public de la Convention nationale*, 27 Messidor, An II (15 July 1794), AN W 426.

38. Aulard, *La Société des Jacobins*, VI: 219.

39. The following quotes are from *Rapport de la Mission d'Alexandre Rousselin, Commissaire Civil National du Comité de Salut public de la Convention Naitonale, à Troyes, Département de l'Aube, sur ses operations dans cette Commune et sur les troubles qui y ont existés* (Troyes: Sainton, n.d. [1794]).

40. This is an early example of the politics of vengeance examined in Stephen Clay, "Justice, vengeance et passé révolutionnaire: les crimes de la terreur blanche," *Annales historiques de la Révolution française* 350 (2007): 109–33. See also Howard G. Brown, *Ending the French Revolution: Violence, Justice, and Repression from the Terror to Napoleon* (Charlottesville: University of Virginia Press, 2006).

41. *Acte d'accusation par Antoine-Quentin Fouquier, Accusateur-Public du Tribunal Révolutionnaire*, 2 Thermidor, an II (20 July 1794), AN W 426.

42. *Procès-verbal de la Séance du tribunal-criminel-révolutionnaire*, 2 Thermidor, an II (20 July 1794), AN W 426.

43. *Extrait du registre des audiences du tribunal révolutionnaire*, 2 Thermidor, an II (20 July 1794), AN W 47 (3140).

44. Unless otherwise noted, this account of the trial is based on *Histoire du Terrorisme exercé à Troyes par Alexandre Rousselin et son comité révolutionnaire pendant la tyrannie de l'ancien comité de Salut public suivi de la Réfutation du rapport de la mission dudit Rousselin, avc les pieces justificatives* (Troyes: Sainton, An III [1795]). Although clearly biased, none of the official documents generated by the trial contradict its more complete account.

45. François-Alphonse Aulard, ed., *Recueil des Actes du Comité de Salut public avec la corresponance officielle des Représantants en mission et le registre du Conseil executive provisoire*, vol. 15, 8 July 1794—*9 Août (20 Messidor an II–22 Thermidor an II)* (Paris: Imprimerie nationale, 1903), 431.

46. Louis-Marie Prudhomme, *Histoire générale et impartiale des erreurs, des fautes et des crimes commis pendant la Révolution française*, 6 vols. (Paris: n.p., 1797), V: 414.

47. R. R. Palmer's venerable *Twelve Who Ruled: The Committee of Public Safety during the Terror* (Princeton, NJ: Princeton University Press, 1941) is still the best account of the interpersonal rivalries on the Committee.

48. On this period from Robespierre's perspective, Peter McPhee's account is exemplary. See his *Robespierre*.

49. Cited by Gilles Dussert, *Vadier: le grand inquisiteur 1736–1828* (Paris: Imprimerie nationale, 1989), 178.

50. Cited by McPhee, *Robespierre*, 198.

51. Cited by Palmer, *Twelve Who Ruled,* 368 and McPhee, *Robespierre*, 205, 209

52. Cited by Hamel, *Histoire de Robespierre*, III: 557.

53. Cited by Andress, *The Terror*, 325.

54. Aulard, *La Société des Jacobins*, VI: 213.

55. Edmond Biré, *Journal d'un bourgeois de Paris pendant la Terreur*, 5 vols., vol. 4, *La chute des Dantonistes 5 Novembre 1793–6 Avril 1794* (Paris: Perrin, 1897), 333.

56. Edme-Bonaventure Courtois, *Rapport fait au nom des comités de salut public et de sûreté générale sur les événemens du 9 Thermidor, an II* (Paris: Imprimerie nationale, 1796), 30–31.

57. Biré, *Journal*, IV: 213, 329.

58. Cited by Hamel, *Histoire de Robespierre*, III: 573.

59. Méhée de La Touche [Rousselin], *La Vérité toute entier*, 59.

60. Cited by Tackett, *The Coming of the Terror*, 330.

61. Cited by Villiaumé, *Histoire*, III: 317.

62. *Arrêté du Comité de Sûreté générale*, 18 Thermidor, an II (5 August 1794), AN F7 4775/2.

63. Alexandre Rousselin, *Lettre au Comité de Sûreté générale*, n.d., AN F7 4775/2.

64. Cited by Henri Wallon, *Histoire du Tribunal Révolutionnaire de Paris*, 5 vols. (Paris: Hachette, 1881), V: 262–63.

65. In the two previous paragraphs, the first quote is cited by Wallon, *Les représentants du peuple en mission*, III: 362. The rest are from François-Alphonse Aulard, ed., *Recueil des Actes du Comité de Salut public avec la corresponance officielle des Représantants en mission et le registre du Conseil executive provisoire*, vol. 16, *10 Août 1794—20 Septembre 1794 (23 Thermidor an II–4e jour des Sans-culottides an II* (Paris: Imprimerie nationale, 1904), 127–28, 131.

66. Michel Biard's investigation of the representatives on mission effectively uses this terminology. See his *Missionnaires de la République. Les représentants du peuple en mission (1793–1795)* (Paris: CTHS, 2002).

67. Dominique-Joseph Garat, *Mémoires de Garat*, ed. Eugène Maron (Paris: Poulet-Malassis, 1862), 331.

68. *Arrêté du Comité de Sûreté générale*, 1 Nivôse, an III, AN F7 4775/2.

69. *Réimpression de l'ancien Moniteur seule histoire authentique et inaltérée de la Révolution française depuis la reunion des états-généraux jusqu'au consulat (Mai 1789–Novembre 1799) avec des notes explicatives*, vol. 23 (Paris: Henri Plon, 1842), 384.

70. For a recent look at this phenomenon, see Stephen Clay, "The White Terror: Factions, Reactions, and the Politics of Vengeance," in *A Companion to the French Revolution*, ed. Peter McPhee (London: Wiley, 2012), 359–77.

71. Jean-Bernard Albert, *Compte rendu à la Convention nationale par le représentant du peuple Albert, sur le département de l'Aube, le 29 ventôse an III* [19 March 1795] (Troyes: Sainton, 1795), 9.

72. *Adresse de la Municipalité de Troyes, à ses concitoyens*, 4 Germinal, An III [24 March 1795], AN, D 51/2.

73. Cited by Alexandre Tuetey, ed., *Répertoire général des sources manuscrites de l'histoire de Paris pendant la Révolution française* (Paris: Imprimerie nouvelle, 1910), IX: lxvi.

74. Tuetey, *Répertoire général*, IX: lxvi.
75. Pierre-Jean-Baptiste Nougaret, *Histoire des prisons de Paris et des départemens, contenant les Mémoires rares et précieux. Le tout pour servir à l'histoire de la révolution française: notamment à la tyrannie de Robespierre, et de ses agens et complices*, 4 vols. (Paris: Courcier, 1797), III: 69, 82.
76. Prudhomme, *Histoire générale*, V: 414.

CHAPTER 4

1. This is according to Nicolas Ruault, *Gazette d'un Parisien sous la Révolution: Lettres à son frère 1783–1796*, ed. Anne Vassal and Christiane Rimbaud (Paris: Librairie Académique Perrin, 1975), 386.
2. Reproduced in the *Réimpression de l'ancien Moniteur* (Paris: Henri Plon, 1862), XXVI: 348
3. Martyn Lyons venerable and flawed *France Under the Directory* (Cambridge: Cambridge University Press, 1975) is still the best general account.
4. Since the bicentennial, there has been considerable debate about this period beginning with Bronislaw Baaczko, *Comment sortir de la Terreur. Thermidor et la Révolution* (Paris: Gallimard, 1989) and François Furet, "La Terreur sous le Directoire," in *The Transformation of Political Culture 1789–1848*, ed. François Furet and Mona Ozouf, vol. 3, *The French Revolution and the Creation of Modern Political Culture* (Oxford: Pergamon Press, 1989), 173–86 to Howard G. Brown, *Ending the French Revolution: Violence, Justice, and Repression from the Terror to Napoleon* (Charlottesville: University of Virginia Press, 2006) and most recently Marc Belissa and Yannick Bosc, *Le Directoire: La république sans la démocratie* (Paris: Fabrique, 2018).
5. Bernard Gainot disagrees with this analysis. See his *1799, un nouveaux jacobinism?* (Paris: Éditions du CTHS, 2001).
6. On the role of elections, the best general study is Malcolm Crook, *Elections in the French Revolution: An Apprenticeship in Democracy, 1789–1799* (Cambridge: Cambridge University Press, 1996).
7. Cited by Hortensius de Saint-Albin, "Preface" to Alexandre Rousselin de Corbeau de Saint-Albin, *Championnet: Général des armées de la République française ou les campagnes de Hollande, de Rome et de Naples*, 2nd ed. (Paris: Poulet-Malassis et de Broise, 1861), 6.
8. See Catherine Kawa, *Les ronds-de-cuir en Révolution: Les employés du Ministère de l'intérieur sous la Première république (1792–1800)* (Paris: CTHS, 1996).
9. Laura Mason has been working on the significance of Babeuf for years and will soon produce her definitive interpretation. In the meantime, see her "Thermidor and the Myth of Rupture," in *The Oxford Handbook of the French Revolution*, ed. David Andress (Oxford: Oxford University Press, 2015), 521–37.

10. Quoted in François-Alphonse Aulard, ed., *Paris pendant la Réaction thermidorienne et sous le directoire: Recueil de documents pour l'histoire de l'esprit public à Paris*, vol. III, *Du 1er Ventôse an IV au 20 Ventôse an V (20 Février 1796–10 Mars 1797)* (Paris: Léopold Cerf, 1899), 212–23.

11. Quoted by Cuneo d'Ornano, *Hoche*, I: 254

12. Quoted by Cuneo d'Ornano, *Hoche*, I: 296.

13. Louis Marie de La Révellière-Lépeaux, *Mémoires de Larevéllière-Lépeaux*, 3 vols. (Paris: Plon, 1895), I: 337–38.

14. Georges Duruy, ed., *Memoirs of Barras: Member of the Directorate*, 4 vols., trans. C. E. Roche (New York: Harper & Bros., 1896), III: 38.

15. See Isser Woloch, *Jacobin Legacy: The Democratic Movement under the Directory* (Princeton, NJ: Princeton University Press, 1970).

16. Quoted in a *Manuscrit sur Rousselin de St. Albin*, n.d., AN 171AP/3.

17. Duruy, *Memoirs of Barras*, III: 379.

18. *Compte-rendu par le général Bernadotte, ex-ministre de la guerre, de l'administration de ce département, depuis le 15 messidor an 7, jusqu'au 29 fructidor suivant: présenté aux consuls de la République, le 1er germinal an 8* (Paris: Imprimerie de la République, 1800), iii.

19. Quoted by Jean-Paul Garnier, *Barras: Le Roi du Directoire* (Paris: Librairie Académique Perrin, 1970), 278.

20. Quoted by Dunbar Plunket Barton, *Bernadotte: The first phase 1763–1799* (London: John Murray, 1914), 411.

21. The quotes in this and the previous paragraph are from Duruy, *Memoirs of Barras*, IV: 18–19.

22. To see these events from the lens of Bonaparte, see Philip Dwyer, *Napoleon: The Path to Power* (New Haven, CT: Yale University Press, 2009) and Steven Englund, *Napoleon: A Political Life* (Cambridge, MA: Harvard University Press, 2004).

23. Quoted by Léonce Pingaud, *Bernadotte, Bonaparte et les Bourbons (1797–1844)* (Paris: Plon, 1901), 44.

24. Quoted by Barton, *Bernadotte*, 444.

25. Quoted by Walter Scott, *The Life of Napoleon Buonaparte, Emperor of the French*, 9 vols. (Edinburgh: Longman, Rees, Orme, Brown and Green, 1827), IX: Appendix III.

26. Alphonse de Beauchamp, ed., *Mémoires de Joseph Fouché, duc d'Otrante, ministre de la police générale*, 2 vols. (Paris: Le Rouge, 1824), I: 97–98.

27. To compare Rousselin's actions to those who did come to support Bonaparte, see Isser Woloch, *Napoleon and His Collaborators: The Making of a Dictatorship* (New York: Norton, 2001).

28. L. Calinau, *Dictionnaire des Jacobins vivans, dans lequel on verra les hauts faits de ces messieurs* (Hamburg: n.p., 1799), 157–58.

29. Alexandre Rousselin, *Lettre au citoyen Lagarde, secrétaire générale du Directoire exécutif*, n.d. [Germinal, an VI], AN AFIII 515.

30. The quotes in this and the previous paragraph are from Albert-Augustin-Antoine-Joseph Duhot, *Rapport au nom des commissions d'instruction publique et d'institutions républicaines, sur une motion d'ordre de Laloy, concernant la vie du général Hoche, présentée au Conseil par Alexandre Rousselin* (April 26, 1798).

31. The quotes in this and the two previous paragraphs are from Rousselin, *Vie de Lazare Hoche*, x, 2–4, 6–7.

32. The quotes in this and the previous paragraph are from Alexandre Rousselin, *Notice sur Chérin, Général de division, chef de l'état—major général de l'armée du Danube, mort à Arau le 20 prairial à quatre heures de l'après midi, par suite de la blessure reçue dans la journée du 15 en avant de Zurich* (Paris: Imprimerie nationale, 1799), 6–7.

33. Alexandre Rousselin, *Notice historique sur Marbot, général divisionnaire* (Paris: Desenne, 1800), 5–6.

34. Alexandre Rousselin de Corbeau de Saint-Albin, *Vie de Championnet*, 2nd ed (Paris: Poulet-Malassis et de Broise, 1861 [1860]), 20.

35. Alexandre Rousselin, *Vie de Lazare Hoche*, expanded 4th ed. (Paris: Henry, Belin, et Cie., 1800), 328.

36. Cited by Saint-Albin, "Preface," 12–13.

37. Cited by Françoise Wagener, *L'Impératrice Joséphine (1763–1814)* (Paris: Flammarion, 1999), 114.

38. Letter of March 28, 1810 cited by André Gavoty, *Les Amoureux de l'Imperatrice Joséphine* (Paris: Fayard, 1961), 148.

39. Ernest d'Hauterive, ed., *La police secrete du premier empire: Bulletins quotidiens addresses par Fouché à l'empereur*, new series published by Jean Grassion (Paris: Librairie historique R. Clavreuil, 1964), vol. 5, 288.

40. Quoted by Gavoty, *Les Amoureux de l'Imperatrice Joséphine*, 147–49.

41. Benjamin Constant, *Correspondance générale*, vol. 3 *(1795–1799)*, ed. C. P. Courtney and Dennis Wood with Peter Rickard (Tübingen: Max Niemeyer Verlag, 1993), 400.

42. In opposition until 1815 when he rallied even before the Hundred Days, Constant used the time to refine his political ideas and begin his first (and most famous) novel, *Adolphe*. He also developed close ties with German intellectuals like Johann Wolfgang Goethe and Friedrich von Schiller. With the Restoration of the Bourbon monarchy, Constant was appointed to the Council of State. He was elected to the legislature in 1817. Although his own ideas were an amalgam of Rousseau, German romanticism, and French Revolutionary ideals, Constant became associated with liberalism, a political perspective that Rousselin also came to endorse. On Constant's evolving ideas, see K. Steven Vincent, *Benjamin Constant and the Birth of French Liberalism* (London: Palgrave-Macmillan, 2011).

43. Benjamin Constant, *Correspondance générale*, vol. 5 *(1803–1805)*, ed. Dennis Wood and Adrianne Tooke with Peter Rickard (Tübingen: Max Niemeyer Verlag, 2007), 199.

44. Benjamin Constant, *Correspondance générale*, vol. 4 *(1800–1802)*, ed. Dennis Wood and Adrianne Tooke with Peter Rickard (Tübingen: Max Niemeyer Verlag, 2006), 77, 445, 480 and Constant, *Correspondance générale*, V: 73.

45. Constant, *Correspondance générale*, IV: 480.

46. Benjamin Constant, *Correspondance générale*, vol. 8 *(1810–1812)*, ed. Paul Delbouille and Robert Leroy with Eckart Pastor and Martine Willems (Berlin: de Gruyter, 2010), 168.

47. See Thierry Lentz, *La conspiration du général Malet* (Paris: Perrin, 2012) for a fuller account of this incident.

48. The quotes in this and the previous paragraph are from Alexandre Rousselin de Saint-Albin, "La conjuration de Général Malet," in *Documents relatifs à la Révolution française extraits des oeuvres inédites de A. R. C. de Saint-Albin*, ed. Hortensius de Saint-Albin (Paris: E. Dentu, 1873), 121, 123, 127, 156.

49. Cited by Charles Nauroy, *Le curieux* 2: 25 (December 1885), 28.

50. A few accounts say 1806, but 1807 is more likely based on hints in Barras's correspondence.

51. Alphonse de Roserot, ed., *Mémoires de Madame Chastenay 1771–1815*, 2 vols., 2nd ed. (Paris: Plon, 1896), II: 488.

52. Duruy, *Memoirs of Barras*, IV: 20–21.

53. Captain Corbeau was jailed for 18 months in 1793–94 after a diplomatic mission. Upon release, he returned to duty, serving in the German lands where he became a lieutenant-colonel in command of a battalion. Removed from his post in 1795, he returned to the army the following year and was placed in charge of the military supply depot at Auxonne thanks to the influence of General and deputy Jean-Charles Pichegru. Corbeau retired to Paris in August 1800 to devote himself to the study of the influence of religion and morals on social development. He published *State Formation in Modern History, preceded by a History of the Jews* in 1813.

54. Cited by Nauroy, *Le curieux* 2: 25 (December 1885), 27 and the adoption papers in Archives de Paris, D4U1 52.

55. These documents are cited in "Rousselin de Saint-Albin: Documents généalogiques," in the Robert Mennevé Collection, Isabelle C.P. Lacorne Family Archives, 58–59.

56. It was written by his brother in law, deputy Achille de Juvenal. Quoted in Saint-Albin, "Preface," *Vie de Championnet*, 3.

57. Alexandre-Charles Rousselin Corbeau de Saint-Albin, "Histoire de Jean-Baptiste Kléber," in Saint-Albin, *Documents relatifs à la Révolution française*, 116.

58. This mythic version of Rousselin's family background was the one I encountered when I first wrote about him more than twenty-five years ago.

59. Saint-Albin, *Documents relatifs à la Révolution française*, 269–70.

60. Cited by Marcel Reinhard, *Le grand Carnot: L'organisateur de la victoire 1792–1823*, 2 vols. (Paris: Hachette, 1952), II: 312.

61. The quotes are from Saint-Albin, "Preface," 13.

62. For a general account and reference to a wealth of other versions in the bibliography, consult Philip Dwyer, *Citizen Emperor: Napoleon in Power* (New Haven, CT: Yale University Press, 2013).

63. The Additional Act was signed on 22 April 1815 and approved on 1 June. The quotes are adapted from "The Act Additional," The Waterloo Association, https://www. napoleon-series.org/research/government/legislation/c_additional.html.

64. Cited by Reinhard, *Le grand Carnot*, II: 310–11.

65. Alexandre-Charles Rousselin-Corbeau de Saint-Albin, "Notes biographiques et satiriques sur la conduit du grand Carnot à la fin de l'Empire," Bibliothèque Thiers, Fonds Masson 161, 289–312, 304–305.

66. Cited by Henri Carré, *Le grand Carnot (1753–1823)* (Paris: Éditions de la table ronde, 1947), 326.

67. Cited by Reinhard, *Le grand Carnot*, II: 312.

68. Duruy, *Memoirs of Barras*, IV: 357.

CHAPTER 5

1. The 1814–1816 period as a major turning point for this generation of activists is discussed in the appendix.

2. The themes of continuity and change are evoked powerfully in Isser Woloch, *The New Regime: Transformations of the French Civic Order, 1789–1820s* (New York: Norton, 1994).

3. On the survival of Bonapartism as a political ideology, see Robert S. Alexander, *Bonapartism and Revolutionary Tradition in France: The Fédérés of 1815* (Cambridge: Cambridge University Press, 1991).

4. Quoted in Frederick B. Artz, *France under the Bourbon Restoration 1814–1830* (Cambridge, MA: Harvard University Press, 1931), 89.

5. Irene Collins, *The Government and the Newspaper Press in France 1814–1881* (Oxford: Oxford University Press, 1959) is still the standard account of the state's relations with the press.

6. These quotes are cited by his son Hortensius de Saint-Albin, *Documents relatifs à la Révolution française*, 7.

7. Thiers soon embarked on writing a popular, multivolume history of the French Revolution that earned him membership in the Académie française in 1834. He served two stints as prime minister during the 1830s and became the first president of the Third French Republic.

8. Rousselin de Saint-Albin is not included in the list of members in the records of the legion of honor, but all contemporary documents list him as a member.

9. The best account of this era remains Guillaume de Bertier de Sauvigny, *The Bourbon Restoration*, trans. Lynn Case (Philadelphia: University of Pennsylvania Press, 1966).

10. Léon Thiessé, *M. Étienne: Essai biographique et littéraire* (Paris: Firmin Didot, 1853), CXXXV.

11. The quotes in this and the previous paragraph are cited by Thiessé, *M. Étienne*, CXXXV–CXXXVI.

12. Benjamin Constant, "The Liberty of Ancients Compared with that of Moderns," (1816) available at Libertarianism.org, https://www.libertarianism.org/publications/essays/liberty-ancients-compared-moderns (accessed 28 December 2016).

13. Scholarly attention to Romanticism and its importance both political and literary is both deep and wide. To understand the complexities of choices and approaches, Carol E. Harrison provides a different perspective in *Romantic Catholics: France's Postrevolutionary Generation in Search of a Modern Faith* (Ithaca, NY: Cornell University Press, 2014).

14. Quoted in Louis Petit de Julleville, ed., *Histoire de la langue et de la Littérature française des origines à 1900*, 8 vols. (Paris: Armand Colin, 1908), VII: 690.

15. The Charter is reprinted in Irene Collins, ed., *Government and Society in France: 1814–1848* (London: Edward Arnold, 1970), 10–15.

16. Both quotes are from Antoine Jay, *Plaidoyer pour le sieur Bidault, Éditeur responsible du Constitutionnel, pronounce devant la Cour d'assises du department de la Seine, le 29 Juin, dans l'affaire de la souscription nationale* (Paris: Baudouin frères, 1820), 3–4.

17. Quoted in Ralph Menning, ed., *The Art of the Possible: Documents on Great Power Diplomacy 1814–1914* (New York: McGraw-Hill, 1996), 22.

18. Both quotes are from *Extrait du Rapport [du Ministère de l'Intérieur] sur les Journaux du 2 Decembre 1822*, n.d. [December 1822], AN F18 329A.

19. *Rapport de police du Ministère de l'Intérieur*, 31 July 1823, AN F18 329A.

20. Léon Thiessé, *Lettres normandes ou correspondence politique et littéraire* (Paris: Bureau des lettres Normandes, 1820), X: 267–68.

21. Quoted in Eugène Hatin, *Histoire politique et littéraire de la presse en France*, 8 vols. (Geneva: Slatkine, 1967 [1861]), VIII: 450.

22. The report is found in AN F18 261 and is quoted by Claude Bellanger, Jacques, Godechot, Pierre Guiral, and Fernand Terrou, eds., *Histoire générale de la presse française*, vol. 2, *De 1815 à 1871* (Paris: Presses universitaires de la France, 1969), 150.

23. Quoted by Collins, ed., *Government and Society in France*, 12.

24. Quoted in Bertier de Sauvigny, *The Bourbon Restoration*, 185.

25. Duc de Broglie, *Souvenirs, 1785–1870*, 4 vols. (Paris: Calmann Lévy, 1886), II: 231 quoted in Irene Fouzzard, "The Government and the Press in France, 1822 to 1827," *English Historical Review* 66 (1951): 51–66, 53.

26. From a speech delivered on 12 December 1826 and quoted by Sherman Kent *The Election of 1827 in France* (Cambridge, MA: Harvard University Press, 1975), 12.

27. The references to the article are from *Le Constitutionnel* (15 August 1822) on Gallica.

28. *Lettre de Morgan de la Cour royale d'Amiens au Garde des Sceaux*, August 1822, AN BB30 221.

29. Quoted in *Lettre du préfet du Bas-Rhin au Ministre-Sécretaire d'État de l'Intérieur*, 21 April 1822, AN F18 329A.

30. *Lettre confidentielle des Préfets du Bas-Rhin et Haut-Rhin*, 6 March 1825, AN F18 329A.

31. *Le Constitutionnel* (26 January 1820).

32. *Le Constitutionnel* (25 January 1820).

33. Nicolas-François Bellart, *Lettre du procureur de la Cour Royale de Paris au Garde des Sceaux*, 23 January 1820, AN BB18 996.

34. Thiessé, *Lettres normandes*, X: 60–61.

35. *Le Constitutionnel* (23 April and 14 May 1820).

36. *Le Constitutionnel* (2 February 1821)

37. Thiessé, *Lettres normandes*, X: 60–61.

38. *Lettre du procureur du roi du tribunal de première instance de la Seine au Garde des Sceaux*, 7 September 1822, AN BB30 221.

39. Benjamin Constant, "Lettre," *Le Constitutionnel*, 15 September1822.

40. Four, *Lettre du procureur du roi du tribunal de première instance de la Seine au Garde des Sceaux* dated 7 September, 16 September, 14 October, and 2 December 1822 are all found in AN BB30 221.

41. *Lettre du Parquet du tribunal de première instance de la Seine à Son Excellence Monseigneur le garde de sceaux de France*, 24 July 1823, AN BB30 222.

42. *Rapport de police du Ministère de l'Intérieur*, 31 July 1823, AN F18 329A.

43. Quoted in *Procès fait au Constitutionnel comme prévenu de tendance à porter atteinte au respect du à la religion de l'état* (Paris: Baudouin frères, 1825), 7–8, 11, 14, 17.

44. Quoted in André-Marie-Jean-Jacques Dupin, *Réponse des rédacteurs du "Constitutionnel" à cette assertion de l'acte d'accusation en tendance dressé par M. le procureur général, le 30 juillet 1825, que "jamais le Constitutionnel n'a dit un mot, un seul mot, en faveur des vertus et des bienfaits qui naissent d'une piété éclairée* (Paris: Fain, 1825), 3 and 9.

45. Quoted in Collins, *Government and Society*, 48 and 50.

46. Quoted in *Procès fait au Constitutionnel comme prévenu de tendance à porter atteinte au respect du à la religion de l'état*, 43.

47. *Procès du Constitutionnel: Plaidoyer de M. Dupin* (Paris: Baudouin frères, 1825),129–31.

48. *Procès du Constitutionnel : Plaidoyer de M. Dupin*, 134–35, 195–96.

49. Quoted in Jules Brisson and Félix Ribeyre, *Les grands journaux de France* (Paris: Jouaust, 1862), 285.

50. Quoted in Fouzzard, "The Government and the Press in France, 1822 to 1827," 55.

51. *Le Constitutionnel* (21 May 1825).

52. The quotes in this and the two previous paragraphs are from André-Marie-Jean-Jacques Dupin, *Défense du Constitutionnel prononcée à l'audience de la cour royale, du 17 juillet 1827* (Paris: Baudouin frères, 1827), 3–8.

53. *Rapport du bureau de censure de Paris*, 23 July 1827, AN BB30 269.

54. *Rapport sur les operations du bureau de censure de Paris*, 27 August 1827 and 10 September 1827, both in AN BB30 269.

55. *Rapport sur les operations du bureau de censure de Paris*, 15 October 1827, AN BB30 269.

56. *Rapport sur les operations du bureau de censure de Paris*, 30 September 1827, AN BB30 269.

57. *Rapport sur les operations du bureau de censure de Paris*, 24 September 1827, AN BB30 269.

58. *Rapport sur les operations du bureau de censure de Paris*, 30 September 1827.

59. Quoted in Hatin, *Histoire politique et littéraire de la presse en France*, VIII: 433–34.

60. A consideration of the role of generations in the study of the Restoration is found in the appendix.

61. The quotes in this and the preceding paragraph are from *Le Constitutionnel* (21 May 1827).

62. The quotes in this paragraph are all from Collins, *Government and Society*, 83–85.

63. David Pinkney's *The French Revolution of 1830* (Princeton, NJ: Princeton University Press, 1972) remains the best account.

64. Alexander de Teixera de Mattos, ed. and trans., *The memoirs of François René, vicomte de Chateaubriand, sometime ambassador to England*, 6 vols. (London: Freemantle and Company, 1902), V: 90.

65. All italics are in the original. André-Marie-Jean-Jacques Dupin, *Mémoires de M. Dupin*, 5 vols. (Paris: Plon, 1856), II: 137.

66. The quotes in this paragraph are from Collins, *Government and Society*, 87.

67. Teixera de Mattos, *The Memoirs of François René, vicomte de Chateaubriand*, V: 137.

68. Saint Albin, *Documents relatifs à la Révolution française*, 11.

69. The position of the press in French society and in shaping the government is explored in Jeremy Popkin, *Press, Revolution, and Social Identities in France 1830–1835* (University Park: Pennsylvania State University Press, 2002).

70. Quoted in Saint Albin, *Documents relatifs à la Révolution française*, 9.

71. Quoted in a letter printed in Philippe-Joseph-Benjamin Buchez and Pierre-Célestin Roux, *Histoire parlementaire de la révolution française; ou, Journal des assemblées nationales, depuis 1789 jusqu'en 1815*, 40 vols. (Paris: Paulin, 1834–1838 [1837]), XXXV: xi.

72. The quote is from Louis Lacour, ed., *Mémoires inédits du comte de Lamotte-Valois sur sa vie et son époque (1754–1830)* (Paris: Poulet-Malassis et de Broise, 1858), 313.

73. The quotes in this paragraph are from the *Mémoire du Sieur Charles Antoine Nicolas, comte DELAMOTTE-Valois* (Paris: Moreau, 1823), 6, 12–13.

74. Saint Albin, *Documents relatifs à la Révolution française*, 11.

75. Pierre Josserand, ed., *Mémoires d'un bourgeois de Paris par le Docteur Véron*, 2 vols. (Paris: Guy le Prat, 1945), II: 158.

76. Quoted in Buchez and Roux, *Histoire parlementaire de la révolution française*, XXXV: xi.

CHAPTER 6

1. The three quotes are cited by George Duruy, "Introduction aux Mémoires inédits de Barras," *Revue des deux mondes* 122 (1894): 292–317, 292–93, 298.

2. Only after the Revolution of 1848 did the Saint-Albin family take possession of the documents.

3. Henri Fournier le jeune, *Lettre au Paul Grand*, 2 October 1832, AN 171AP 3.

4. Cited by Duruy, "Introduction," 304. The italics are in the original.

5. *Saint-Albin contre Malet. A Messieurs le Premier Président, le Président et Messieurs les Conseillers composant la première Chambre de la Cour royale* (Paris: Veuve Dondey-Dupré, 1836), 8–9.

6. Cited by Jules Claretie, ed., *Oeuvres de Camille Desmoulins*, 2 vols. (Paris: Charpentier, 1874), II: 392.

7. Cited by Claretie, ed., *Oeuvres de Camille Desmoulins*, II: 395.

8. Cited in *The Century Monthly Illustrated Magazine*, vol. 33 *November 1897–August 1898* (New York: Macmillan, 1898), 113–26, 123.

9. Alexandre Rousselin, *Vie de Lazare Hoche*, expanded 4th ed. (Paris: Henry, Belin, et Cie., 1800), 7; Saint-Albin, *Documents relatifs à la Révolution française*, 53–54, 115, 328; Alexandre Rousselin, *Notice historique sur Marbot, général divisionnaire* (Paris: Desenne, 1799), 9; and Alexandre Rousselin de Corbeau de Saint-Albin, *Vie de Championnet*, 2nd ed (Paris: Poulet-Malassis et de Broise, 1861 [1860]), 21.

10. The quotes are cited by Géorges Averel, *Lundis révolutionnaires 1871–1874: Nouveaux éclairissements sur la Révolution française à propos des travaux historiques les plus récents et des faits politiques contemporains* (Paris: Ernest Leroux, 1875), 175–77.

11. Charles Bousfield, ed. and trans., *Memoirs of Count Horace de Viel Castel: A Chronicle of the Principal Events, Political and Social, during the Reign of Napoleon III from 1851 to 1864*, 2 vols. (London: Remington and Co., 1888), I: 137–38.

12. The quotes are from Armand de Pontmartin, *Derniers Samedis*, 2nd series (Paris: M. Levy, 1892), 82–84.

13. The quotes in this and the previous paragraph are from Joseph-Marie Quérard, *Les supercheries littéraires dévoilées*, 5 vols. (Paris: l'Editeur, 1845–56), IV: 179–92, 180–82.

14. Geoffroy de Grandmaison, *Un Demi-Siècle de Souvenirs* (Paris: Librairie académique Perrin, 1898), 11, 36–39.

CONCLUSION

1. The quotes from Quérard's apologies are reproduced in a "Notice biographique sur A. R. Corbeau de Saint-Albin," in Saint-Albin, *Documents relatifs à la Révolution française*, 1–18, 2–3.
2. Saint-Albin, *Documents relatifs à la Révolution française*, 116.
3. "Renseignements démandé par la Direction générale [de police] sur M. de Saint-Albin," 23 February 1815, cited in the Robert Mennevé Collection, Isabelle C. P. Lacorne Family Archives, 483.
4. Saint-Albin, *Documents relatifs à la Révolution française*, 12.

APPENDIX

1. Robert Darnton, *What Was Revolutionary about the French Revolution?* (Waco, TX: Markham Press, 1990).
2. Rousselin's impact was very different than those of ordinary citizens like those delineated by Alain Corbin, *The Life of an Unknown: The Rediscovered World of a Clog Maker in Nineteenth-Century France*, trans. Arthur Goldhammer (New York: Columbia University Press, 2001) and Daniel Roche, ed., *Journal of My Life by Jacques Menetra*, trans. Arthur Goldhammer (New York: Columbia University Press, 1986).
3. Morris Slavin, *The Hébertistes to the Guillotine: Anatomy of a "Conspiracy" in Revolutionary France* (Baton Rouge: Louisiana State University Press, 1994); Albert Soboul, *The Sans-Culottes: The Popular Movement and Revolutionary Government, 1793–1794*, trans. Remy Inglis Hall (Princeton, NJ: Princeton University Press, 1981 [1959]); and Richard Cobb, *The People's Armies: The* Armées Révolutionnaires: *Instrument of the Terror in the Departments April 1793 to Floréal Year II*, trans. Marianne Elliott (New Haven, CT: Yale University Press, 1987 [1961, 1963]).
4. Timothy Tackett, *The Coming of the Terror in the French Revolution* (Cambridge, MA: Harvard University Press, 2015); and Marisa Linton, *Choosing Terror: Virtue, Friendship and Authenticity in the French Revolution* (New York: Oxford University Press, 2013) meld all three concerns.
5. Michael L. Kennedy, *The Jacobin Club of Marseilles, 1790–94* (Ithaca, NY: Cornell University Press, 1973) and *The Jacobin Clubs in the French Revolution*, 3 vols., (Princeton, NJ: Princeton University Press [vols. 1–2] and New York: Berghahn Books [vol. 3], 1982–2000); Samuel Guicheteau, *La Révolution des ouvriers nantais. Mutation économique, identité sociale et dynamique révolutionnaire (1740–1815)* (Rennes: Presses Universitaires de Rennes, 2008); Dominique Godineau, *The Women of Paris and Their French Revolution*, trans. Katherine Streip (Berkeley: University of California Press, 1998 [1988]); and Katie Jarvis, *Politics in the Marketplace: Work, Gender, and Citizenship in Revolutionary France* (Oxford: Oxford University Press, 2019).

6. On such politics, see Mona Ozouf, *Festivals and the French Revolution*, trans. Alan Sheridan (Cambridge, MA: Harvard University Press, 1988 [1976]) and Lynn Hunt, *Politics, Culture, and Class in the French Revolution* (Berkeley: University of California Press, 1984).

7. Isser Woloch, *Jacobin Legacy: The Democratic Movement under the Directory* (Princeton, NJ: Princeton University Press, 1970); *Napoleon and His Collaborators: The Making of a Dictatorship* (New York: Norton, 2001); and *The New Regime: Transformations of the French Civic Order, 1789–1820s* (New York: Norton, 1994).

8. David A. Bell, *Lawyers and Citizens: The Making of a Political Elite in Old Regime France* (Oxford: Oxford University Press, 1994); Louis Bergeron and Guy Chaussinand-Nogaret, *Les "Masses de granit": Cent mille notables du Premier Empire* (Paris: Éditions de l'EHESS, 1979); Adeline Daumard, *Les bourgeois et la bourgeoisie en France depuis 1815* (Paris: Aubier, 1987), Jeff Horn, « *Qui parle pour la nation?* » *Les élections et les élus de la Champagne méridionale, 1765–1830* (Paris: Société des études robespierristes, 2004); and Hervé Leuwers, *L'Invention du "Barreau français" (1660–1830): La construction nationale d'un groupe professionnel* (Paris: Éditions de l'EHESS, 2006).

9. The quotes in the previous sentence are from Alan B. Spitzer, *The French Generation of 1820* (Princeton, NJ: Princeton University Press, 1987), xiii and 267 and Jean-François Sirinelli, *Génération intellectuelle : Khâgneux et normaliens dans l'entre-deux guerres* (Paris: Fayard, 1988).

10. François Furet, *Interpreting the French Revolution*, trans. Elborg Forster (Cambridge and Paris: Cambridge University Press and Éditions de la Maison des Sciences de l'Homme, 1981 [1978]), 62; Keith Michael Baker, *Inventing the French Revolution: Essays on French Political Culture in the Eighteenth Century* (Cambridge: Cambridge University Press, 1990), 11; Patrice Gueniffey, *Le Nombre et la raison: la Révolution française et les élections* (Paris: Éditions de l'EHESS, 1993), 24.

11. Nicolas Charles, "La Terreur. Entretien avec Jean-Clément Martin," *Historiens et géographes* (May 2019) : 2–6, 2.

12. Hervé Leuwers and Michel Biard, "Analyser la 'terreur' dans l'historiographie anglophone," has contributions from Marisa Linton, Peter McPhee, and Timothy Tackett. It appeared in *Annales historiques de la Révolution française* 392 (2018): 141–65. The subject was also a major point of discussion at the conference celebrating Timothy Tackett's contributions to the field held in September 2017. See Micah Alpaugh, Robert Blackman, and Ian Coller, eds., "Becoming Revolutionaries: Papers in Honor of Timothy Tackett," *H-France Salon* vol. 11, no. 16 (2019), https://h-france.net/h-france-salon-volume-11-2019/.

13. Emotional response also fueled the contemporary conspiracy theories studied by Morris Slavin, *The Hébertistes to the Guillotine: Anatomy of a "Conspiracy" in Revolutionary France* (Baton Rouge: Louisiana State University Press, 1994) and more broadly in the work edited by Peter Campbell, Thomas Kaiser, and Marisa

Linton, eds., *Conspiracy in the French Revolution* (Manchester: Manchester University Press, 2007).

14. Tackett, *The Coming of the Terror in the French Revolution*, 3. The quotation is from Bronislaw Baczko, "The Terror before the Terror? Conditions of Possibility, Logic of Realization," in *French Revolution and the Creation of Modern Political Culture*, ed. Keith Michael Baker and Colin Lucas, 4 vols. (Oxford: Pergamon Press, 1987–1994), IV: 19–38, 30.

15. For an introduction to the field, see Jan Plamper, *The History of Emotions: An Introduction* (New York: Oxford University Press, 2017).

16. The difference between what can and cannot be done based on the availability of certain sources is highlighted succinctly by Timothy Tackett in "Living in Paris in the French Revolution: The Story of an Ordinary Citizen," in *French History and Civilization*, vol. 9, *Festschrift in Honor of Peter McPhee*, ed. Briony Neilson and Julie Kalman, (2020), 1–11. .

17. Jean-Luc Chappey's *La société des Observateurs de l'Homme, (1799–1804). Des anthropologues au temps de Bonaparte* (Paris: Société des études robespierristes, 2002) shows how alternative intellectual networks were politicized under Bonaparte in ways reminiscent of Rousselin, Constant, de Staël, and their circle.

18. The metaphor of a "fever" of Revolutionary politics described in the venerable account of Crane Brinton has considerable merit. *The Anatomy of Revolution*, rev. ed. (New York: Vintage, 1965).

19. These contributions are discussed at length in Alpaugh, Blackman, and Coller, "Becoming Revolutionaries."

20. I first encountered these emotional differences in 1989 which were much remarked upon by contemporaries when doing research for my doctoral dissertation that became « *Qui parle pour la nation?* ».

21. Stephen Clay, "Vengeance, justice and the reactions in the Revolutionary Midi," *French History* 23, no. 1 (March 2009): 22–46.

22. Hervé Leuwers, *Camille et Lucile Desmoulins : Un rêve de république* (Paris: Fayard, 2018) and *Un juriste en politique : Merlin de Douai (1754–1838)* (Arras: Artois Presses Universitaires, 1996) ; Dominique Margairaz, *François de Neufchâteau. Biographie intellectuelle* (Paris: Publications de la Sorbonne, 2005); Pierre Serna, *Antonelle. Aristocratie révolutionnaire, 1747–1817* (Paris: Félin, 1997) ; and Michael Sydenham, *Léonard Bourdon: The Career of a Revolutionary, 1754–1807* (Waterloo: Wilfrid Laurier University Press, 1999).

23. Richard Cobb, *The People's Armies* and *The police and the people: French popular protest, 1789–1820* (Oxford: Clarendon Press, 1970); Godineau, *The Women of Paris and Their French Revolution*; George Rudé, *The Crowd in the French Revolution* (Oxford: Oxford University Press, 1967); and Soboul, *The Sans-Culottes*.

24. Noteworthy recent biographies of Robespierre or Napoleon Bonaparte include: Philip Dwyer, *Citizen Emperor: Napoleon in Power 1799–1815* (New Haven, CT: Yale University Press, 2013) and *Napoleon: The Path to Power* (New Haven,

CT: Yale University Press, 2009); Steven Englund, *Napoleon: A Political Life* (New York: Scribner, 2004); Alan Forrest, *Napoleon: Life, Legacy, and Image: A Biography* (New York: St. Martin's Press, 2012); Patrice Gueniffey, *Bonaparte 1769–1802*, trans. Steven Rendall (Cambridge, MA: Belknap Press of Harvard University Press, 2015 [2013]); Hervé Leuwers, *Robespierre* (Paris: Fayard, 2014); Jean-Clément Martin, *Robespierre, la fabrication d'un monstre* (Paris: Perrin, 2016); Peter McPhee, *Robespierre: A Revolutionary Life* (New Haven, CT: Yale University Press, 2012); and Ruth Scurr, *Fatal Purity: Robespierre and the French Revolution* (New York: Vintage, 2006).

25. On bureaucrats see Clive H. Church, *Revolution and Red Tape: The French Ministerial Bureaucracy 1770–1850* (Oxford: Clarendon Press, 1981) and Catherine Kawa, *Les ronds-de-cuir en Révolution : Les employés du Ministère de l'intérieur sous la Première république (1792–1800)* (Paris: CTHS, 1996).

26. Marie-Claude Delieuvin, *Marc-Antoine Jullien, de Paris, 1775–1848 : théoriser et organiser l'éducation* (Paris: L'Harmattan, 2003): Eugenio Di Rienzo, *Marc-Antoine Jullien de Paris (1789–1848), una Biografia Politica* (Naples: Éditions Guida, 1999); and Robert R. Palmer, *From Jacobin to Liberal: Marc-Antoine Jullien, 1775–1848* (Princeton, NJ: Princeton University Press, 1993). See also Paul Hanson, "From Jacobin to Liberal," *Historical Reflections/Réflexions Historiques* 37, no. 3 (2011): 86–100.

27. Palmer, *From Jacobin to Liberal*, 60, 139, and 226.

28. Bronislaw Baczko, *Comment sortir de la Terreur. Thermidor et la Révolution* (Paris: Gallimard, 1989); Howard G. Brown, *Ending the French Revolution: Violence, Justice, and Repression from the Terror to Napoleon* (Charlottesville: University of Virginia Press, 2006); Stephen Clay, "Justice, vengeance et passé révolutionnaire: les crimes de la terreur blanche," *Annales historiques de la Révolution française* 350 (2007): 109–33, François Furet, "La Terreur sous le Directoire," in *The Transformation of Political Culture 1789–1848*, ed. François Furet and Mona Ozouf, Vol. 3 of *The French Revolution and the Creation of Modern Political Culture* (Oxford: Pergamon Press, 1989), 173–86, and Ronen Steinberg, *The Afterlives of the Terror: Facing the Legacies of Mass Violence in Postrevolutionary France* (Ithaca, NY: Cornell University Press, 2019).

29. See Pierre Serna, *La République des girouettes: 1789–1815 et au-delà une anomalie politique : La France de l'extrême centre* (Seysel: Champ Vallon, 2005).

Selected Bibliography

Alexander, Robert S. *Bonapartism and Revolutionary Tradition in France: The Fédérés of 1815*. Cambridge: Cambridge University Press, 1991.

Andress, David (ed.). *The Oxford Handbook of the French Revolution*. Oxford: Oxford University Press, 2015.

Andress, David. *The Terror: The Merciless War for Freedom in Revolutionary France*. New York: Farrar, Straus, and Giroux, 2005.

Antoine, François, Jean-Pierre Jessenne, Hervé Leuwers, and Anne Jourdan (eds.). *L'Empire napoléonnien: une expérience européenne?* Paris: Armand Colin, 2014.

Baczko, Bronislaw. *Comment sortir de la Terreur. Thermidor et la Révolution*. Paris: Gallimard, 1989.

Baker, Keith Michael. *Inventing the French Revolution: Essays on French Political Culture in the Eighteenth Century*. Cambridge: Cambridge University Press, 1990.

Belissa, Marc, and Yannick Bosc. *Le Directoire : La république sans la démocratie*. Paris: Fabrique, 2018.

Bell, David A. *Lawyers and Citizens: The Making of a Political Elite in Old Regime France*. Oxford: Oxford University Press, 1994.

Bell, David A *The Cult of the Nation in France: Inventing Nationalism, 1680–1800*. Cambridge, MA: Harvard University Press, 2001.

Bergeron, Louis, and Guy Chaussinand-Nogaret. *Les "masses de granit" : Cent mille notables du Premier Empire*. Paris: Éditions de l'EHESS, 1979.

Bernet, Jacques, Jean-Pierre Jessenne, and Hervé Leuwers (eds.). *Le lien politique local dans la grande nation. Vol. 1 of Du Directoire au Consulat*. Lille: Centre de Recherche sur l'Histoire de l'Europe du Nord-Ouest, GRHIS, Préfecture de la région Haute-Normandie, 1999.

Bertier de Sauvigny, Guillaume de. *The Bourbon Restoration*. Trans. Lynn Case. Philadelphia: University of Pennsylvania Press, 1966.

Biard, Michel. *Les Lilliputiens de la centralisation. Des intendants aux préfets, les hésitations d'un « modèle français »*. Seyssel: Champ Vallon, 2007.

Biard, Michel (ed.). *Les Politiques de la Terreur, 1793–1794*. Rennes: Presses Universitaires de Rennes and the Société des études Robespierristes, 2008.

Biard, Michel. *Missionnaires de la République. Les représentants du peuple en mission (1793–1795)*. Paris: CTHS, 2002.

Biard, Michel. *Terreur et Révolution française*. Paris: UPPR, 2016.

Biard, Michel, and Hervé Leuwers (eds.). *Danton : Le mythe et l'histoire*. Paris: Armand Colin, 2016.

Biard, Michel, and Marisa Linton. *Terreur! La Révolution française face à ses démons*. Paris: Armand Colin, 2020.

Blackman, Robert. *1789: The French Revolution Begins*. Cambridge: Cambridge University Press, 2019.

Brinton, Crane. *The Anatomy of Revolution*. Rev. ed. New York: Vintage, 1965.

Bluche, Frédéric. *Danton*. Paris: Librarie Perrin, 1984.

Bourdin, Philippe, and Bernard Gainot (eds.). *La République directoriale : Actes du colloque de Clermont-Ferrand (22, 23 et 24 mai 1997)*. 2 vols. Paris: Société des études robespierristes, 1998.

Brown, Howard G. *Ending the French Revolution: Violence, Justice, and Repression from the Terror to Napoleon*. Charlottesville: University of Virginia Press, 2006.

Brown, Howard G. *War, Revolution, and the Bureaucratic State: Politics and Army Administration in France, 1791–1799*. Oxford: Oxford University Press, 1995.

Campbell, Peter, Thomas Kaiser, and Marisa Linton (eds.). *Conspiracy in the French Revolution*. Manchester: Manchester University Press, 2007.

Chappey, Jean-Luc. *La société des Observateurs de l'Homme, (1799–1804). Des anthropologues au temps de Bonaparte*. Paris: Société des études robespierristes, 2002.

Church, Clive H. *Revolution and Red Tape: The French Ministerial Bureaucracy 1770–1850*. Oxford: Clarendon Press, 1981.

Clay, Stephen. "Justice, vengeance et passé révolutionnaire: les crimes de la terreur blanche." *Annales historiques de la Révolution française* 350 (2007): 109–33.

Clay, Stephen. "The White Terror: Factions, Reactions, and the Politics of Vengeance." In *A Companion to the French Revolution*, ed. Peter McPhee, 359–77. London: Wiley, 2012.

Clay, Stephen. "Vengeance, Justice and the Reactions in the Revolutionary Midi." *French History* 23, no. 1 (March 2009): 22–46.

Cobb, Richard. *The People's Armies: The armées révolutionnaires: instrument of the Terror in the departments April 1793 to Floréal Year II*. Trans. Marianne Elliott. New Haven, CT: Yale University Press, 1987 [1961, 1963].

Cobb, Richard. *The Police and the People: French Popular Protest, 1789–1820*. Oxford: Clarendon Press, 1970.

Collins, Irene. *The Government and the Newspaper Press in France 1814–1881*. Oxford: Oxford University Press, 1959.

Corbin, Alain. *The Life of an Unknown: The Rediscovered World of a Clog Maker in Nineteenth-Century France*. Trans. Arthur Goldhammer. New York: Columbia University Press, 2001.

Crook, Malcolm. *Elections in the French Revolution: An Apprenticeship in Democracy, 1789–1799*. Cambridge: Cambridge University Press, 1996.

Darnton, Robert. *The Literary Underground of the Old Regime*. Cambridge, MA: Harvard University Press, 1982.

Darnton, Robert. *What Was Revolutionary about the French Revolution?* Waco, TX: Markham Press, 1990.

Daumard, Adeline. *Les bourgeois et la bourgeoisie en France depuis 1815*. Paris: Aubier, 1987.

Davidson, Denise Z. *France after Revolution: Urban Life, Gender, and the New Social Order*. Cambridge, MA: Harvard University Press, 2007.

Delieuvin, Marie-Claude. *Marc-Antoine Jullien, de Paris, 1775–1848 : théoriser et organiser l'éducation*. Paris: L'Harmattan, 2003.

Desan, Suzanne. *The Family on Trial in Revolutionary France*. Berkeley: University of California Press, 2004.

Desan, Suzanne, Lynn Hunt, and William Max Nelson (eds.). *The French Revolution in Global Perspective*. Ithaca, NY: Cornell University Press, 2013.

Di Rienzo, Eugenio. *Marc-Antoine Jullien de Paris (1789–1848), una Biografia Politica*. Naples: Éditions Guida, 1999.

Dwyer, Philip. *Citizen Emperor: Napoleon in Power 1799–1815*. New Haven, CT: Yale University Press, 2013.

Dwyer, Philip. *Napoleon: The Path to Power*. New Haven, CT: Yale University Press, 2009.

Edelstein, Melvin. *The French Revolution and the Birth of Electoral Democracy*. London: Routledge, 2017.

Englund, Steven. *Napoleon: A Political Life*. New York: Scribner, 2004.

Forrest, Alan. *Napoleon: Life, Legacy, and Image: A Biography*. New York: St. Martin's, 2012.

Forrest, Alan, and Matthias Middell (eds.). *The Routledge Companion to the French Revolution in World History*. London: Routledge, 2015.

Furet, François. *Interpreting the French Revolution*. Trans. Elborg Forster. Cambridge and Paris: Cambridge University Press and Éditions de la Maison des Sciences de l'Homme, 1981 [1978].

Furet, François. "La Terreur sous le Directoire." In *The Transformation of Political Culture 1789–1848*, ed. François Furet and Mona Ozouf, 173–86. Vol. 3 of *The French Revolution and the Creation of Modern Political Culture*. Oxford: Pergamon Press, 1989.

Gainot, Bernard. *1799, un nouveaux jacobinism?* Paris: Éditions du CTHS, 2001.

Godineau, Dominique. *The Women of Paris and Their French Revolution*. Trans. Katherine Streip. Berkeley: University of California Press, 1998 [1988].

Gross, Jean-Pierre. *Fair Shares For All: Jacobin Egalitarianism in Practice.* Cambridge: Cambridge University Press, 1997.

Gueniffey, Patrice. *Bonaparte 1769–1802.* Trans. Steven Rendall. Cambridge, MA: Belknap Press of Harvard University Press, 2015 [2013].

Gueniffey, Patrice. *La politique de la Terreur : Essay sur la violence révolutionnaire 1789–1794.* Paris: Fayard, 2000.

Gueniffey, Patrice. *Le Nombre et la raison : la Révolution française et les élections.* Paris: Éditions de l'EHESS, 1993.

Guicheteau, Samuel. *La Révolution des ouvriers nantais. Mutation économique, identité sociale et dynamique révolutionnaire (1740–1815).* Rennes: Presses Universitaires de Rennes, 2008.

Hanson, Paul R. *Contesting the French Revolution.* Chichester, UK: Wiley-Blackwell, 2009.

Hanson, Paul R. "From Jacobin to Liberal." *Historical Reflections/Réflexions Historiques* 37, no. 3 (2011): 86–100.

Harrison, Carol E. *Romantic Catholics: France's Postrevolutionary Generation in Search of a Modern Faith.* Ithaca, NY: Cornell University Press, 2014.

Horn, Jeff. *Economic Development in Early Modern France: The Privilege of Liberty, 1650–1820.* Cambridge: Cambridge University Press, 2015.

Horn, Jeff. « *Qui parle pour la nation?* » *Les élections et les élus de la Champagne méridionale, 1765–1830.* Paris: Société des études robespierristes, 2004.

Horn, Jeff. *The Path Not Taken: French Industrialization in the Age of Revolution, 1750–1830.* Cambridge, MA: MIT Press, 2006.

Hunt, Lynn. *Politics, Culture, and Class in the French Revolution.* Berkeley: University of California Press, 1984.

Hunt, Lynn. *The Family Romance of the French Revolution.* Berkeley: University of California Press, 1992.

Israel, Jonathan I. *Revolutionary Ideas: An Intellectual History of the French Revolution from The Rights of Man to Robespierre.* Princeton, NJ: Princeton University Press, 2014.

Jarvis, Katie. *Politics in the Marketplace: Work, Gender, and Citizenship in Revolutionary France.* New York: Oxford University Press, 2019.

Jessenne, Jean-Pierre (ed.). *Brumaire dans l'histoire du lien politique et d'Etat-nation.* vol. 3 of *Du Directoire au Consulat.* Lille: Centre de Recherche sur l'Histoire de l'Europe du Nord-Ouest, GRHIS, Préfecture de la région Haute-Normandie, 2001.

Jordan, David P. *The Revolutionary Career of Maximilien Robespierre.* New York: Free Press, 1985.

Kawa, Catherine. *Les ronds-de-cuir en Révolution : Les employés du Ministère de l'intérieur sous la Première république (1792–1800).* Paris: CTHS, 1996.

Kennedy, Michael L. *The Jacobin Club of Marseilles, 1790–94.* Ithaca, NY: Cornell University Press, 1973.

Kennedy, Michael L. *The Jacobin Clubs in the French Revolution*. 3 vols. Princeton, NJ and New York: Princeton University Press (vols. 1–2) and Berghahn Books (vol. 3), 1982–2000.

Leuwers, Hervé. *Camille et Lucile Desmoulins : Un rêve de république*. Paris: Fayard, 2018.

Leuwers, Hervé. *L'Invention du "Barreau français" (1660–1830) : La construction nationale d'un groupe professionnel*. Paris: Éditions de l'EHESS, 2006.

Leuwers, Hervé. *Robespierre*. Paris: Fayard, 2014.

Leuwers, Hervé. *Un juriste en politique : Merlin de Douai (1754–1838)*. Arras: Artois Presses Universitaires 1996.

Leuwers, Hervé, and Michel Biard (eds.). "Analyser la 'terreur' dans l'historiographie anglophone." *Annales historiques de la Révolution française* 392, no. 2 (2018): 141–65.

Leuwers, Hervé (ed.) with Jacques Bernet and Jean-Pierre Jessenne. *L'intégration des citoyens dans la grande nation*. Vol. 2 of *Du Directoire au Consulat*. Lille: Centre de Recherche sur l'Histoire de l'Europe du Nord-Ouest, GRHIS, Préfecture de la région Haute-Normandie, 2000.

Lewis, Gwynne. *Second Vendee: The Continuity of Counter-Revolution in the Department of the Gard 1789–1815*. Oxford: Oxford University Press, 1978.

Linton, Marisa. *Choosing Terror: Virtue, Friendship and Authenticity in the French Revolution*. New York: Oxford University Press, 2013.

Lucas, Colin. *The Structure of the Terror: The Example of Javogues and the Loire*. Oxford: Oxford University Press, 1973.

Lyons, Martyn. *Napoleon Bonaparte and the Legacy of the French Revolution*. New York: St. Martin's Press, 1994.

Lyons, Martyn. *France Under the Directory*. Cambridge: Cambridge University Press, 1975.

Margairaz, Dominique. *François de Neufchâteau. Biographie intellectuelle*. Paris: Publications de la Sorbonne, 2005.

Martin, Jean-Clément. *La Vendée et la France*. Paris: Seuil, 1987.

Martin, Jean-Clément. *La Terreur : Vérités et légendes*. Paris: Perrin, 2017.

Martin, Jean-Clément. *Robespierre, la fabrication d'un monstre*. Paris: Perrin, 2016.

McPhee, Peter. *Liberty or Death: The French Revolution*. New Haven, CT: Yale University Press, 2016.

McPhee, Peter. *Robespierre: A Revolutionary Life*. New Haven, CT: Yale University Press, 2012.

Ozouf, Mona. *Festivals and the French Revolution*. Trans. Alan Sheridan. Cambridge, MA: Harvard University Press, 1988 [1976].

Palmer, Robert R. *From Jacobin to Liberal: Marc-Antoine Jullien, 1775–1848*. Princeton, NJ: Princeton University Press, 1993.

Palmer, Robert R. *Twelve Who Ruled: The Year of Terror in the French Revolution*. Princeton, NJ: Princeton University Press, 1941.

Pinckney, David. *The French Revolution of 1830*. Princeton, NJ: Princeton University Press, 1972.

Popkin, Jeremy. *Press, Revolution, and Social Identities in France 1830–1835.* University Park: Pennsylvania State University Press, 2002.

Reiss, Tom. *The Black Count: Glory, Revolution, Betrayal, and the Real Count of Monte Cristo.* New York: Broadway, 2012.

Roche, Daniel (ed.). *Journal of My Life by Jacques Menetra.* Trans. Arthur Goldhammer. New York: Columbia University Press, 1986.

Schechter, Ronald. *The Genealogy of Terror in Eighteenth-Century France.* Chicago: University of Chicago Press, 2018.

Scurr, Ruth. *Fatal Purity: Robespierre and the French Revolution.* New York: Vintage, 2006.

Serna, Pierre. *Antonelle. Aristocratie révolutionnaire, 1747–1817.* Paris : Félin, 1997.

Serna, Pierre. *La République des girouettes : 1789–1815 et au-delà une anomalie politique: La France de l'extrême centre.* Seysel: Champ Vallon, 2005.

Serna, Pierre (ed.). *Républiques soeurs: Le Directoire et la Révolution atlantique. Actes du colloque de Paris, 25 et 26 janvier 2008.* Rennes: Presses Universitaires de Rennes, 2009.

Serna, Pierre, Antonino De Francesco, and Judith Miller (eds.). *Republics at War, 1776–1840: Revolutions, Conflicts, and Geopolitics in Europe and the Atlantic World.* London: Palgrave-Macmillan, 2013.

Sirinelli, Jean-François. *Génération intellectuelle : Khâgneux et normaliens dans l'entre-deux guerres.* Paris: Fayard, 1988.

Slavin, Morris. *The Hébertistes to the Guillotine: Anatomy of a "Conspiracy" in Revolutionary France.* Baton Rouge: Louisiana State University Press, 1994.

Soboul, Albert. *The Sans-Culottes: The Popular Movement and Revolutionary Government, 1793–1794.* Trans. Remy Inglis Hall. Princeton, NJ: Princeton University Press, 1981 [1959]).

Spitzer, Alan B. *The French Generation of 1820.* Princeton, NJ: Princeton University Press, 1987.

Steinberg, Ronen. *The Afterlives of the Terror: Facing the Legacies of Mass Violence in Postrevolutionary France.* Ithaca, NY: Cornell University Press, 2019.

Sutherland, Donald. *The Chouans: The Social Origins of Popular Counterrevolution in Upper Brittany, 1770–96.* Oxford: Oxford University Press, 1982.

Sydenham, Michael. *Léonard Bourdon: The Career of a Revolutionary, 1754–1807.* Waterloo: Wilfrid Laurier University Press, 1999.

Tackett, Timothy. *Becoming a Revolutionary: The Deputies of the French National Assembly and the Emergence of a Revolutionary Culture (1789–1790).* Princeton, NJ: Princeton University Press, 1996.

Tackett, Timothy. *The Coming of the Terror in the French Revolution.* Cambridge, MA: Harvard University Press, 2015.

Tackett, Timothy. *When the King Took Flight.* Cambridge, MA: Harvard University Press, 2003.

Tocqueville, Alexis de. *The Old Régime and the French Revolution.* Trans. Stuart Gilbert. New York: Penguin Books, 1955 [1856].

Vincent, K. Steven. *Benjamin Constant and the Birth of French Liberalism.* New York: Palgrave Macmillan, 2011.

Vovelle, Michel. *The Revolution Against the Church: From Reason to the Supreme Being.* Trans. Alan José. Columbus: Ohio State University Press, 1991 [1988].

Walton, Charles. *Policing Public Opinion in the French Revolution: The Culture of Calumny and the Problem of Free Speech.* New York: Oxford University Press, 2009.

Woloch, Isser. *Jacobin Legacy: The Democratic Movement under the Directory.* Princeton, NJ: Princeton University Press, 1970.

Woloch, Isser. *Napoleon and His Collaborators: The Making of a Dictatorship.* New York: Norton, 2001.

Woloch, Isser. *The New Regime: Transformations of the French Civic Order, 1789–1820s.* New York: Norton, 1994.

Index

For the benefit of digital users, indexed terms that span two pages (e.g., 52–53) may, on occasion, appear on only one of those pages.

Admirat, Henri, 76
Albert, Jean-Baptiste, 95–96
Amar, Jean-Baptiste, 73–74, 85–86, 88–89, 92, 100
Amnesty, 100
Angoulême, duc d', 155–56
Anti-clericalism, 11, 43–44, 52–53, 142, 183
Antonelle, Pierre-Antoine, 192
Army of the Ardennes, 49
Arcis (Aube), 68
Aube (see Troyes)
Averal, Georges, 177

Bara, Joseph, 41–42
Babeuf, Gracchus, 102–3, 192–93
Bailleul, Antoine, 136
Bailleul, Jean-Chalres, 136
Barère, Bertrand, 19, 44, 49, 61, 67, 74, 88–89, 91, 174
Barras, Paul, 73–74, 75–76, 86, 87, 88–89, 91, 102–6, 107, 109–10, 111, 118–20, 126–27, 128–29, 173, 175–76, 179, 193
　Memoirs, 126, 170–73, 175, 176–77, 179

Barras, Marie-Pélagie Templies de, 171–72
Bar-sur-Aube, 51–52
Beauharnais, Alexandre de, 118–19
Beauharnais/Bonaparte, Joséphine (Marie-Josèphe-Rose Tascher de la Pagerie), 109–10, 118–20, 170–71, 193
Bellart, Nicolas-François, 147, 149–50
Bernadotte, Jean-Baptiste, 106, 116–17, 119, 120, 123–24
Berry, duc de, 141, 144
Biard, Michel, 189, 190
Billaud-Varennes, Jacques-Nicolas, 31–33, 74, 83–84, 85, 87, 88–89
Biography/biographers, 10
Biré, Edmond, 87
Blanc, Louis, 175
Bô, Jean-Baptiste, 61–62, 64, 67–68, 77, 79, 80, 81, 88–89, 94–95, 96–97
Boissy d'Anglas, François-Antoine, 174
Bonald, vicomte de, 153–54
Bonaparte, Joseph, 108, 110
Bonaparte, Joséphine (see Beauharnais, Joséphine)
Bonaparte, Louis, 155

Bonaparte, Lucien, 109–10

Bonaparte, Napoleon, 99, 147, 188–89, 192

    Leader, 105–6, 155–56, 169

    Legacy, 99, 130, 172

    Personal relationships, 105, 118–20, 170–71, 176

    Return from Elba, 128–31, 133–34

    Seizure of power, 107, 108, 109–12

Bonapartism/Bonapartists, 132, 133–34, 135–36, 138, 155, 160, 171, 176, 178, 182

Bonaparte, Roland, 1–3

Bordeaux, 39, 192–93

Bordeaux, duc de, 141

Bourbon, House of (see Restoration)

Bourdon, François-Louis, 86, 87, 88–89, 192

Bramand, Paul-François, 53–54

Brest, 24, 25

Broé, Jacques-Nicolas de, 150

Brienne, 62

Brissot, Jacques-Pierre, 23, 36–37, 39

Brissotins (see Girondins)

Broglie, duc de, 144, 154–55

Brunswick, Duke, 24–25, 29–31, 66–67, 121

Buchez, Philippe-Joseph-Benjamin, 163–64

Caen, 39

Cambon, Pierre-Joseph, 88–89

Carnot, Lazare, 84, 85, 86, 88–89, 128–29, 130–31, 174, 193–94

Carrier, Jean-Baptiste, 63–64, 86, 88–89, 95–96, 127

Cauchois-Lemoire, Augustin-François, 137–38, 158, 159–60

Caulaincourt, Armand-Augustin-Louis, marquis de, 147

Censorship, 117, 122, 130, 138, 141–45, 147–58, 162

Chamber of Deputies, 121–59

Championnet, Jean-Étienne, 116, 123–24, 175–76

Chardin, Jean-Siméon, 174

Charles X, 128–29, 144–45, 149, 152, 155–60

Chastenay, Louis-Marie-Victoire de, 126–27

Chateaubriand (vicomte de), François-René, 123, 158–59

Chaumette, Pierre-Gaspard 174

Chauvet, 170

Chenier, André, 174

Chenier, Joseph-Marie, 174

Chérin, Louis-Nicolas-Hyacinthe, 106–7, 113, 115, 116–17, 123–24, 175–76

Chevassut, Alexandre, 134–35

Choiseul, duc de, 153–54

Clarke, Henri, 120

Clary/Bernadotte, Desirée, 109–10

Cobb, Richard, 188

Codant, Charles, 51–52

Collège d'Harcourt, 8–13

Collot D'Herbois, Jean-Marie, 63, 72, 76, 83–85, 87–89

Commissioners of the Committee of Public Safety, 43–44, 49–64, 77, 81, 96–97, 134–35, 178, 189–91

Committee of General Security, 40–41, 68, 70, 73, 76, 78–80, 89–90, 93, 95, 97, 100

    Opposes Robespierre, 84, 85–86, 87, 88–89, 90–91

Committee of Public Safety, 38–40, 43–44, 49–50, 56, 58–59, 61, 68, 70–76, 78–80, 83–85, 91, 93, 174, 187–91

    Divisions of, 84, 86–89, 100

Condorcet, marquis (MarieJean-Antoine-Nicolas de Caritat), 25–26

Conspiracies (see plots)

Constant, Henri-Benjamin, 120–23, 126–27, 130, 133, 139–40, 148–49, 154–55, 157, 190–91, 193

Constitution(s)/Charter, 23, 96, 101, 106, 130, 136–37, 139, 141–43, 158

Constitutionnel, Le, 6, 129–30, 134–43, 163–67, 170, 171

   Censorship, 142–45, 148–54

   Circulation, 135, 137, 149, 162, 165

   Closure, 135–37

   Opposition, 142–43, 145–48, 152–54, 155–56, 158, 160

   July Monarchy, 160–62

Cophignon, Jean, 152–54

Corbeau de Saint-Albin, Antoine-Pierre-Laurent, 8–9, 26–27, 44, 96, 105, 127–28, 134, 175–77, 183

Corbeau de Saint-Albin, Antoine-Laurent de, 183

Corbière, comte de, Jacques-Joseph, 142

Corday, Charlotte, 1–3, 41–42, 175, 181

Cordeliers Club/Cordeliers, 18, 19, 20–24, 27, 29, 35, 37, 68–72, 188

Corruption, 10, 11, 60, 68, 70–72, 82, 84–85, 92–93, 114–15, 145

Cotta, 146–47

Counter-revolution/counter-revolutionnaries, 26–27, 40–42, 45, 56, 61, 192–93

Courtat, 171

Courtois, Edme-Bonaventure, 87–89

Couthon, Georges, 76, 78–80, 83, 84, 89–91, 97, 100, 174

Custine, comte de (Adam Philippe), 27

Damaison, Étienne, 172

Danton, Georges-Jacques, 1–5, 14, 16, 31, 68, 81, 105, 128–29, 173–77

   Death, 72–74, 81–82

   Declining influence, 67–68

   Friends (Dantonistes), 68–69, 77–80, 82, 83, 85–92, 102–3

   Indulgents, 71–74, 83–84

   Politician, 14, 16, 20–23, 25–26, 28–30, 34, 35, 41, 58–59, 163

   Terror, 38, 39, 49, 52, 106

Danton, Madame (Antoinette-Gabrielle Charpentier), 20–21

Darnton, Robert, 187

D'Aubigny, Vilate, 72

David, Jacques-Louis, 174

David-Delisle, Alexandre-Edme, 82, 90–91

Dechristianization/vandalism, 44, 47, 52–58, 60–61, 63, 75, 77, 79

Democratic ideals, 11, 35–36

Democratic politics (popular politics), 25–26, 68, 71–72, 100, 101, 139–40, 188

Denunciation(s), 22, 41, 47–48, 53, 54, 56, 73, 76–83, 93–96, 100–3, 105, 169, 190–91

Desmoulins (of Troyes), 54–55

Desmoulins, Camille, 3, 4–5, 14, 16–17, 20–22, 25, 66, 69–70, 72, 105, 128–29, 173–75, 192

   Activist, 14–16, 22, 25, 26

   Death, 72–74

   Journalist, 16–18, 68–70

Desmoulins, Lucile (Anne-Lucile-Philippe Laridon Duplessis), 19, 25, 74–75, 192

Directory/Directors, 101–2, 104, 106, 107–9, 111–13, 115, 121, 188–89

Dubois-Crancé, Edmond-Louis, 86–89

Dubouchet, Pierre, 45–49, 63

Ducos, Roger 109

Duhot, Albert-Augustin-Antoine-Joseph, 113

Dumas, René-François, 79–80, 82–83

Dumoulin, Évariste, 136–37, 159–60, 162

Dumouriez, Charles, 35

Dupin, André-Marie-Jean-Jacques, 147, 150–52, 153–55, 159–60

Dupin, Charles, 157–58
Duplessis, Anne-François, 5, 173–74
Duruy, Georges, 1–3, 172–75, 182
Dutacq, Armand, 164
Duval, George, 14–16

Education, 8–13, 130–31
Emotions, 3, 5–6, 8, 33, 39, 41, 66–67,
    88, 99, 114, 140–41, 168–69, 188,
    190–91, 194
Enlightenment texts, 9, 11, 149–50
Estates-General, 13–14
Étienne, Charles-Guillaume, 136, 138–39,
    154–55, 158, 162, 165
Eugènie, Empress, 182

Fain, Armand-Louis-Jean, 134–35, 150
Fauchet, Jean-Antoine-Joseph, 174
Fauchon, Edme, 45–46
Fécamp, 150
Federalism/Federalist Revolt, 39, 63, 82,
    84, 90–91, 101
Festival of the Supreme Being
    (see Robespierre)
Finot, Louise, 55–56
Fleurus, 84
Fleury, 51–52, 60
Fouché, Joseph, 49–50, 60, 63, 86–89, 91,
    111, 120, 123, 126–30, 173, 193
Fouquier-Tinville, Antoine-Quentin, 71,
    74, 82–83, 93
François de Neufchâteau, Nicolas-Louis,
    40–41, 192
Freemason lodge, 16–17, 20–21
Fréron, Louis-Marie-Stanislaus, 18,
    29, 86–87
Furet, François, 189

Gachez, François, 50, 59, 60, 62, 79–80, 94
Garat, Dominique-Joseph, 22–23, 40,
    95, 123

Garnier, Antoine-Marie-Charles, 50, 77,
    82–83, 87–91, 93, 95
Gémond, François, 134–35
General will, 11, 28–29, 43, 59, 64, 98
Generation(s), 3, 11, 45, 139, 157–58, 169,
    188–89, 193–94
Geneva, 119–21, 127
Geoffroy, 76
Girardin, Émile de, 164
Girondin(s) (Brissotins), 23, 25–26,
    33–39, 63–64, 68, 102, 105
Godineau, Dominique, 188
Gohier, Louis-Jérôme, 109, 119
Gorsas, Antoine-Joseph, 36–37
Grain requisition, 44, 46, 75, 91, 104
Grand, Paul, 171–72
Grand, Pierre, 171
Grandmaison, Geoffroy de, 179
Guadet, Marguerite-Élie, 36–37
Guélon, Augustin, 77, 79–80, 82–83,
    92, 191
Guétry, André, 117–18
Guffroy, Armand-Joseph, 88–89, 95–96
Guicheteau, Samuel, 188
Guizot, François, 158
Guyot (Troyes), 58–59

Hanriot, François, 37
Hébert, Jacques-Réné/Hébertists, 29,
    37, 68–69, 71, 78, 79–80, 83–84,
    88–89
Hoche, Lazare, 99, 104–6, 112–16, 118–19,
    171, 174–76
Holy Alliance, 141–42
Huchet, Charles Angélique François,
    comte de la Bédoyère, 135–36
Huez, Widow, 55

Jacobin Club/Jacobins, 14, 26–27, 44,
    74–77, 91, 95–97, 188
    Post-1794, 102–3, 107–12, 116–17

Paris, 18, 19, 22–23, 25, 29, 40–41, 48, 67–68, 71, 75–76, 78, 80, 88, 89–90, 92

Jansenism, 10–12, 151–52

Jarvis, Katie, 188

Javogues, Claude, 87

Jay, Antoine, 134–35, 141–42, 154–55, 162

Jeanbon Saint André, André, 84, 88–89

Jones, Colin, 188

Joubert, Barthélemy-Catherine, 116

Jourdan, Jean-Baptiste, 108–9

Jubinal, Achille, 182

Jullien, Marc-Antoine, 63–64, 134–35, 168–69, 192–93

July Monarchy, 160–61, 164–65, 175, 181, 183–84

Kennedy, Michael L., 188

Kléber, Jean-Baptiste, 128, 175–76

Laborde, Alexandre-Louis-Joseph de, 131

Lafayette, marquis de (Marie-Joseph Paul Yves Roch Gilbert du Motier), 18, 20–22, 161, 168–69

Lafitte, Jacques, 161

Lamotte-Valois, Charles-Antoine-Nicolas, comte de, 51, 162–63, 187

Lanjuinais, Jean-Denis, comte de, 134–35

Lasteyrieand, Charles-Philibert de, 131

Law of 22 Prairial, 78–80, 86, 93

Le Bas, Joseph-François, 89

Lecointre, Laurent, 88–89

Legendre, Louis, 73, 76, 87–90, 92, 95

Legion of Honor, 138, 164–65

Legislative Assembly, 25–26, 29

Lepelletier, Louis-Michel, 41–42, 174

Lerouge, Alexis, 50–51

Liberal/liberalism, 6–7, 106, 133, 138, 140, 154–58, 160, 166, 178, 187–90, 192–93

Lindet, Robert, 72, 84, 88–89

Linton, Marisa, 189–90

Louis XVI, 13–14, 20, 22–23, 128–29, 133–34

Louis XVIII, 128–29, 141–42, 170

Louis-Philippe d'Orléans, 143, 158, 161–62, 166, 168–69, 171–72, 182

Lucas, Colin, 190

Lyon, 39, 62–63, 88, 96, 120, 127, 151

Maillard, Stanislaus-Marie, 32

Malet, Aristide de, 172–73

Malet, Claude-François de, 123–26, 172–73, 175–76

Malet (widow), 125, 172–73

Marat, Jean-Paul, 1, 18, 29, 33–35, 37, 41–42, 46–47, 163
    Bust, 47, 95–96, 175, 181

Marbot, Jean-Antoine, 116–17, 175–76

Marcandier, Roch, 18

Marceau-Desgraviers, François-Séverin, 174

Marescot, Armand-Samuel, 108–9

Marie-Antoinette, 22, 134–35

Marseille, 24–25, 31–32, 39

Martignac, Jean-Baptiste Gay de, 156

Martin, Jean-Clément, 189

Massena, André, 116, 123–24

Matton, Pierre-Joseph-Marcelin, 5, 173–74

Maure, Nicolas, 45, 79, 83, 94–95

Maximum, 96, 100–1

Méhul, Étienne, 117–18

Melun, 45, 95

Merlin de Douai, Philippe-Antoine, 192

Michelet, Jules, 174–75

Millard, Bonaventure-Jean-Baptiste, 50–51

Mirabeau, comte de (Honoré-Gabriel Riqueti), 14

Moderation/moderates, 3, 4, 39, 45, 48, 51, 60–61, 68–70, 72, 91–92, 95–96, 104–5, 179, 183–84

Montagnards, 35, 37, 39, 45

Montpezat, Marie-François-Joséphine de Trémolet de, 126, 175–76

Moore, John, 25

Morality, 10, 11, 147, 150

Moulins, Jean-François-Auguste, 109

Nation/nationalism, 29–30, 41–42

National Assembly, 13–14, 16

National Convention, 35, 37–41, 43–46, 48, 50–51, 61, 64, 70, 73, 78, 80, 85–88, 89–92, 95–96, 100, 101, 113, 128–29, 188

National Guards/national guardsmen 21–22, 24–25, 29–32, 35, 37, 59, 60–62, 74, 77, 89, 124–25, 152–53

Necker, Jacques, 121

Networks, 66–68, 74–75, 78–79, 81–84, 88, 94, 97–98, 126, 132, 191

Newspaper(s)/press, 11, 17–18, 21–22, 40–41, 57–58, 68–70, 80, 89–90, 102–3, 129–30, 134–35, 137, 143–45, 148–57, 158–60, 162–63, 187–88

Neuwied, 104–5

Nougaret, Pierre-Jean-Baptiste, 163–64

Orléans, Marie-Amélie, 143, 182

Osselin, 102, 111

Paine, Thomas, 35

Palmer, R.R., 192–93

Panard, 174

Paré, Jules-François, 26, 40, 44, 49, 67, 76, 102–3

Parent, Nicolas, 56

Paris, 8, 20, 24–25, 120–21, 123, 127, 152–53, 161, 191

Commune, 20, 22–23, 25, 29, 37–39, 69–70, 89, 92–93, 174–75

Palais royal, 14–15, 135, 159–60

Popular politics, 6, 14–16, 18, 21–23, 26, 27, 39, 160, 187–88

Sections, 25–26, 29, 32, 34, 36–37, 73, 187–88

September Massacres, 29–34

Pasquier, Étienne-Denis, 170

Payan, Claude, 86

People, The 29–31, 33, 36–37, 39, 43, 45–47, 50, 58–59, 62, 70, 73–76, 81, 83–84, 94, 96–97

Périer, 159–61

Philadelphes, 123–26

Philippeaux, Pierre, 72

Pichegru, Jean-Charles, 105–6, 173, 175–76

Pichon, Citizen, 47

Pilon, Nicolas, 56

Plots (conspiracies), 29–31, 35, 43–45, 66, 82, 84–85, 89–91, 105, 111, 123–26, 170–73

Polignac, prince de, 158–60

Pontmartin, Armand de, 178

Popular politics (see democratic politics)

Popular society/societies, 44, 47, 48, 54–57, 60–61, 75–77, 82–83, 187–90

Portalis, Joseph-Marie, comte de, 156–57

Pottofeux, Pierre-Polycarpe, 79

Press (see newspapers)

Prieur de la Côte-d'Or, Claude-Antoine, 84, 88–89

Provins (Seine-et-Marne), 43–49, 63, 189–92

Prudhomme, Louis-Marie, 102, 192–93

Public opinion, 29–30, 33–34, 40–42, 57–59, 64, 70, 72, 88, 101, 104, 139, 140, 150, 154–55, 192–93

Public spirit, 45, 49, 50–51, 58, 85–86

Purge(s) (administrative), 39, 50, 58, 60–61, 63, 68–69, 71, 77, 83–84, 86–89, 95–96

Quérard, Joseph-Marie, 163–64,
178–79, 182–83

Rapinat, Jean-Jacques, 117–18
Renault, Cécile, 76, 78–79, 84–85
Representatives on mission, 36–37, 43–50,
58–59, 61–64, 67–68, 79, 83, 86, 88,
94–96, 189–90, 191
Republic/republicanism, 11, 35, 40–43,
50–51, 62–63, 101–2, 116–17, 121,
124–25, 133–34, 160, 189, 192, 193
Republic of Virtue, 35–36, 58–59, 72,
75–76, 84–85
Restoration (1814-1830), 128, 131, 133–34,
138, 141–43, 154–57, 160, 166, 169,
170–71, 183–84, 191–92
Revolutionary Army, 44, 50, 55, 59,
60–62, 74–75, 77, 162–63,
187–91
Revolutionary Tribunal, 29, 37, 44,
59, 61, 63, 66, 71, 73–75, 78–80,
82–86, 89–93, 97, 100, 102,
163–64, 191
Revolutionary violence, 3–5, 28–34, 52,
71, 88, 101, 106–7, 169, 189, 190,
193, 194
Richelieu, duc de, 136–37
Robert (Aube), 77–78
Robespierre, Augustin, 89
Robespierre, Charlotte, 88
Robespierre, Maximilien, 4–5, 16,
19, 63–64, 69–71, 74–77, 81,
89, 192–93
Coup against (9 Thermidor), 67,
88–89, 174–75
Festival of the Supreme Being,
76, 85–86
Ideas, 35, 72
Scapegoated, 84–86, 88, 93, 96–98,
100, 102, 168–69
Terror, 68, 73–74, 79–91, 97, 163, 175
Roland, Marie-Jeanne (Madame), 26

Roman history, 9–10, 31, 43, 46–47, 78,
112–14, 121–22, 126, 139–40
Romanticism, 106, 114, 117–18,
122, 140–41
Rousseau, Jean-Jacques, 11, 41–42, 121
Rousselin, Alexandre
Administrative work, 34, 38, 39–40,
67–68, 70, 74–75, 80, 89, 92–93, 99,
102–3, 107–11, 119, 130–32, 166, 176,
179–80, 193–94
Biographer, 106–7, 112–18, 175–79
Censoring sources, 6, 8, 27, 171–73,
183–84, 191
Denunciation, 76–77, 79–80, 91, 95–97,
111–12, 162–64, 175, 176
Denunciation of Girondins, 36–39,
80, 163
Éducation, 8–13, 18, 118, 166, 183
Émigrés, 41, 111, 121–22
Father, 126–27, 138, 161, 164–67,
181–84, 190
Friends, 105, 118–23, 191
Historian, 3, 33, 112–13, 114, 118,
121–22, 170–75, 176–77, 179–81,
183–84
Imprisoned, 76–77, 91–93, 95–97, 100,
102, 111–12
Journalist, 40–41, 43, 46, 48, 57–58,
67–68, 70, 89–91, 129–32, 134–38,
141–43, 145–46, 148–49, 151,
152, 154, 156–57, 161–69, 177, 178,
188, 193–94
July Monarchy, 161, 162, 168
Justifying actions, 68, 75–76, 80–82,
161, 163–64, 168, 182–85
Legacy, 102, 169–70, 173–74, 176–77,
179–80, 181, 183–85, 187, 193–94
Liberalism, 6–7, 101–2, 133, 140,
157–58, 166, 169–70, 178, 180,
183–84, 193
Library, 150, 169, 174–75
Military supply, 104–5, 106–7

Rousselin, Alexandre (*cont.*)
  Missions, 4, 44–64, 67–68, 70, 76, 79,
    93, 94, 104, 162–63, 178–79, 182–83,
    187–92
  Opposition to Napoleon Bonaparte,
    6, 117, 118, 123, 125, 155–56
  Noble, 127–28, 133–34, 166, 178, 179,
    183, 193–94
  Police spy, 39–40, 93, 120, 121–22, 188
  Popular politics, 14, 43, 67, 92, 160,
    169–70, 187–88, 192
  Reputation, 99, 102–3, 111–12, 118,
    128, 131, 162, 168–70, 177–80,
    183–84, 191
  Republicanism, 101–2, 111–12, 114,
    117–18, 125, 132, 138, 192, 193
  Resisting the Terror, 4, 72–74, 182–84, 189
  Secretary, 1–3, 18–19, 23, 27, 29, 105–6, 188
  September Massacres, 31–34
  Survivor, 99, 133–34, 169–70, 192
  Terrorist, 4, 6–7, 48–49, 96–97, 126–27,
    132, 162–64, 168–70, 176–79, 182–83,
    187, 193
  Trial, 82–83
  Upbringing, 8, 183
  Vice-consul, 119–20
Rousselin, Amélie Sophie-Eléonore
    Marc, 143, 182
Rousselin, Clémentine (Marie-Gaspardine-
    Justine-Clémentine de Montpezat),
    126–27, 138, 163, 170–71, 183
Rousselin, François-Charles, 8, 96, 128,
    163, 178–79
Rousselin de Saint-Albin, 182
Rousselin de Saint-Albin, Louis-Philippe
    de Corbeau, 143, 161, 178, 182
Rousselin de Saint-Albin, Horténse-
    Joséphine, 143, 182
Rousselin de Saint-Albin, Marie-
    Philibert-Hortensius, 126–27,
    135–36, 161, 163–65, 167, 173,
    175–77, 179, 181–84

Rousselin de Saint-Albin, Marc, 182
Rousselin (Corbeau), Nicole-Antoinette,
    8, 96, 127, 128, 179
Roux, Pierre-Célestin, 163–64
Royalism/royalists, 31–32, 48, 56–57, 70,
    73, 101, 104–6, 126, 157
Royer-Collard, Pierre-Paul, 156–57
Ruault, Nicolas, 89

Saint-Albin, Cécile, 181
Saint-Albin, Marie, 181
Saint-Quentin, 145
Saint-Just, Louis-Antoine, 73, 74, 84–86,
    89, 173–74
Saladin, Jean-Baptiste-Michel, 93
Sans-culottes, 36, 43, 45–46, 70, 95, 96
  Paris, 70, 83–84
  Provins, 45–47
  Troyes, 49, 50–51, 53, 57–59, 61, 64,
    75–76, 80–81, 94
Schecter, Ronald, 189
Scott, Walter, 175
Seine-et-Marne (see Provins)
Sénart, Gabriel-Jérôme, 79–80
Serna, Pierre, 194
Sibille, Auguste, 53
Sieyès, Emmanuel-Joseph, 108–9,
    115, 155
Sirinelli, Jean-François, 188–89
Slavin, Morris, 188
Soboul, Albert, 188
Spitzer, alan, 188–89
Staël, Erik Magnus, von Holstein, 121
Staël-Holstein, Anne Louise Germaine,
    de, 99, 120–23, 193
Stevenson, Sara Y., 174
Strasbourg, 145–47, 155
Sue, Eugène, 165
Sulkowski, Joseph, 119
Symbolic politics, 22, 28, 29, 41–42,
    46–47, 51–54, 56–57, 61–62,
    69–70, 85–86, 188

Tackett, Timothy, 190, 191

Talleyrand-Périgord, Charles-Maurice, 9–10, 119–20, 161, 168–69

Tallien, Jean-Lambert, 63–64, 70, 72, 86–89, 100, 170

Talma, François-Joseph, 105

Talma, Julie, 105, 121–23

Tartuffe, 150–51

Tax on the rich, 45, 50–51, 55, 58–59, 61, 63, 77, 96–97

Terror, The, 3–5, 8, 29–34, 40–41, 43, 47–48, 50, 52, 55–59, 64–65, 68, 71, 78, 83–84, 87, 88–91, 93–98, 100–2, 188–90

Théot, Catherine, 85–86

Thermidorean Reaction, 96

Legacies, 100, 102, 108, 138, 160, 168–69, 189–90, 191

Thibaudeau, Antoine-Claire, 72, 128–29

Thiers, Adolphe, 137–38, 154–55, 158–60, 165, 175

Thiessé, Leon, 138–39, 142, 148

Tissot, 136

Thuriot, Jacques, 85–89

Toulon, 39, 62

Troyes (Aube), 49–64, 68, 77, 94–96, 162–63, 178–79, 187, 189–91

Denunciations by, 67, 77, 79–80, 91, 95–98, 100, 189–90

Sections, 55, 59–62, 75, 80–83

Ultra-terrorist, 79–81, 86–89, 91

Vadier, Marc-Guillaume, 73–74, 85–89

Valence, 26–27

Vandalism (see dechristianization)

Vendée (war in), 45, 49–50, 84, 101, 104, 114–15

Vengeance, 24–25, 31, 36–37, 43, 51–52, 56–57, 64, 95–97, 100–1, 129, 163, 169

Vergniaud, Pierre, 36–37

Véron, Louis-Désiré, 165

Viel, Horace de, 177–78

Villèle, Jean-Baptiste de, 152–54, 156–58

War, 23–24, 28–31, 34–35, 39, 62–63, 96, 100, 101, 104–10, 115, 116, 119–20, 123–25, 169

White Terror, 96, 98, 99, 100

Woloch, Isser, 188–89